In the name of...

Written by
Manjiri Gokhale Joshi

In the name of...
Manjiri Gokhale Joshi

©Manjiri Gokhale Joshi

Published in 2025

© Published by

Qurate Books Pvt. Ltd.
Goa 403523, India
www.quratebooks.com
Tel: 1800-210-6527,
Email: info@quratebooks.com

All rights reserved
No part of this publication may be reproduced, stored in a retrieval system, or transmitted in any form or by any means, electronic, mechanical, photocopying, recording or otherwise, without the prior permission of the author.

ISBN: 978-93-58986-67-9

To the tragic memory of every human being on the face of the earth who was killed, or endured suffering in the name of race, religion, caste, scriptures, or tradition.

"There are undoubtedly many learned men among the followers of every religion. Should they free themselves from prejudice, accept the universal truths – that is those truths that are to be found alike in all religions and are of universal application, reject all things in which the various religions differ and treat each other lovingly, it will be greatly to the advantage of the world."

– *Swami Dayanand Saraswati (1824-1883)*

"Be it for good or for evil, we cannot do without religion. Religious thoughts are in our blood. If we try to flee from it, it will pursue us."

– *Justice Mahadev Govind Ranade (1842-1901)*

When God created heaven and earth, he so ordered things that each part might perform its function peacefully without clashing with any other. The Koran tells us that "It is not allowable (i.e., possible) for the sun to reach the moon, nor does the night overtake the day, but each, in an orbit, is swimming."

(Koran: 36:40)

"I would say, no, I hadn't met God. Just so you know, God lives in our hearts. He cannot be seen, but his presence is felt."

Rakesh Sharma, the first Indian to travel to space in 1984, when asked if he had met God in space.

Credits

Editor - Neetu Katyal

Author photograph - Shraddha and Shailesh Bhamre

Marathi translation - Aditi Bhave, Kalyani Kulkarni

Translation editor - Dr Mrinal Dhongde

Translation reviewer: Purnima Sathe

Audio recording (English): Tanvi Joshi

Audio recording (Marathi): Purnima Sathe

Table of Contents

Credits..5
Chapter 1: In the name of LOVE...9
Chapter 2: In the name of TRADITION 15
Chapter 3: In the name of LINEAGE...25
Chapter 4: In the name of NATIONALISM 31
Chapter 5: In the name of SOBRIETY 39
Chapter 6: In the name of COLOUR...49
Chapter 7: In the name of a STATUE and a MINARET 58
Chapter 8: In the name of HISTORY..66
Chapter 9: In the name of RACE...74
Chapter 10: In the name of HONOUR 81
Chapter 11: In the name of RITUALS...89
Chapter 12: In the name of SURVIVAL..99
Chapter 13: In the name of HEAVEN...106
Chapter 14: In the name of the COW and the PIG 114
Chapter 15: In the name of REVENGE...124
Chapter 16: In the name of DIVERSITY.......................................136
Chapter 17: In the name of RELIGION 146

Chapter 18: In the name of the DEMI-GODS 154

Chapter 19: In the name of the SPIRIT 162

Chapter 20: In the name of PEACE 171

Chapter 21: In the name of POLITICS 178

Chapter 22: In the name of DUTY 187

Chapter 23: In the name of a DOUBLE HELIX 195

Chapter 24: In the name of HOLY TEXTS 200

Chapter 25: In the name of LOVE again 212

Glossary 217

Chapter 1:

In the name of LOVE

In the pitch-dark cinema hall, Ira gingerly ascended the creaky stairs, her eyes darting between the moving tiny globule of light from the usher's electric torch and the ascending rows of movie-goers who were already in their seats. Her vision significantly marred by the printed yellow and brown floral chiffon scarf half covering her face, Ira made her way across the obstacle race course of bumpy knees and big toes sticking out of sandals as the title song blared across the darkened, populous shared space. She pressed her palm down on the edge of the stained, crimson velvet covered seat to stop it from folding back, whilst the fingers of her other hand were still entwined around the *dupatta*, veiling her nose and lips. She plopped into the empty seat.

There was a time before Ira was compelled to sneak into a darkened cinema hall and use an erstwhile nonchalantly tossed colourful accessory, the *dupatta*, as the means to her anonymity. But today, as she crept into the cinema, Ira was least interested in the melodrama unfolding on the screen. The two seats to her left were thankfully empty – maybe a couple would turn up later, she thought. As she settled into her seat, her back resting on the torn crimson backrest, from the seat on her right emerged a small glass bottle of ice-cold *Thumbs up* with a plastic straw stuck in it. Without taking her eyes off the screen, and enervated by her secret journey, she sipped the sweet black liquid and returned the bottle. Next came turmeric infused yellow popcorn, packed in a palm-sized plastic pouch ripped open at the corner. Without taking her eyes off the screen, Ira popped a few between her parted lips and handed the pouch back.

The blaring music waned and the last of the titles, in giant, fluorescent colours proclaiming the movie superstar's name "In and as…" dissolved. Two little girls dressed as boys in tight-fitting khaki shorts and identical white shirts cavorted around a woman dressed in a bright pink saree with orange polka dots, her forehead glistening with a coin-sized red dot and her jet-black eyes enhanced with thick black eyeliner. The woman expertly sprinkled red powder in the parting of her oiled, black glossy hair, peering into an ornate oval mirror on the wall. As the onscreen mother squealed at her children in a mock-berating tone and the boys squealed back in girly voices, Ira squinted towards her left. Safe in the knowledge that her co-viewers were now glued to the antics on screen, Ira finally looked to her right. Omar held out his left palm for Ira to slip in hers. For as far back as she could remember, this was always a sign of Omar, saying,

"OK, let's get on with it."

As seven-year-olds, Ira and Omar were picked to play Mary and Joseph in their school nativity play. Ira in a pale blue gossamer gown, stitched by the neighbourhood Dorabjee tailor, was about to drop the blue-eyed, blonde doll in her arms as she struggled to not trip over the floor length garment. Omar held out his palm and Ira gratefully held on to it. With his free hand, Omar slightly lifted the skirt of her trailing gown and the little holy couple calmly walked across the stage, the children's choir singing,

"Hark the holy angels sing, a New King's born today. Mary's boy child, Jesus Christ, was born on Christmas day…" Ira's parents and her Grandma Saguna in her crisp, white *nauvari* (traditional nine-yard-saree) applauded proudly in the audience. Just a few rows behind, Omar's mother Sakinabi and her driver Kartar Singh (always by her side, especially when she had to deal with conversation in English), beamed and clapped expeditiously, delighted to see Omar in a protagonist role on stage, whatever it was he was supposed to be doing. Omar's father Mushtaque Siddiqui was absent, traveling on business.

A few years later, in 1984, petrified that a mob would attack Kartar Singh on account of his turban following the anti-Sikh sentiment resulting from Indira Gandhi's assassination, Omar had held out his hand again. Ira clutched it tight, and the 10-year-olds ran safely home from school.

This was also the year that their class teacher decided to do her bit for national integration by dressing her wards in finery representing each of the States of India. Endorsing stereotypes to the hilt, the teacher relegated the "dark-skinned" ones to the southern States, failing to acknowledge that the southern States had their share of fair skinned population, and the rest of India had both fair and dark people.

But these were innocent faux pas that people took in their stride during the 1980s. Pale-skinned Omar and Ira were conveniently given the snow-capped picturesque northern State of Kashmir to represent, for sadly, their cosmopolitan classroom had no children from violence-ridden Kashmir. Omar's mother had gladly lent his sister Rabia's bright green, sequined, knee-length *kurta* to Ira for this performance.

Debating partners, representing their school in the Model United Nations Assembly (MUNA), after hours of library research, waxing eloquent on what that time seemed in a different world far away, was the Israel-Palestine question, Ira and Omar always brought the trophies home. They were then elected Head Boy and Head Girl.

From being the one who always made Ira laugh, Omar became the one who could make her cry, explode in anger and blush. Working towards building careers, they were in no rush to announce their relationship, especially to their families. Getting married was to be planned several years later, their nonchalant existence assured that the friendship that blossomed into romance would culminate in a lifetime of passionate love.

Today, in that darkened public space, underneath the whir of a dusty ceiling fan circulating nicotine infused air, Omar's slim strong palms tenderly encircled the turmeric-stained tips of Ira's fingers. Ira's palm concealed beneath the folds of the soft brown and yellow chiffon, fervently urged the long-awaited moments to stay. What they had assumed as the only way to be, spirited cajolery over endless cups of steaming tea, walks along a never empty Mumbai beach with their elbows barely touching, gulping down tangy *pani puri* served in bowls made of brown, dried leaves and dreamy afternoons of ardour in a secret haven, was in peril of being shrivelled down to a few stolen frenzied moments of passion.

For the first time since they could both remember, Omar and Ira had not met or spoken for over two months. Far from welcome in the Dixit household anymore, Omar had finally managed to reach Ira on her home phone with help from his cousin Nikhat and set up this rendezvous.

On previous movie dates, the two would board the train together at Dadar West. Ira would refuse to sit by herself in the "Ladies First Class" compartment, unperturbed by the men staring resentfully. The two of them caught the fresh air at the entrance, their feet planted firmly apart for balance, chatting away, a palm clutching the overhead handlebars with practiced ease. As the men stared, Omar would shake his head disapprovingly and attempt to block their view of Ira with his then slight frame.

"Omar, nobody is ogling! They are unhappy I've taken up a seat a man could have used, which I haven't, we are standing!", Ira would jest, tossing her hair in her characteristic manner. Holding back the urge to caress her dark tresses, Omar would instead dig into his pocket to produce the result of hours in the booking queue. If the tickets were not booked in advance, especially for the blockbuster films, Ira would have to hover around while Omar haggled with the wily black marketeers deftly making their way outside the cinema, their shifty eyes expertly sifting the "advance booking" movie goers from those "desperate to not disappoint" their girlfriends.

Irrespective of when the tickets were procured, Omar and Ira were always in their seats in time for the trailers, to giggle at the government sponsored birth control ads, whose chosen mode of depicting a sexual encounter was showing a couple boating in the Mahabaleshwar lake. They anticipated the roaring yawn of the 20th Century Fox lion and the echoing crunch of a giant, juicy red Shimla apple being eaten on a 70mm screen to advertise the supernatural dental strengthening power of a toothpaste brand.

After the three-hour saga ending with police sirens wailing after the hero had single-handedly vanquished a band of villains with his bare hands, even as his pretty maiden viewed the proceedings nervously twisting the edge of her flowing scarf or saree, Omar and Ira would remain seated. They only rose to step out of the cinema after the names of the unsung technical team had rolled away.

But today, 20 minutes earlier, unconcerned with the screen ending which went something like "And this was just the beginning..." as the couple held hands and floated away into the horizon, Omar slipped out of the cinema. The pungent fragrance of those precious, stolen moments still nuzzling her pert nose, Ira had slipped away 10 minutes earlier, armed with a polythene bag containing the black *burkha* Omar had borrowed from Nikhat, and the promise to meet at their secret spot behind the "Valentine's Day - 1993" red-themed party venue. Their passionate encounters could have continued thanks to the anonymity offered by this garment.

But, two months later, in April of 1993, Ira was on her first international flight, her blue, faded jeans and wine-coloured cardigan, a contrast to the conventional black beads around her neck. Her dulled mind, a union of unease and despondence, Ira's muddle of thought was taken over by dizziness and a wave of nausea. As the aircraft taxied on Terminal 3, a hundred voices in unison were drumming in her ears-

"We, The People of India

Having solemnly resolved to constitute India into a Sovereign, Socialist, Secular, Democratic Republic and to secure to all its citizens: Justice, social, economic, and political.

Liberty of thought, expression, **belief, faith,** *and* **worship...***"*

Mrs. Albuquerque, half Portuguese, half Goan, teaching Civics at their School, was convinced that the Indian Constitution and its Preamble, should be read aloud at the school assembly along with the Bible. She had marched into the school principal's office and impressed the importance of national pride upon the Nun. Apart from memorising chemistry formulae, poems on the English countryside and world war dates for their exams, Omar, Ira, and the schoolhouse captains were promptly given an additional task - of learning the Constitution's Preamble by rote and saying it aloud during assembly, so that the entire school could repeat after them.

"Liberty of thought, expression, **belief, faith,** and **worship**..." Masking her yawn with her fingers covered in fading henna design, she looked outside the window - her first ever glimpse of the grey London horizon. Something she had only read about in her favourite Enid Blyton and Agatha Christie books, the English countryside, should have beckoned her, cheered her.

Still sleepy, Ira opened her handbag to retrieve her boarding pass and passport. A yellowed post-it note dropped into the aisle. It was Omar's scribbling of the Preamble on one side and his first ever expression of love for Ira on the other. Stamped upon by co-passengers in a rush to get off the tiring flight, Ira left the "Liberty of thought, expression, **faith, belief** and **worship**" behind on the aircraft and stepped out into the cold London air, to put her best foot forward…for a new life.

Chapter 2:

In the name of TRADITION

December 5, 2017 – Twenty-five years after her breezy existence ended, Ira was on a flight from London Heathrow, accompanied by Sameer, his head tonsured, holding onto the precious urn of ashes.

Ira had hoped that the series of traumatic experiences would conclude with the funeral. Shattered by the loss of their only son, Ira's in-laws had not insisted on tradition, concurring that the ordeal of the years gone by should now end. Now, it was Sameer, who insisted that his father's ashes be scattered in the Ganga like "all good Hindus in the UK were doing". The tonsuring of his head, as the son of the deceased, was one such gesture resulting from his newfound fascination with religion. A custom to show respect and mourn the death of a father in ancient times, it was rare to find any Maharashtrian Hindu shaving off all their hair anymore. Maharashtrians living in urban India (especially Brahmins) were prone to taking the shortest, most practical route and simply getting back to work.

This was also the reason that despite the migrant population from Mumbai, Pune and surrounding cities, there was no temple built by Maharashtrians in the UK. Sameer's web search had not yielded a Maharashtrian Hindu funeral direction company. But, during the 20 days since Sriram's death, Sameer had combed the internet for Hindu traditions and found this custom, head shaving, and much more.

Besides, Sameer's chief advisor on this subject now, was the funeral director-cum-priest Harshad *bhai* bumbling morbidly through the eulogy and lengthy Sanskrit narration of verses for the departed soul. By his own admission, it had been four decades since Harshad *bhai's* departure from India. He did not know anyone in the state of Maharashtra; and the state's capital Mumbai, for him, was just the tinsel town, where Bollywood film stars lived. But his credentials, advertised boldly on his website, (albeit with spelling mistakes) spoke of his extensive self-proclaimed, in-depth knowledge of handling all funerals from Tamil and Gujarati to Punjabi and Sikh. The words "Marathi" as the language spoken or "Maharashtra" as the region of India was missing on his website, but he had assured the grief-stricken Sameer that he was well equipped to handle everything, given his six years of experience in the business of funeral direction.

Through the funeral, Harshad *bhai* made sweeping generalizations on what "all Hindus always did" referring to Sameer as the "eldest son of the departed" and Dr. Ira Godse as just, "the widow".

The first meeting between Sameer and Harshad *bhai* had seen the latter insisting on a range of archaic "death of husband" customs from various parts of ancient India like she wear a plain, white saree, cover her head, first put on and then break glass bangles, wipe off the red dot on her forehead, get someone to snatch away the black and gold marital beads around her neck and so on.

Sameer had thankfully followed Ratnaprabha's advice and deleted these from the agenda. Ratnaprabha did not want another spectacle of her family and reason for sustained community gossip, once again caused by her poor son. Harshad *bhai* had also presented a list of "funeral *pooja* items" that Sameer was to procure. Unfamiliar with the Gujarati language, Sameer had gratefully accepted his "kind" offer to procure these items at a "special price just for Sameer, given his tragic loss." Harshad *bhai* said he would arrange for the *prasad* (holy snacks) that his friend, "a special *pooja* caterer" would do for a special price. Ira watched this long-drawn, increasingly flamboyant affair, a far cry from the brief, dignified farewell that the Dixit family gave her beloved grandma Saguna in Mumbai barely two years ago, conducted by her erudite priestess maternal aunt Pratibha. Too weary to protest, Ira had mutely witnessed the opulent saga. But when Harshad *bhai* tried to wheedle his way into "end-to-end management of the urn of ashes from London to the holy city of Varanasi", Ira tried to reason,

"Sameer, your father had never been to India since we got married in 1993. If you choose to immerse his ashes in a water body within England, we could try to seek permission to do it here. We don't know what he would have wanted, but this is just clearly what the funeral director wants…"

"Mum, this is what I want! Harshad *bhai* told me that Daddy's soul will not attain salvation till his ashes are scattered in the holy river. He will organize it as an extra service as part of his package."

The words "service" and "package" did not seem alien to Sameer but to Ira, with her ancestry deep in priesthood, they reeked of everything generations in her family had fought against. They had held their ground against the notion that the priest, solely on the pretext of his knowledge of the ancient scriptures, would be the fulcrum on which faith, religion, society, and custom would rest and thus, control the decisions and behaviours of families, especially when they were most vulnerable during tragic situations.

"Hinduism does not force you to do anything, people who want you to believe they are the interpreters would want you to, so that they can retain control over you," is what the priestess Pratibha and her grandma had always told Ira. But Sameer was in no mood to listen. Consumed by the rapid onslaught of sudden and half-baked information that had eluded him till recently, Sameer was gradually being indoctrinated into versions of Hinduism and outdated Brahmanical traditions that a host of other influencers wanted him to.

Ira had visited Varanasi as a tourist. She had read lately that it was now a tragic farce of the holy city – the succession of live pyres burning on the picturesque ghats, leaving behind pollutants in the river that people bathed in, a place crawling with local touts taking foreign tourists for a ride. Given Sameer's upbringing, his belief was about to be punctured, which Ira was afraid would cause him further trauma. It was then that Ira suggested that she and Sameer should travel to India together with the ashes.

Among the many aspects of living in the UK she had come to respect, was the British ability to lay down a process for everything, including the transfer of ashes to another country, and ensuring that everyone follows it. "Given the increased threat of terror attacks", the website stated the precise permitted material for the urn along with the documents to be carried to ensure that security and customs in both countries accorded due respect and did not insist on opening the urn.

Still a film aficionado, Ira noted what a contrast this smooth experience was to *"Saransh"*, the heart-wrenching 1984 Hindi film that depicted a father's ordeal of trying to claim his young son's ashes from custom officials in Mumbai, following his tragic death in a New York mugging incident. Sriram had not liked the cinema and had refused to enter one. Besides, Bollywood movies were not released that often in England then. Ira had still tried to catch a film occasionally, offering her respite from a life that had spun so much out of control. A year after she had moved to England, her teary eyes had followed the haunting image of the little girl in a red coat in "Schindler's List", humanizing the suffering she had read about in textbooks.

Through the funeral that refused to end, Harshad *bhai* extolled the virtues of a man he had never met in a Gujarati British accent. It wasn't that extreme a situation, but when Ira had first realised the gravity of Sriram's ailment and its aggravation by his mother's draconian dominance and over-protection, she likened her fate to a 1970 movie titled *"Khilona"*. As was common among families, refusing to accept any shortcoming in their offspring, the "cure" to anything in Indian society was typically – marriage. The bride, by magic, was supposed to bring about transformation in a situation that the parents had been unable to address, in Sriram's case, for 28 years. Sriram was never abusive or violent. On his good days, he could be described as gentle, well-mannered, polite, always following the rules. Unfortunately, on his bad days, of which there were many, he was quiet, withdrawn, and uncommunicative. His family chose to dismiss these saying,

"Sriram is under the weather today." This British term, best used to describe a mild cough or cold brought about by the change of weather, was among the many aspects Ira eventually accepted as Godse adaptations to life in Britain, only when it suited them.

So, right from a surprised Ira seeing just her father-in-law when she first arrived at Heathrow airport, to missing many of Sameer's school events and birthdays, "under the weather" it was for Sriram. His parents tried to compensate for their son's absence. Despite her petty, devious ways and dogmatic adherence to archaic customs, Ratnaprabha was a doting, hands-on grandmother. Even after Ira finally got her medical degree and Sriram slipped in and out of redundancy and temporary jobs, Prabhakar never once failed to make generous gifts in cash and kind.

"Maybe that's what my grandmother was thinking," Ira had consoled herself, especially during the early years of berating her fate. For it was Saguna, having realised that Omar was not good news after all, who had swung into action with her extensive community contacts and zeroed in on Sriram Godse, the son of a doctor from the UK. The reason cited in the turbulent Dixit family conference was,

"They are not like us; you won't be able to adjust."

"Going to school with whom the Brahmins called *itar jaati* (other castes) was permissible, inviting them over for Diwali was an act of compassion, and attending Muslim festivals and weddings was a supposed sign of progressiveness. But the thought of marriage to one, was best not touched!" Ira had retorted, her light-brown eyes flashing, during one such discussion about Ira's potential matrimonial matches.

Apart from brokering the marital alliance, Saguna's astute move was getting Prabhakar Godse to commit that they would not just "allow" Ira to study in the UK but would support her medical education. Ratnaprabha agreed, citing that being Brahmins after all, education runs in their blood.

They were relieved that socially awkward, melancholy Sriram, who had never had a relationship or had even dated, had bagged the "fair, slim, convent-educated" bride within the caste, an aspiration of every Brahmin parent at that time in urban Maharashtra. There was also the matter of their surname – Godse. Sharing a surname with Gandhi's assassin had been especially difficult in the 50s and 60s, the reason why Prabhakar preferred to embrace the anonymity offered by British life and ceased contact with the extended Godse family. By the 90s, the surname was not an issue.

Like other migrants who moved countries in the 1960s, thanks to infrequent trips home and expensive international calls, they blindly and strictly practiced an archaic version of their religion. The India they had left behind was unrecognizable, its cities, especially Mumbai, was a cosmopolitan blend of languages and religions. The country was unified not by the erstwhile independence movement, but a curious aspirational anglicization in language, attire, and new national obsessions – Bollywood and cricket.

In the name of TRADITION

Sriram spoke very little. When he first met Ira in Mumbai, fluent in English, well-read and sporting a pair of jeans and a sleeveless blue top as she got home from college to see the three Godses sipping tea in their living room, Sriram described her in a single wondrous word,

"Anglicised!" The fourth Godse (Sriram's sister Swati) was an enigma. During the wedding preparations, there was fleeting mention of Swati not being able to make it to India at such short notice. During her first Diwali in the UK, suffering from morning sickness that never seemed to leave her, Ira had been miserable. She was still getting used to assisting Ratnaprabha with her relentless household chores. Ratnaprabha had made an array of traditional Diwali delicacies. There was no compromise on the variety of sweets and savouries, but the tiny portions had Ira wondering if there was more in the kitchen. When morning sickness would leave her, she would get ravenously hungry and be ever so conscious of dipping into the little portions of food cooked daily. The ancestral Koknastha Brahmin traits of meticulousness and frugality (given their history of humble beginnings and eternal dependence on donations from benefactors of knowledge) were known. But Ira had never experienced frugality; and in the Godse household, she did, daily. Ratnaprabha insisted that as a new bride, Ira must dress in a silk saree, put on some of her wedding jewellery and draw the traditional *rangoli* designs outside their doorstep to welcome the Goddess of wealth to their home.

Not a fan of draping a heavy silk saree when she was nine-months pregnant, uncomfortable, and itchy, Ira obliged for the duration of the *Laxmi pooja* as Ratnaprabha laid out her own limited jewellery, and a few pounds in bowls next to her mini temple for the family to thank the Goddess of wealth for all that they were blessed with. Ira didn't mind the *rangoli* bit. It gave her a creative outlet and reminded her of the elaborate *rangoli* designs their cleaner Rakma *mavshi* made at their doorstep back in Mumbai. Used to wandering about in Mumbai, at college and then out with friends, the other big change was being cooped inside with the windows shut. The *rangoli* assignment gave Ira a chance to get a bit of fresh air. Engaged in embellishing the white *rangoli* design with bright turmeric yellow lotus curves and expertly serrated powdery green leaves, Ira had not noticed the nip in the air. Ira trooped back into the house proud of her artwork and announced to her in-laws, who she now referred to as *Aai* (mother) and *Baba* (father) as she was told to and as Sriram did.

"*Aai, Baba,* Sriram, come and see my *rangoli*. Let's keep it till *bhau beej* so that Swati *tai* can see it when she visits." Ira realised she had done something grossly wrong. Ratnaprabha had rushed on to the doorstep with a jug of water and splashed it across her intricate design shouting,

"This is England. You cannot be drawing *Swastikas* outside the doorstep. The neighbours are already hostile, they are wondering how Asians can afford such a house. Now they will think we are Nazis!" Baffled, it took the normally sharp-witted Ira a few moments to understand what the fuss was all about. The most favourable ancient symbol of the Hindus, the *Swastika*, in its mirrored form had been used by Hitler as the emblem of the Nazi party, their interpretation of the Aryan race. Ira had last seen the mirrored *Swastika* in her history textbook years ago in school, but had never ever, until now, associated the omnipresent Hindu *Swastika* with it.

"It's ok Ratna, the *Swastika* is used so commonly in India. Your prayer books have it too. Ira would not know that it is a sensitive issue," Prabhakar tried to reason. Nervously twisting the edge of her peacock blue silk saree, Ira mumbled softly, "Sorry."

Ratnaprabha, having washed off the *rangoli* completely, stormed back into the house shrieking,

"And Swati does not visit, even on *bhau beej, rakhee* or any other day. She, nor her black child are welcome here!" Sriram's face clouded at the mention of Swati. Without a word, he stepped away, locking himself in his room the rest of the evening, not even emerging for the auspicious *Laxmi pooja* which Ratnaprabha had expected the newlyweds to perform together as a couple.

In one instant, Ira was told to shut out the chapter of Sriram's beloved sister Swati. Except for the quaint annual *bhau beej* tradition of a brother presenting a gift to his sister after the *ovalni* ceremony, every other tradition was followed in the Godse house. Most critical among these were the days of fasting. Growing up, Ira had observed Omar and his family fasting through Ramadan. It was Omar's personal affair and would never interfere with anything else their bunch of friends did. While Ira sipped tea during their dates (flatly refusing to eat in his presence), she had never seen

In the name of TRADITION

Omar touching even a drop of water. That is why, the delicious *shirkorma* that Sakinabi used to make for *Eid* and send along for the Dixit family, tasted so much sweeter. Saguna had stopped fasting since she was diagnosed with diabetes. She had proclaimed that she did not need the fear of God to be able to exercise self-restraint. That did not stop her from ordering the cook Shanta *Kaku* to put in extra dollops of *tup* (clarified butter) in the *sabudana khichadi* she got packed for her trusted driver Abdul and his family during Ramadan. As with everything Saguna did, the gift came with valuable advice, "Abdul, tell Fauzia that she must eat her portion of the *khichadi* too, especially before she begins her day. You are in an air-conditioned vehicle all day and the children rest after school. But there is no respite for Fauzia with all her chores in this sweltering Mumbai heat. *Sabudana khichadi* is not just a tasty snack for us Maharashtrians to indulge in. When my grandmother and mother used to fast in the name of various Gods, this was the only meal they had in the day. And that is why, the *khichadi* is packed with the energy burst of the starchy sago, potatoes, butter, sugar, salt, peanuts, and coconut."

But years later, Ira was to fall in line with the Hindu calendar in the Godse kitchen, the holy days marked out, traditions to be followed, fasts to be observed, potatoes for the *khichadi* to be boiled separately, the salt, sugar, and oil for the fasting food to be stored on separate shelves and whatever else. Why this was to be done in the 90s in the United Kingdom, nobody knew, and nobody asked. Apparently, it is what Ratnaprabha Sathe's own family (before she married Prabhakar Godse in 1952) had always done and expected her daughter-in-law to do.

In this orthodox household, where fear reigned supreme, of breaking tradition, of a surname shared with an assassin, of the external English world which never accepted the migrants, had grown Sriram and Swati. Compounded by unnamed fears manifest due to his undiagnosed ailment, Sriram's fears died with him. At the funeral, Swati, who had retaliated with her fearlessness, sat mutely at the back of the chapel of rest, stone-faced, dressed in a long white kurta and leggings, having come to pay homage to her estranged, beloved brother. Next to her sat Leila in a formal black knee-length dress, her hair pulled back, her arm wrapped tightly around her mother. And thus, had ended the saga of the funeral.

Ira, Sameer and Sriram's urn of ashes stepped out of Mumbai's *Chhatrapati Shivaji Maharaj* International airport. The majestic, state of the art Terminal 2, its rows of immigration counters and tasteful pieces of art, were a proud entry into India, a far cry from the derelict infrastructure and deplorable corruption of the customs officials of a decade ago. Named after Chhatrapati Shivaji Maharaj, the brave 17th century Maratha king who fought against the Mughal invasions, the airport was the pride of Mumbai and one of the few acts in his name that this demi-God would have been proud of. But the image of India Ira wanted Sameer to see, soon dissolved. The journey from the airport to the Dixit home in Dadar West (which was a straight, one-hour route) took four, long hours.

"It is December 6th Madam, what do we do!" exclaimed the North Indian cab driver in Hindi.

"Oh! December 6th, 1992, the anniversary of Babri Mosque - Ayodhya," Ira sighed.

"No Madam, the Ayodhya dispute is in court. Looks like there will be a temple after all. But it doesn't affect our traffic," the taxi driver rolled down the glass and shouted an expletive in Hindi.

"Sorry Madam," he turned to look back at his clearly "foreign returned passengers" and launched into an explanation, "December 6th, 1956, is when Ambedkar died, and today, like they do every year, over 150,000 rowdy followers of the man are congregating at Dadar's Shivaji Park."

Ira sighed again, remembering a news article. She echoed softly,

"Oh yes. Members of the historically oppressed "lower" *dalit* caste had good reason to honour the memory of the pioneer who gave India its Constitution, his community of followers reserved places in education and jobs and a new religion in retaliation to the Hindu caste system that had relegated them to the lowest rung of society - Buddhism. These followers had not read his teachings. The annual usurping of trains and buses leading to Dadar, the filth on the streets, the rowdiness and noise is what remained, festering against the resentment harboured by the erstwhile "higher castes" for the positive discrimination they now faced due to the reserved seats in education and government jobs."

Having caught just part of the exchange given his shaky Hindi, Sameer's curiosity was piqued. "Dr. Ambedkar?"

Ira exhaled, "Yet another beacon of Maharashtra who rose to international fame, now reduced to a demi-God by elements fissuring division in his name". Sameer ran a quick web search and proclaimed, "Oh, there is a bust of Dr. Ambedkar at the London School of Economics (LSE) as he got one of his three doctorates from there."

"Once we are back from Varanasi, I'll show you where his home was and reminders of the other demi-Gods. The freedom fighter Savarkar, who is said to have escaped England by swimming across the English Channel, Phalke, who pioneered India's first motion film, Tilak and Gokhale, who established the education societies and all of them, have a connection with England…" Ira smiled wryly, but during the few seconds when she had thought that her son was back with his mother, he disappeared snapping,

"Mum! Harshad *bhai* said a widow should not move out so soon and avoid wearing red, green, and yellow. Anyway, I'm not interested in all these people who pandered to the Muslims. It is time to show some courage, like Nathuram Godse did in killing the man who pampered Muslims the most and gifted them a country and millions of rupees that funded their terrorism. Besides, I've booked myself in a hotel in Pune next week. I need to go and see Nathuram Godse's shrine…"

Chapter 3:

In the name of LINEAGE

Barely adjusting to the shock of a new relationship, not just with her silent, disengaged husband, but also a new country and the orthodox aspects of her own religion, Ira had discovered she was pregnant. On November 15, 1993, on the very day of *bhau beej* when Swati did not visit her brother, Sameer was born. The grandparents were delighted. Though not ideal given the child rearing, Ratnaprabha consented to Ira appearing for her A-level examinations the following year, and then enrol in a university to study medicine. She made it clear that she was meeting her side of the commitment, the promise her husband had made to Ira's grandmother, of supporting her medical education, if Ira followed all the traditions expected in the Godse household.

Despite a father who slipped in and out of depression, a domineering grandmother and a mother who was stretched to the bone, Sameer excelled at academics. On the joyous day of his university graduation, he introduced his family to Cahya. The grandparents maintained a cold distance, Ira was delighted. This was 2015 and the opinions of families did not count as much. With the spirited Cahya in their lives and Sameer in a well-paying job in London, these were the happiest years of Ira's life in the UK. Cahya introduced the Godses to the aspects of English life that they were always afraid to experience. One Friday evening, Cahya had sat at the dinner table at the Godse's house with her laptop, trying to book tickets for a revival of 'Evita'. Ira quickly agreed and with a little goading from Sameer, so did his grandfather.

"All of this must be quite expensive, and I won't be able to understand the accents. I'll be home with Sriram." Ratnaprabha announced her decision to stay at home, clearing away the bowls of homemade creamy Mango *Shrikhand* that they had just devoured. Ira had tried reasoning with her mother-in-law, hoping for Prabhakar's intervention. Prabhakar walked away into the living room. Sameer gave his mother a knowing stare and clicked his tongue. Cahya calmly entered the card details.

Prabhakar had thoroughly enjoyed the evening at the Dominion theatre, least concerned with the observation that they seemed to be the only people of colour in the audience. Ira was enchanted by the music, the grandiose, technical sophistication of the sets and for three memorable hours, to be transported to the life of the heroine in Argentina. As the cast exited after the final bows amidst the standing ovation, Ira put her arm around Cahya's shoulders, "That was wonderful Cahya and Sameer, thank you!" Taken aback and faintly embarrassed, Cahya smiled.

"Oh Mum!" Sameer gave Ira a stern look for this public display of affection, smiling to himself.

A few Fridays later, Sameer and Cahya concocted a meal of oven-grilled vegetables, roasted potatoes in rosemary and red wine sauce and risotto. At the table, they laid out resplendently with the exotic vegetarian recipes Cahya had downloaded, there was a separate plate for Sriram with his rice and *aamti*. Ratnaprabha always knew and Ira had come to realise that anything out of the ordinary, even a diversion from standard dinner, would trigger Sriram. If the routine was maintained, he was fine. Whether this was because the Godses only ate their simple vegetarian dinner and always had lentil curry or due to Sriram's mild autism, which Ira suspected much later, was never known. In any case, it was just easier to have the routine in place.

Cahya also joined the family for what was the closest to an outing - to listen to India's Prime Minister (PM) Narendra Modi speak to 60,000 Indians, the British PM David Cameron, and his saree-clad wife at Wembley Stadium in November of 2015. Never interested in politics but agreeing to tag along, Sameer stepped out of the stadium mesmerised by the collective passionate singing of India's national anthem amidst thousands of undulating dots of light across the stadium. The adulation of the people for their "statesman like leader" did not stop with the flashing of the mobile phone lights.

Amidst this sea of humanity, Sameer briefly encountered Raghav Swami. On hearing Sameer's full name, the man gave him a broad smile, "Mr. Sameer Godse, you speak such good Marathi despite growing up in the UK! Do visit when you come to India. You have a bright future in politics. Here is my card. And I'm writing down my personal mobile number." On a glossy business card streaked with saffron, Raghav scribbled his mobile number and patted Sameer on the back. Sameer politely smiled back and put the card into his wallet.

Though impressed by the emotive fervour, Sameer was far too engrossed in building his career, and in Cahya to care about Indian politics or what happened to religion - the Hinduism his family practiced, the Buddhism Cahya practiced or anyone else's.

But, on March 22, 2017, Cahya was speaking to Sameer on the phone while walking to Westminster station when the line got disconnected. Startled by a news alert, he tried calling back. Sameer died a thousand deaths, furiously texting Ira that Cahya was at Westminster and not reachable. Six had been killed and 49 injured as a van rammed into innocent bystanders. After 90 minutes, Cahya called from London Euston. She had missed the terrorist attack by a whisker, having boarded the train a few minutes prior. Through tears of relief, Sameer blurted,

"What gives this community the license to unleash such mindless terror!"

Two months later, Sriram was asked to visit his firm's Manchester office to collect a client's signature due to a pressing deadline. On that fateful May evening, he emerged from Manchester Victoria station, his thoughts as always on the next steps of the precisely outlined schedule. His head characteristically tilted at an angle, his now greying closely cropped hair accentuating his high forehead, Sriram had taken a few steps across the tarmac when he was jolted by the explosion.

Perplexed by the disruption in his accurate travel plan, his deep-set, sea green eyes darted frantically at the mayhem. All that registered was that people were running. His head abuzz, Sriram dropped the briefcase containing the signed documents and ran. Confused by the hyperactivity, his mind propelled him to escape towards a haven safer than the pandemonium.

Like the people screaming in terror, scampering towards the exit, Sriram ran too - but towards the Manchester Arena instead of away.

Inside the arena, he was engulfed by a wave of humanity screaming for help, children scrambling over chairs to be let out, limbs strewn, bodies of concert goers frozen at grotesque angles. Dizzy at the sight of blood, trembling, Sriram sank to the floor. For months later, he was consumed by the guilt of not being able to help, breaking out in sweat during nightmares, weeping in his room or apparently apathetic to anyone's attempts at conversation. With no visible injury, Sriram had been classified as "walking injured" and dispatched home.

Compounded by his undiagnosed mild autism, series of traumatic instances of bullying over the years, the loss of Swati - the only person who he was deeply attached to, Sriram suffered from post- traumatic stress disorder (PTSD), which ultimately led to his suicide in November, on Sameer's birthday. No-one realised the collateral damage caused by the horrific suicide bomb attack killing mainly children.

Devastated at seeing him crumble, was Ratnaprabha's unlikely outburst,

"For the terror unleashed by Muslims across the world, Muslims do not deserve this pandering, India gifting them Pakistan along with 55 crores of rupees instead of the *Akhand* Bharat that could have been and the liberties that the UK and US have given them." For the first time, Ira heard Ratnaprabha utter the term "*Akhand* Bharat" (Undivided India). Through a film of tears, Prabhakar reprimanded his wife with a tight squeeze of the edge of her saree. Ratnaprabha went quiet. But through her tirade at the 22-year-old Libyan terrorist, supposedly avenging deaths in Syria and blowing up the Manchester Arena, Sameer has caught on to something. Ira sat quietly, signing the paperwork that Cahya and Sameer had placed before her. With the sorrow had come a sense of relief, especially after the traumatic last six months. "This is euthanasia orchestrated by God", she thought, "whichever God one believes in, or not."

Sameer had grown up hearing stories about Ira's illustrious extended family of ancestors - India's first woman doctor, the founders of nursing institutions, social reformers who championed widow remarriage and more. From his father of course, Sameer had heard nothing. When young Sameer was put to bed by his grandfather, whenever Ira was working late evenings,

Prabhakar would read to him from a children's story book. In the sleepy afternoons, his grandmother would tell him exciting tales about the model king Ram, his army of monkey followers and how he conquered Sri Lanka to rescue his virtuous wife, queen Sita. But about where the Godses came from, he was told nothing. All family folklore seemed to start in 1964, the year his grandparents migrated to the UK. His aunt Swati was never mentioned. No photographs of her were allowed around the house. During the 13 days after his father's death (when his grandmother told him that they should keep an oil lamp burning day and night), Sameer scoured the internet for everything one could find about this surname. When he stepped out of his room for a meal, he asked, "Are we related to Nathuram Godse?"

"We are not, no relation at all," Prabhakar snapped.

"You may have all hidden it from me all these years, afraid as we Hindus have been, of everything, especially the Muslims who killed my father, but I know there is a cosmic connection. Nathuram Godse was hanged on November 15, 1949, for Gandhi's murder. On November 15, 1993, I was born as his reincarnation and on November 15, 2017, my father died and that was the sign from above for me, to rise and revive the memory of this great man and stop the appeasement of Muslims and the terror they have unleashed on the world," Sameer's voice rose in a passionate call to action. Sporting an uneven stubble having not shaved since Sriram's death as per the traditions that he had now suddenly started following, Ira shuddered at the transfiguration. The grandparents, aghast, attempted to reason.

"Of course we share a surname with Nathuram Godse. But we are not related. And suppose, given the deep claws of your internet, which seems to dig unknown graves and provide all the answers to your questions, if you do find an ancestor who links us, we are not interested in pursuing the connection. It helps no-one," Prabhakar shook his head vigorously, his dark brown eyes flashing.

"When I married your *Ajoba* (grandfather) in 1954, no family was willing to show the courage to give their daughter in marriage to a Godse. There was severe backlash against Brahmins after Gandhi*ji*'s assassination. When you go to Mumbai, your grandparents will tell you that the Dixit home faced its tense moments as well, especially given its proximity to *Savarkar Bhavan*. But that is history, please leave it there." Ratnaprabha tossed the rice

In the name of LINEAGE

and lentil mixture together on her plate, picked up a tiny pinch of salt and tousled it in with the rice grains. Since Sriram's demise, the light, un-spiced *varan* (lentil) and plain, white boiled *bhaat* (rice) had been the meal in the household. Ratnaprabha slowly put a tiny ball of *varan bhaat* into her mouth. She gazed at the Marathi calendar on the wall and spoke slowly,

"With poverty and the weddings of my sisters to deal with, my father thought that marrying off a daughter to a Godse with good prospects, was a compromise he should make. Gandhi*ji*'s assassination was being consigned to history books. But in 1964, Nathuram's brother Gopal Godse was released from prison, having served his sentence for his role in the conspiracy. There was a celebration in Pune where Lokmanya Tilak's grandson, Ketkar declared that he had heard about the conspiracy six months prior and had alerted the then Chief Minister of Mumbai-Kher. Once again, all hell broke loose. The case was re-opened."

"And then, I thought it was best to leave India and the associations with that surname. We avoided contact with other Godses. Leave them." Prabhakar concluded, thumping the walking stick that he now had to use.

Chapter 4:

In the name of NATIONALISM

Fascinated that he was finally getting to hear something related to his ancestry, Sameer would not let go of his intense internet search. Besides, every new finding was receiving laudatory responses from Sameer's new mentor. For unbeknownst to anyone, Sameer had been having a series of conversations with the enigmatic saffron-clad Raghav Swami."

During their lengthy calls, Raghav had managed to convince Sameer about the "cosmic design" behind the November 15 occurrences. Raghav had also told him that his saffron army was waiting to garland their emerging charismatic leader.

"Mr. Sameer Godse, take yourself back to the magical atmosphere of the Wembley Arena, where I first caught a glimpse of you. Amidst that crowd of 60,000 patriots, my third eye spotted the powerful energy that your countenance radiates. When you told me your surname, it was just a reiteration of my mystical talent in identifying inspirational leaders. When you told me about the tragic martyrdom at the hands of Muslims of your late father, Nathuram's namesake on the date of your birth, my arms rose in prayer to Lord Rama himself. The legal war for our beloved Lord Rama to reside in his rightful place of birth in Ayodhya continues. One day, the jubilation of that temple will warm the hearts of true Hindus. My Lord has told me in my dream, that a certain boy, tall, fair, handsome, well spoken, will build another temple for Nathuram, not just in India but also in England!"

The trauma of his father's death, the lure of visibility and Raghav's clever imagery had mesmerised Sameer. His obsessive web searches confirmed the rising popularity of Godse supporters in pockets.

Trapped in the scorching flames of indoctrination, Sameer was now seeking validation from his grandfather. Pursing his lips, his white fingers trembling, Sameer rose and began pacing the room, blurting,

"Do you people know that the word "Godse" was banned in the Indian Parliament since 1956, and it took an appeal from an MP, Hemant Godse (who also claims he is not related to Nathuram) and finally, in 2015, the word Godse was permitted to be used as long as it is not in context of Nathuram!"

Prabhakar sighed, reluctantly accepting that brushing away history would not work for Sameer, and said,

"Pre-independence, Brahmins – moderates and pacifists, had their differences. The Ranades, Gokhales, Joshis, and Agarkars believed that the way forward was through collaboration with the British on legal and administrative matters, and education. Others, the Chapekar brothers, Savarkar, even Tilak and later Apte, Godse, believed in the radical way. They still overcame their differences and came together to support the freedom struggle. It is thanks to their pursuit of encouraging men (and the intense effort on tackling severe social barriers to educate women) to learn English, study law and medicine that we, so many of us Indians, are here in England today." Sameer was in no mood to listen to the stories of the glorious achievements of the moderates. He had heard enough of these from his mother and his great-grandmother during his India trips. His voice rose,

"Nathuram Godse's ashes are preserved in an urn in Pune. It was his wish that they be immersed in the *Sindhu* (Indus) river that flows through Pakistan after Pakistan becomes part of India again one day. The Gandhi who gave in to every Pakistani demand and even went on to fast so that they get given a pot of money which they used to kill Hindus for...even Gandhi's ashes were not allowed to be immersed in Pakistan! We sit here, inert against the terror of Islam. There are people trying to preserve the dream of *Akhand* Bharat; he dreamt of what *Ajji* you referred to. Don't think I didn't notice. There are calls for a temple of Nathuram to be built in Gwalior and Meerut, but people are afraid to even praise him in public. I'm not afraid, I was born to fulfil these dreams!"

Ratnaprabha and Prabhakar had lost everything, a daughter to a scandal, Sriram to this mindless bombing, and now Sameer, trying to rake up a connection. In a desperate attempt to hold him back, Prabhakar asked,

"What does Cahya think of this? You wanted to get engaged. You were due for a promotion at work? You were both saving to buy a house. In fact, we held back your birthday money so that we can contribute towards your house. This house, of course, is yours. But we understand and appreciate that you and Cahya would want to live in a house of your own." Sameer scoffed,

"Oh, the Buddhists are the worst pacifists. Cahya gives me some mumbo jumbo about how Gandhi practiced the essence of Buddhism and his nonsense about how "An eye for an eye makes the world go blind!" Pausing dramatically, Sameer, flipped open his laptop, pointed to his recent research and continued his passionate speech,

"Nathuram Godse had no problem with Gandhi. In fact, he followed Gandhi's call to boycott western education and dropped out. But later, Gandhi sided with the Muslims, giving them everything they wanted and emasculating the Hindus. This is what the world is doing today. *Ajoba*, you have been paying taxes in the UK since the 1960s. You tell us how so many Hindu doctors contributed to building the NHS. From the taxes we pay, the UK government subsidizes university education, offers student loans. Fine, I availed of a student loan as well. But I worked hard at university, I pay taxes too. And I don't know anyone in our Hindu social circle who doesn't. But look at the ilk of the Manchester bomber. Student loan money used to build bombs! The world needs to know the difference between them and us and we need to show some teeth like our ancestors did.

Given all her mixed baggage, what will Cahya know about the purity of race and religion that we Brahmins have! She wanted to come to India for the holy immersion. I told her Hindu women don't go traveling with unrelated men till they are married. Harshad *bhai* told me this is not in our culture. Even Mum came to England only after she was married to Daddy!" Ira looked up at Sameer. His shocking statements stank of radicalization and patriarchy that even Ira's grandmother had disapproved of. His secular, egalitarian upbringing seemed to have vanished. Even more painful was the nonchalant dismissal of the girl he deeply loved, leaving nothing more to be said. Tears streaming down her cheeks, Ira got up saying she had to pack. Sameer's comment about the "purity of his Hindu Brahmanical lineage" continued to ring in her ears.

The distinctions among religion, tradition, what the scriptures said, what self-proclaimed messengers chose to interpret and what followers understood were now being buried, propelled by a single force more powerful than all of them put together – *politics*.

After the immersion of Sriram's ashes in the river in Varanasi, Sameer and Ira visited the temple. Had it not been for Ira's palms clasped in a firm *Namaste*, her head shaking and her firm assertion of *"Nahin, dhanyawaad"* (No, thank you) to every person who approached them, Sameer would have been caught in the web of rituals, flowers, hotels, and many other "authentic" aspects of Hinduism being touted. Given his unmistakable British accent, the price of everything on offer had tripled, which had been the main reason that Ira had wanted to accompany him to Varanasi.

In the evening, they experienced what brings so many tourists to Varanasi. On the deck of a bright blue wooden boat, mother and son sat along with 30 other visitors. As the sun set on the Ganga, a row of priests ascended onto platforms by the riverside, each waving a tower of oil lamps in rhythm to the 45 minutes of holy chants, the *Ganga-Aarti*, as hundreds of visitors watched. Ira was mesmerised by the Sanskrit words sung in such unison, the terracotta lamps afloat in the dark swirls of the river witness to the fierce saffron-yellow of the priests' oil lamps offered to the tiny twinkles in the sky, as if beckoning the sea of humanity, to be one. The aesthetic orchestration of this experience was sure to transport both believers and non-believers to tranquillity. As he sat beside her on the gently rocking wooden boat, sullen and silent, Ira mouthed a silent prayer to thank the Almighty for having Sameer in her life.

The morning after they returned to Mumbai, he set off to Pune, refusing to let Ira accompany him, and clamping down consideration of a stay with her aunt Pratibha in Pune, curtly declaring he was on a "mission" and not to "socialise." He had booked a hotel for two nights for what he described as his "pilgrimage to visit Nathuram Godse's shrine".

But after just a night, he checked out and returned to Mumbai. During Sameer's past rare visits to India, Ira's parents Damodar and Priyamvada had tried to pamper their only grandchild. Brimming over with pride at his excellent university grades and then a coveted London job, the subject of

Sameer held prime place during Priyamvada's social interactions. In the past, Sameer had been warm and communicative and enjoyed the attention. This time, he refused to touch Priyamvada's *Chilli Paneer* and *Chicken Manchurian*, spicy, deep fried popular Indo-Chinese inventions that his *Aaji* in London, had no idea existed! Damodar's suggestions of shopping at the city's bustling malls or dinner to sample Mumbai's eclectic global fare, were dismissed.

He was naturally very close to his paternal grandparents. With the Dixits, given the limited contact, he would not speak his mind. On this trip, he was polite but cold. Ira gently asked him why he was rejecting their affection. Sameer exploded,

"*Ajji* and *Ajoba* in England are devastated. I've lost a father and I'm angry with the single community that is causing these disasters. You are not behaving like a Brahmin widow. I told you what Harshad *bhai* had said. Instead of telling you what is apt as per custom, your parents want to take us to sample Lebanese fare at an upmarket Mumbai restaurant!" Exasperated with Sameer's misguided take on this Brahmin custom, especially fuelled by a British immigrant, self-styled, commercially-driven priest's views on what an "ideal widow" should do, Ira made another attempt to show Sameer the essence of Hinduism. She called out,

"Abdul *chacha*, could you unlock *Ajji's* library please? I want to show Sameer something."

Saguna's faithful driver had been advised to stop driving after his eye surgery. Saguna had promptly given him a new set of responsibilities within the house. In the months that followed her passing, Damodar had continued his wages and funded his son's college tuition. Abdul led them to the library. Next to the photographs of the community's greats, there was now Saguna's picture in her crisp, white nine-yard saree. A thin sandalwood garland speckled with tiny pink flowers hung from the frame. Without being asked to, Abdul brought in a dust cloth and wiped down the intricately carved armrests of the deep brown wooden chairs. He then pulled out a large, grey-blue checked handkerchief from his pocket, quietly wiped the edges of the gilt edged, curvaceous frame of Saguna's image. Sameer ignored him while Ira's eyes followed Abdul's quiet shuffling out, as he wiped away what Ira knew to be a silent tear in the name of her grandmother. She turned to Sameer,

"Sameer, I'm no Sanskrit scholar as you know, but Saguna *Panji* was, and I'm going to tell you what she told me and practised all her life. Our scriptures, the *Vedas,* do not say that a woman should not be educated. Child marriage was prevalent in the 1800s because life expectancy was so low, especially among women who died during childbirth, given the lack of medical advancement. Somewhere along, the priest class (yes, the Godses, Dixits and the entire community) had generations who had the knowledge of Sanskrit and thus access to religious texts." Attempting to bring perspective to Sameer's recent glorification of violence and his loathing of the "moderates", Ira opened a yellowed page of a text showing the outline drawings of four men. "Look Sameer, the caste system was prescribed to specify the vocation of each community. The *Brahmins* imparted knowledge and guided the community, the ones with physical strength *(Kshatriyas)* protected territory, the ones with entrepreneurial spirit *(Vaishyas)* excelled in trade and the *Shudras* did all the work that involved manual labour. A father passed on skills to his children and over time, these compartments became watertight."

As Ira explained how practices with the intent of maintaining good hygiene and sanitation (at a time when sanitizers did not exist), then hardened into the evil of untouchability, Damodar walked into his mother's favourite room. He flipped open a metallic chair stacked against the wall, dusted off the seat with a kerchief and sat down, close to Sameer. Abdul appeared as if by magic at the doorway, dust cloth in hand. Damodar shook his head. Ira silently raised her palms to thank him in a namaste. Abdul shuffled away. Picking up where Ira left off, Damodar spoke of how the caste system was then exploited by several members of the Brahmin community.

"It suited their purpose and with exclusive access to the texts, they preached a host of evils, in the name of the texts that they knew others could not read! Apart from the horrific untouchability, which unfortunately is still prevalent in parts of rural India today, the system caused suffering to women, especially widows. My own grandmother and others, widowed in her generation, were forced to shave off their hair, wore a deep maroon garment that covered them from head to toe all their lives, were debarred from all auspicious ceremonies and were often ill-treated and exploited by their own families," Damodar got up pointing to the photographs adorning the walls. "These gentlemen, Jyotiba Phule, Vishnu Shastri Pandit, Mahadev Ranade, fought for and implemented widow re-marriage, girls' education and making women self-sufficient in the 1860s.

They were the true followers of the Hindu religion and my mother brought us up this way! The 13th day Hindu ceremony preaches that one should honour the memory of the departed, pray for peace and insists that the people left behind should resume their day-to-day activities. We have lost a son-in-law too, Sameer. We can only try and help you and Ira resume your life without your father," Damodar smiled lovingly at his grandson.

Sameer mumbled something about having to pack for Meerut soon and walked away.

The next morning, Sameer was on a flight to Delhi, which would be followed by a three-hour drive to Meerut. He had refused Damodar's offer to drop him off at the airport and responded to Ira's attempt at an embrace with an awkward pat on her arm. Ira turned back from the door, sighing,

"Let's give him a few weeks *Baba*. Once we are back in London, he'll have his work and Cahya, his routine." Ira had willed everything to be fine. Until, she encountered, held in place by a spoon on the gleaming black glass tabletop, a sheet of paper with Sameer's cursive writing in blue ink.

"Mum, I went to Pune to search for my Godse roots. There is no shrine, no temple to Nathuram, no guided tour or guidebook. In fact, the *Shaniwar Peth* address I had procured where Nathuram lived in a single room and ran a tiny tailoring business, does not even have a signboard that he lived there. It is the same with the place where Nathuram and his business partner Narayan Apte ran the offices of two newspapers. These places have been replaced by mundane, ordinary commercial establishments. The people in these shops don't bother honouring the memory of the two who gave their lives for the cause of *Akhand* Bharat!

Sad. I then went to the Ajinkya Developers office at Shivaji Nagar. There are pizza places, up-market stores selling international brands right there. Ajinkya is the grandson of Nathuram's brother Gopal Godse who passed away in 2005. I was told Ajinkya was traveling. He runs his real estate business there.

Even if I were to travel to Pune again and try to meet anybody from the family, they are unlikely to maintain ties. My grandparents ran away from the legacy to hide in England over 50 years ago, never bothered keeping in touch and still insist there is no relation. Why would anyone bother with us?

Anyway, when I asked, an office attendant took me to the inner room and showed me the glass case displaying the single urn containing Nathuram Godse and Narayan Apte's ashes. Also on display is the frayed white shirt that Godse wore to Gandhi's final s*abhaa* on January 30th, 1948. Next to this rests the volume of the *Bhagwat Geeta* he carried in his hands when he was hanged.

The attendant told me that the family and a few others come to pay homage on November 15th, the day of martyrdom every year. He showed me the illuminated map of *Akhand Bharat* (with Pakistan and Bangladesh very much part of the complete India) and Nathuram Godse's photo in the centre—these are all used for the ceremony. At least this was something. But overall, this city where both Godse and Apte came from, is not interested in honouring them.

Bustling malls, restaurants, burgeoning industry and educational institutions, people seem to be just interested in getting on with their livelihoods.

There is no active movement to build a temple. There is nothing to be done in Pune. But I have been fortunate enough to have been handpicked by Raghav Swami to fulfil the mission in Gwalior and Meerut where people are showing more courage and are actively doing something to keep Nathuram alive. I am privileged to have been chosen as the emerging leader of this journey. In fact, I have been asked to deliver the keynote address at the rally they are holding to kick off the movement. Don't bother looking for me. In fact, you should return to London at the earliest and look after your-in-laws like a good Hindu widow is duty bound.

Sameer."

The note slipped out of Ira's fingers as she sank to the floor.

Chapter 5:

In the name of SOBRIETY

London, Friday, January 12th, 2018.

Ira was back at work. She had not heard from Sameer since the note he left behind. He did not answer her calls. She continued to track his social media posts and text him every two days. Both indicated that he was still in India. He had become unresponsive to Cahya's attempts to reach him.

Like every week, since she and Sameer moved out of the Godse house years ago, she made the trip to Croydon to meet her in-laws. The schedule had been as such - Prabhakar would pick Sameer up from the bus stop after school. The doting Ratnaprabha would have Sameer's favourite snack ready for him. Upon finishing work, Ira would join them for the evening meal. Sameer looked forward to these evenings more than any other, having the entire family listen to him as he narrated stories of his adventures at school that week and enjoying his grandmother's delicious, Maharashtrian dishes.

By the time Ira arrived, Ratnaprabha would have a steaming pot of the sweet jaggery, sour tamarind and spicy combination of the *masale bhaat* (spiced rice) on the kitchen platform.

Nestling in its shadow, would be her tiny traditional container of homemade *tup* (clarified butter). Sameer had been told; this was a must at Maharashtrian weddings. Sameer's arrival every Friday was of no less importance than a wedding in the family! With the meal nearly ready, Ira would scrub her hands and face in the downstairs bathroom, wash her feet and enter the kitchen to lay the table. Ira had learned to cook from her mother-in-law, but the norms of laying out a proper Maharashtrian *thali* meal were ingrained into her by her grandmother.

On the morning of a *Gudi Padwa* festival lunch when Ira was eight, Saguna had likened the silver plate to the clock. At the stroke of 12, you served a pinch of salt. At 11, went the slice of lemon, at 10, went a knob of the fresh coconut, green chilli, and coriander chutney with just a dash of lemon juice, sugar and salt. At 9, went the finely chopped cucumber *Koshimbir*, with just the gentle touch of peanut powder and the cumin seed seasoning. On the right side of the plate, at the stroke of 1 went the turmeric potato vegetable at 2, the pulses. The bowl of lightly spiced *taak* made from fresh yoghurt was placed off centre between the nine and ten. The *masale bhaat* mould went at the stroke of six, the *papads* and sticky rice crispy *kurdais* sprinkled at the stroke of 3.

Years later in the Godse kitchen, Ira served the meals just as they should be. Little Sameer engaged with the clock metaphor as he relished the hot fluffy *puris* that his grandmother rolled out on her wooden *polpaat* and Ira deep fried. Even if Sriram ate with his son and now estranged wife Ira, his plate at his corner of the dining table always had his white rice and bowl of *aamti*, the only way he would have it.

Sameer's grandmother's delicacies were among the many dishes he would never taste elsewhere. The "Curry houses" sprouted across the UK served mainly North Indian or Bangladeshi fare. He didn't particularly like what his English friends relished at the local "Lord's Curry house" they frequented– bright orange curries with roughly cut, large chunks of vegetables drowning in oodles of oil, and a small dash of salt and spice. But what he went to the "Curry houses" for, were lamb *kebabs* and chicken wings, which were strictly prohibited in the Godse home. In fact, Sameer had never let his grandmother get wind of his other culinary favourites including the hearty full English served at his university cafeteria, piping hot sausages and greasy bacon, and how he relished steak.

In the pantheon of God images and mini statues in Ratnaprabha's little temple in the corner of her kitchen, was a lovely tiny brass likeness of the boy Krishna with his favourite pet – *Kamdhenu*. Through her stories,

Ratnaprabha had impressed upon Sameer how the cow *Kamdhenu* fulfilled all of Krishna's wishes, and how it was a sin to harm cows. Always the bearer of an alternate view, due to her upbringing that encouraged evaluation of practices, Ira had sat Sameer down during a "juice break" punctuating one of their weekend shopping trips during his childhood,

"Sameer, this is not to question your grandmother's faith. But I always tell you what my grandmother taught me, to try and understand why we do something before we do it. Like your grandmother does, mine also told me delightful tales of the little prankster Krishna stealing butter from the milkmaids in Gokul. If you look closer at these stories, selling milk-based products seems to be the primary occupation in this community of cowherds. So naturally, killing for short-term gain was to be avoided for the long-term welfare of this community. By nurturing cows, feeding them well and treating them with affection, the community was building strong resources like *Kamdhenu* (*Kaam* means desire and *Dhenu* means cow in Sanskrit), who would continue to produce milk and ultimately help them realise all they desired. It does not mean that those who eat beef are doing anything wrong. With the cold climate that England and other countries in this part of the world have, very few vegetables grow here. Years ago, it was not possible to import vegetables. In those years, it is but natural that nurturing livestock was a predominant source of income and meat was the main form of food available," explained Ira, smiling at Sameer's wide eyes soaking in everything he was being told. She tousled his soft, dark curls and concluded,

"One last thing, Sameer. When you go to your friends' birthday parties and when you grow up and go out with friends on your own, you should know about the dishes commonly eaten here. It is very important for you to blend in, not judge the people around you and not have them judge you. Your grandmother will not approve, but I would like you to taste all types of food and decide what you like." Having absorbed the gist of his Mum's attempt at balancing conflicting standpoints, the bright-eyed, fast growing little boy downed his juice and ran off to the bowling alley.

Diplomatic as he was, he continued to enjoy a vegetarian feast at the Godse home and try out everything conceivable outside of the home. Ira knew how much Sameer valued this time and tried her best to never miss a Friday evening at the Godse house. On good days, Sriram would join in the conversation and even play Sudoku with Sameer, but on "under the weather" days, he would not step out of his room. Over time, Sameer learnt to not ask about his father's presence. But whenever he was present, Sameer would be warm and respectful towards him.

But on that Friday in January of 2018, when Ira made her way to Croydon, the shadow of gloom refused to leave the Godse house. The small, sparsely furnished living room was tidy as usual. The kitchen, usually buzzing with activity, be it a pressure cooker whistling away unleashing the aroma of lentils and rice or the whirr of a blender whipping up fresh garlic and groundnut chutney, was numb, echoing the pain of its chief occupant – Ratnaprabha.

After Ira and Sameer moved out and when Sameer went to university and could not make it home on Fridays, the sole aim of Ratnaprabha's existence had been to cook three hot meals for Sriram. Even on his "under the weather" days, Sriram would not miss mealtime and neither he, nor his mother liked any digression from what was to be eaten at these specific meals. Breakfast was one of four: *poha* (puffed rice), *upama* (semolina spiced version), *sheera* (semolina sweet version) or *sabudana khichadi* (made for Ratnaprabha's various fasts). Lunch was a dry vegetable dish, lightly seasoned with Maharashtrian spices, a mildly spiced lentil curry, a traditional Maharashtrian salad with a hot ghee and cumin seasoning, plain white rice, a *chutney*, and fresh *polis* (thin wheat flatbread) rolled and roasted daily. Dinner was the same as lunch with a different dry vegetable or pulses dish and lentil curry.

On a nail drilled into the wall next to the refrigerator, hung a Marathi version of the English calendar with the Indian festivals marked out on specific dates. As a child, Sameer used to be fascinated with the pen and ink outlines in the squares on specific dates – a baby Krishna with a pot of butter on his birthday, Ganpati, the elephant God on his, and more. Ratnaprabha would diligently follow these squares on her calendar and the customs each demanded. According to this calendar, the *Sankranti* festival fell on January 14, 2018. The woman Ira had known in the last two decades, would have been at the stove stirring a pot of *gul* (jaggery) and *til* (sesame seeds), pouring the hot mixture onto a plate. Upon cooling, the sticky, sweet mixture would be cut into tiny squares, and arranged systematically on a stainless-steel platter, ready to be handed over to each family member on *Sankranti* day with the message of amicability *"Tilgul ghya, goad bola,"* With the exchange of these sweets, let us exchange sweet words throughout the year. Apart from small steel containers for Prabhakar and Ira to share with their work colleagues and Sameer at school, women from the local Indian community would arrive at the Godse house for the traditional *haldi kunku* ceremony on *Sankranti* evening. Paper plates with *tilgul* and a grated fried potato *chivda,* seasoned with dried green chillies, would be passed around amongst the joyous chatter of women, dressed in black and gold sarees. On Ira's first *Sankranti* in 1994, Ratnaprabha had organised the biggest of her *haldi kunku* events to show off her new daughter-in-law to all the Maharashtrian Hindus the Godses knew across the UK. In the years that followed, Ira's British friends from work and the mothers of Sameer's various school friends were invited too.

But in January of 2018, there was silence. With a vacant look in her eyes, Ratnaprabha sat at the dining table.

Like Ira often did on her Friday visits, she arranged the fresh fruit she had brought along in the designated fruit drawer in the refrigerator. She noticed that they were running out of milk and sweetener for Prabhakar's tea. She measured out rice in a small steel bowl and into a colander. To this, she added half a bowl of *mung* lentil, washed the mixture in the kitchen sink and left it to drain at its edge. She heated a few tablespoons of oil in a pan. From Ratnaprabha's round steel tin of assorted spices, she added a tiny spoonful of mustard seeds and a pinch of asafoetida. To the spattering mixture, she added a heaped tiny spoonful of turmeric powder and switched off the flame. Then went in the washed rice and dal, a pinch of salt, the *goda* masala and a spoonful of frozen peas. With all this poured into Ratnaprabha's pressure cooker along with double the quantity of water, the *dal khichadi* was on its way. She nodded at Ratnaprabha, still staring at the calendar on the wall and said,

"*Aai, khichadi,* cooker..." Ratnaprabha nodded out of habit. She was the one who had imparted these cooking lessons to the teenage Ira. Rice, dal khichadi x 3 pressure cooker whistles, potatoes x 5. Ira walked across to the neighbourhood grocery store. Back in 30 minutes, she laid out three plates for a bare, simple meal of khichadi, pickled mangoes, and yoghurt. The three of them ate in silence, for anything they had to say would touch the raw memories of Sriram's death or the piercing pain of Sameer's absence. Ira washed up, placed the plates on the soft muslin cloth, cut out of one of Ratnaprabha's worn-out sarees, and went to pick up her coat to leave.

Prabhakar followed her to the door and murmured,

"Ira, your *Aai* seems to be angry with her Gods. I have never seen her miss her daily prayers, her fasts, her *pooja*s, her customs and her insistence on making the precise, prescribed dish for every Hindu festival." Ira's grief found respite in her work, Prabhakar's in his reading and watching the news. Ratnaprabha only had her religion and her son to occupy her time. Always soft spoken, Prabhakar's voice quivered as he clung on to the only visitor they had in the past four weeks. An old nurse from his workplace had stuck a card under the door offering her condolences as she did not want to disturb him during his time of mourning. When he retrieved the card, he wished she had pressed the doorbell and stepped in for a cup of tea.

"I will come over again next Friday *Baba*. You take care," Ira tightened the belt of her coat and stepped out into the crisp, cold January air and drove to Islington, just a short drive at this time of the night. During the stillness of that evening, she had missed a few calls. She opened her voicemail. The first was Claire. The voice recording was chirpy and long,

"Hello Ira! Hope everything went off as planned in India. It's so good to have you back. Call me back soon. I was about to book us tickets for the Saturday night movie. *"In Between"* is out and I couldn't have watched it without you. I know it's been a tough ride and it's time for you to smile a bit…" Not surprised but touched by Claire's concern, Ira sent her a message saying she'd call her back the next day.

She opened the second voicemail,

"Hello Ira, this is Kritika Sane. We met at your house last year and the year before during the *Sankranti haldi kunku*, remember? My, I will never forget the taste of the soft *tilgul vadis* your mother-in-law made. Do send me the recipe! We've just moved into our new house, please do come over any time between 5 pm and 7 pm on Saturday. Here's the address and oh yes, we girls have decided on a *Sankranti* theme, will look great in the selfies. So, wear black with yellow if you can. Do hope to see you!"

Surprised by the invitation, Ira wondered how Kritika had procured her phone number. Among the additions to Ratnaprabha's *haldi kunku* event over the years, had been women from Maharashtra who had moved to the UK sometime after the turn of the century. This wave of migration was characterized by technology professionals, grown up in the India Ira had left behind to what she observed "anglicise further". But this wave also brought with it a renewed tendency to rigorously practice customs and celebrate festivals with a new dimension – the need to display all that transpired during these interactions on social media.

Apart from her mother-in-law's annual *Sankranti* event, which she had helped organize for most of her adult life, invitations for Ira from the Maharashtrian community were few and far between. This was mainly because several of the men from this diaspora were employed by Indian companies that had set up operations in the UK. The wives of these work colleagues met regularly and the spate of social dos continued. But Sriram did not fall into this category, and as a couple, they did not fit into this framework. Ira had met some of these women at Ratnaprabha's *poojas* and from the social media friend requests that usually followed.

Drained, Ira was unable to visualise herself in a selfie, posing with the band of saree-clad women. She decided to decline the invitation. The next morning, Ira was awoken by the persistent ringing of the telephone. It was Kritika.

"Ira, did you get my message? I've come to your house two years in succession, but you haven't seen our new house! Please come!"

Ira was too tired to point out that she hadn't seen Kritika's old house either, or technically, the Godse house was not hers. Instead, she said politely,

"Thank you for the invitation, Kritika. But sorry, I won't be able to make it this evening. Also, how did you get my number?"

"Oh, I called Ratna *Kaku's* landline to invite her. Prabhakar *kaka* answered and told me she's been unwell and won't be able to make it. So, I asked for you, and he said you were out, but gave me your mobile number. If *Kaku* cannot make it, at least you should," Kritika was very persistent. Ira noticed that years after she and Sriram had separated, the Godses refused to acknowledge the fact. If anyone found out and really dug deep into why Ira and Sameer lived in an apartment, Ratnaprabha's response had been because it was closer to Ira's hospital and Sameer's school. Trying to explain the separation to Kritika two months after Sriram's demise, seemed unnecessary. Instead, Ira said,

"Thanks again Kritika. But I have a friend from work coming over. I'll come over some other time." Kritika would not let go. The return invitation was a box she wanted to tick and get out of the way, having enjoyed the Godse's hospitality two years in succession.

At this, Kritika's shrill voice touched a new high, "Oh, is that the only problem? In India, guests of guests are our guests. Please bring her over and even if it is for a short time, make it! In fact, last year my sister was visiting and Ratna *Kaku* invited her too. My sister was so impressed how Ratna *Kaku* follows every tradition here. She picked up some nuances of the festival from *Kaku*. She's so busy with her job in Bangalore, she doesn't have time for *haldi kunkus*. Now that was true. Whether it was the Dixit home in India or the Godse home in London, somebody's houseguests were always invited. There was nothing more for Ira to say, and she knew Claire would jump at the opportunity to get into one of Ira's outfits and tuck into a delicious Indian snack. So, at 6 pm, dutifully dressed in black and yellow, Claire and Ira stepped into Kritika's home. Dressed in Ira's long black full-sleeved kurta with golden front buttons and embroidery at the neckline, Claire carried herself with style.

Sweeping Ira's shimmering yellow and orange silk *dupatta* across her shoulders, Claire dutifully removed her shoes at the entrance, scanned the room and settled herself cross-legged on the rug laid out at the edge of the living room. The place was teeming with Indian women in black sarees in a range of fabrics – heavy silk *Kanjivarams* with wide, yellow borders, gently flowing chiffons in floral designs, the characteristic *Paithani* with woven gold patterns. The women sported heavy gold necklaces, three-layered strings of pearls, sprigs of artificial flowers and jingling bangles. Soon, Ira was lost in new introductions and inevitable connections from Mumbai. She knew she did not have to worry about Claire. For years, Ira had marvelled at Claire's ability to make her way into an unfamiliar social setting, introduce herself in her booming voice, and eventually endear herself to anyone who was in the room.

"Attribute it to my part Irish, part Scottish genes and that my British grandfather did a stint in India," Claire would laugh whole-heartedly. It was no surprise when half an hour later, Claire was seen balancing a paper-plate with *til gul*, potato *chivda* and a *samosa*, explaining the context of the *Sankranti* festival to Kritika's Spanish neighbour.

"In the olden days, women in India did not step out of their homes. Life was tough with no gadgets, usually large households, cooking in large volumes and pots of drinking water to carry. These *haldi kunku* events were created to give women an opportunity to socialise, dress up and let their hair down a bit. *Sankranti* is celebrated in different regions of India and is known by various names. Scientifically, dark colours absorb and retain heat. As this is a winter festival, black is worn. In fact, this is the only festival where wearing black is allowed, as it is otherwise considered inauspicious. The hostess applies *haldi* (turmeric, an antiseptic) and *kunku* (vermillion powder) on the foreheads of the guests and off we go with the return gift called a *vaan*!" Claire concluded her sermon. Claire had attracted quite an audience.

Ira had done her polite bit of socialising and signalled to Claire that they should get going. They sought out Kritika in the crowd.

"Kritika, I got a Ganesha statue from the *Siddhi Vinayak* temple in Mumbai, and I thought it might be a nice addition to your lovely new home," Ira proffered the gift.

"Oh, that's wonderful. *Siddhi Vinayak* has a special place in our hearts. We had a *pooja* this morning, let's put it in the *dev ghar* (mini temple at home) and you can take the *prasad* too," Kritika led the way into an alcove next to her dining room. Claire followed. Suddenly, Kritika turned to Ira, switched from English to a rapid, conspiratorial whisper in Marathi. Ira handed the gift bag to Kritika and turned to Claire, "We are late. Let's get going," and then turned to Kritika,

"We need to leave Kritika."

Ira and Claire stood in the hallway, joining a row of women who were ready to leave. Kritika had returned with an ornate peacock shaped silver box with the *haldi* and *kunku* powders, and a bulky polythene blue bag. She applied the *haldi* and *kunku* on each woman's forehead and handed them a small silver-orange goody bag containing glass bangles, a packet of red

In the name of SOBRIETY

bindis, a comb, a decorative betel nut, a pouch of uncooked rice, and a set of two small plastic boxes from the neighbourhood supermarket. She did the same for Claire and then, without pausing at Ira, proceeded to the next guest. Seeing Claire's mouth open to remind Kritika that she had missed out Ira by mistake, Ira squeezed her arm and walked away to retrieve their coats. An indignant Claire followed mumbling,

"What was that now? What did I just miss?" Ira continued to walk rapidly and quipped,

"It's a convoluted explanation. We'll need more than the ride to the cinema to get that done. Meanwhile, I don't want to miss the start of the movie!"

Chapter 6:

In the name of COLOUR

Ira continued to message Sameer every few days. She also exchanged messages with Cahya. Cahya was in touch with one of his work colleagues - John. Sameer seemed to be in London and had reported to work but was still not taking calls. After each visit to the Godses, Ira came home despondent. But the overpowering sense of duty meant she just could not wean off. Now, Ira found herself as a residual offspring, with Swati shunned by them. Ira had seen Swati just once, at Sriram's funeral, paying her respects. Given Ira's own distraught state, she had let the moment pass. But like she had felt multiple times, Ira had been tempted to reach out. Ratnaprabha's stern warnings and the connection between the mention of Swati and Sriram's "under the weather" days held her back. But now, worried about their health, and noticing how they had softened their stance on almost everything, she harboured the hope that a reconciliation might just be possible.

But was their estranged daughter interested in building bridges? Tracking down Swati had been easy. Fondly referred to by the Urdu title *"Aapa"*, Swati was a public figure at the forefront of the struggle against domestic violence. Her quotes in the media, awards and apparent cult-like following in Yorkshire, would have been a matter of pride for any parent. But the Godses refused to acknowledge her existence. Having tried to return to her family and shunned, Swati had stopped trying long ago.

Through the painful blur of the funeral, Ira recalled a glimpse of Swati's daughter firmly holding on to her mother's elbow as she offered flowers at her brother's feet. One of the many news articles about Swati mentioned that she was often assisted in her work by her daughter Leila Maria. Leila's own professional social media profile was impressive. Ira sent her a message and a request to meet.

With no response for over a week, and yet another gloomy Friday evening gone by, Ira began to lose hope. As she sat alone, stirring her coffee on a mournful Monday morning, Ira received a call,

"Dr. Godse, this is Patricia Mohan calling on behalf of Leila. I'm afraid there's a lot going on and she has not been able to respond. She has been in court through the week and is scheduled to be in Switzerland for a conference. Would any of these dates work for you?" Two weeks later, a nervous Ira entered the waiting room of Leila's plush oak and leather panelled London office. Having taken the afternoon off from work, Ira was dressed in her standard work outfit, a pair of dark trousers and a crisp striped shirt. She glanced at the wall covered with evocative photographs punctuated with statistics. Dressed in a crisp cream-coloured business suit, appeared Patricia, offering Ira an array of tea and coffee options. As she waited for her *chai* tea, Ira rose to her feet to study the black and white photographs, and the numbers which accompanied them, reeking of the lingering impact of an unjust world.

- Between 2015 and 2017, only one black British student was admitted to Corpus Christi College, University of Oxford. The number of minority ethnic students at top universities rose from 9% in 1995 to 18% in 2017.
- Slavery was abolished in the UK in 1833. The British government paid slave owners a £20 million compensation, equivalent to approximately 40% of the Government's total annual expenditure. Money borrowed to fund the Slavery Abolition Act (1835) was repaid in 2015.
- 12% of incidents in which police use force against people involve black people. The black make up 3.3% of the UK's population.

Ira was soaking in these facts when Patricia came through to lead her into Leila's private office. Leila was on the phone at her Mahogany desk, peering into her sleek laptop, scribbling on a leather-bound notebook. A dark brown, driftwood ashtray nestled between a tall coffee mug and an assortment of paper files, neatly stacked, labelled, and annotated with yellow tags. The taller of the glass cabinets behind Leila sported leather-bound volumes of historic cases and landmark judgements. On the mantelpiece hung Leila's speaker badges at conferences.. Still on the phone, Leila motioned to Patricia. She led Ira to a dark grey leather sofa at the other end of the room. On a low, gleaming glass coffee table sat Ira's steaming mug of tea. Patricia retreated.

On the corner stool stood two beautifully framed pictures – Leila in a white veil and Swati in a bright pink shimmering scarf. Another of Swati, elegant in a green and gold scarf, and Leila stunning in a short, bright pink dress. Swati's resemblance to Sriram was unmistakable – the green eyes, pale skin, jet black hair. She seemed to have inherited her mother's firm jaw, while Sriram had Prabhakar's high, wide forehead. Next to this was a blithe frame of a family on holiday – Leila's hair restrained in a bright yellow band, her arms around a blonde, white man in denim shorts with two children perched on his knees. Ira couldn't resist smiling back at the toothy grins of the sprightly boy and girl.

"Sorry to keep you waiting." Leila pulled a swivel chair and extended her hand with a business-like

"Leila".

Ira took her hand. "Given that I was married to your Mum's brother, I would be *Maami* (aunt), but as we are just a few years apart, do call me Ira!" she smiled warmly. Leila did not return the smile. Polite, but restrained, maintaining her formal demeanour, she placed her palms on her skirt and enquired,

"What can I do for you?" Ira noticed that she had chosen neither of the options to address her – the endearing *Maami* or the familiar Ira. Her response was not surprising. Over the years, Ira had warily consumed pieces of the heart-wrenching saga of Swati's unceremonious departure from the Godse house, her attempt at returning to her parents, the rejection, and the racial slur at the innocent child Leila. Ira had picked up these from snatches of conversation between her in-laws as she went about her chores. But after the shocking admonition during her first Diwali in the UK, she had not mustered the courage to broach the subject. Besides, it was evident that the subject of Swati immediately triggered Sriram into slamming doors and locking himself in his room. It was expected that Leila would resent any overture from the Godses. But what came next, Ira did not expect,

"Look, I don't know why you are here. I don't know anything about the Godses, and I'm not interested. Apart from the deplorable treatment of my mother, the disgusting dismissal of their first grandchild, simply because I have Caribbean genes, they ruined their own son's life. My mother was the only person who understood him and they refused to let her help. Now you show up! What do you want? If this has anything to do with my mother's signature on property papers or any such matter, let's get this over and done with. My mother has ensured that no Asian girl ever must take to the streets because her heartless family values "honour" more than an offspring and I'm inundated with work for cases of discrimination against the Black community in every walk of life. If you believe we want anything to do with the Godses, we don't. So whatever property is to be inherited, keep it for your son. Please send over the papers to Patricia and I'm sure Mum will be pleased to sign off her last connection with her family!" Leila rose to indicate the end of their meeting.

Ira was shocked and instinctively reached out to touch Leila's hand,

"Your grandparents have caused extreme pain. But please don't misunderstand. This has nothing to do with inheritance. Whatever belongs to your grandparents is theirs, I have never thought it is mine. Your Sriram *Maama*, you may have heard, was unable to hold a steady job. And thankfully, whatever I have earned has been enough for me and enough to leave for Sameer. The thought of money did not even cross my mind when I sought a meeting with you. Please give me a few more minutes to explain," Sensing the sincerity in Ira's plea and her hand hesitantly brushing against her sleeve, Leila sat down reluctantly. Ira hurriedly sat down again.

"Maybe you need to rush off and we could meet again if you wish. But let me just explain the reason why I decided to approach you. There is absolutely no doubt that your mother was treated terribly. Personally, I have greatly admired her courage, resilience in carving her niche in the world and even more importantly, what a wonderful job she has done raising you, single-handedly. Your success, if I may take the liberty of saying so, makes me feel extremely proud. Why I did not approach you all these years, is that I was not allowed to, by my in-laws. Why did I have to listen to them? I hope you will understand when you hear the details of our life if we meet again. But what you need to know and I'm especially hoping you will let your mother know, and even arrange for me to meet her, is this. Today, your grandparents are lonely, listless, living by themselves, unable to recover from the death of their only son. Sameer, the grandchild they helped raise, has gone away to India, breaking off from them and from me at a time when they need him the most. Your grandparents just have me. They will not acknowledge it and are probably too weary to initiate anything, but their daughter cannot be far from their thoughts. And for all that dogmatic behaviour, especially by your grandmother, the tragic events have softened their stand on most of the biases that they so held dear. Besides Leila, their closed mindsets have made them irrelevant. They too know now that the cages they built around themselves cannot exist in 2018. Your mother was a victim of this divisiveness in the name of race in the 80s; in our own way, we suffered in the name of religion and class in the 90s and you continue to fight, but believe me, change in the Godse house is inevitable. My fervent wish, seeing the pathetic condition of two hard-working people in their 80s, is that they meet their estranged daughter and granddaughter at least once. I am certain that they would be proud of how well you have done, sadly, with no support from them." Ira put down her teacup and rose to leave. Not risking even a faint smile, she murmured in her characteristic gentle voice,

"Thank you for listening to me Leila".

Leila had not interrupted, and nor had she got up. She was looking at the picture of her mother in the corner, her eyes brimming over with tears that she was determined not to shed.

Ira stepped away saying, "I won't disturb you again Leila. If and whenever you are ready and if Swati *tai* is willing, let us meet. Also, the children look angelic. The best part of growing up in the London of 2018, is that no one asks and no one cares. With a high achieving role model of a mother like you, they are bound to transcend all barriers. My fondest wishes to them."

Leila responded with a silent nod and walked across to the outside door to see Ira off.

On her journey home, Ira allowed herself to hope that she had touched a chord.

Whether that would translate into Leila and Swati reaching out, she did not know. If they still chose not to, Ira could understand. Ira thanked God, who still seemed to be looking over her, whichever one it was: Omar's *Allah*, the Jesus Christ hanging on a cross at their school church, the Godse's ideal King Ram, her grandmother's elephant headed Ganesha, or the serene Buddha that Cahya had gifted her last Christmas. The collective forces of all these Gods had still not succeeded in giving Ira the life she had dreamt for herself all those decades ago. Yet, with no prayer book, rosary, or idol to aid her, she sought peace, immensely grateful for what she still had.

The Godses had lost a son who had been ill most of his life. Sameer, though refusing to communicate, was alive and healthy. Swati had been ill-treated by her own parents, and Leila, Ira had no doubt, had faced immense challenges through her years of growing up. She thought about Leila's struggle to study law on a mother's modest single income, along with the discrimination that came with her half-black, half-brown genes. Once again, Ira felt fortunate to have her in-laws' support through her years of juggling education and the infant, Sameer.

Ira reminisced over how she had first been taught to thank the collection of Gods for her inherent privilege, for what made her still better off than most of the world simply because of her circumstance, instead of dwelling over what she had not succeeded at. This philosophy of acknowledging before complaining came from her grandmother, after the saga which ensued after Ira failed to meet the entry requirements for any of Mumbai's prestigious medical colleges.

In June of 1992, Omar and Ira received their board exam results. Both scored an average percentage in the mid-80s. The mood in the Siddique home had been of immense jubilation. Platefuls of *kababs* emerged from the kitchen for visitors who dropped in to congratulate Omar's proud father, and boxes of colourful sweets had been ordered to be distributed among Mushtaque Siddiqui's business associates and employees. Upon hearing the results, Mushtaque had enveloped Omar in a tight, proprietary hug, proclaiming how nobody in the *khandan* (extended family) had been such a praiseworthy student, especially as most of the cousins on both Mushtaque and Sakinabi's side comprised young men whiling away their time and, thus, barely able to finish school. Omar had overheard Mushtaque's voice booming into the ornate brass handset of the landline proudly installed into the men's drawing room of the house. Seated royally on the deep red and black sofa, his feet resting on the purple and green motifs of the plush Persian carpet, Mushtaque had been guffawing into the phone,

"Yes *Bhai*, all that investment into the convent school is paying off. Now there will be *munafa hi munafa* (profit)." Omar often discounted what his father had to say. This successful businessman had a lot of admirable qualities, one of them being an excellent network that transcended religion, caste, and social strata and of course, genuine fondness for his only son. But when he overheard what he thought was, just part jovial, part serious conversation, on the "return on investment" on Omar's education, he wondered if he was just an invested asset to take the business to the next level, and if his poor older sisters, educated in the local Muslim *madrasas*, were after all, liabilities.

There had been despondence at the Dixit's. Omar's 84% would secure him admission into Mumbai's best commerce, humanities, or law degree college. But it was far too less for Ira's entry into medical college. From Damodar, there was silence at the disappointing results, but from Priyamvada, there was an outburst, especially when their cleaner Rakhma's daughter Laxmi, son-in-law Dagdu and granddaughter Vaishali arrived with *pedhas*. Rakhma bustled into Saguna's study, leading the procession, wiping her streaming eyes with the edge of her brightly coloured *nauvari* saree.

"*Ajji*, how can we ever thank you. Vaishali has got 65%. She will be the first ever girl in our entire slum to be a doctor!" Rakhma moved aside to let Vaishali and her parents touch Saguna's feet.

Saguna, gratified to witness the visible fruit of her sustained social reform, at least among the people in her immediate proximity, asked Abdul to bring tea and snacks for Rakhma's family. Never mincing her words, Saguna reminded Rakhma how upset she had been when Laxmi had been married off to Dagdu at the age of 15. Refusing to accept the explanation that the community demanded early marriages for girls, Saguna had flatly refused to attend the wedding. In barely a year, Vaishali was born and then, two sons. Dismissing her failure to get Laxmi to become financially independent, Saguna had decided to focus on her daughter instead, and had sponsored

Vaishali's education this far. The tea and snacks were consumed. Vaishali departed, carrying her gift, a book by Rama *bai* Ranade, a pioneer of women's nurse training in the 1800s. Shaking her head at the irony, Priyamvada refused to touch the *pedhas* and fidgeted about the room mumbling,

"We sponsor the girl's education, and she will get into medical college with just 65%. With the questionable quality of education at the Municipal schools and of course, her even more questionable English, God knows how she will cope with the medical degree and God forbid, what kind of doctor she will be. And here is Ira, with her 85%, left high and dry, no admission and bleak career prospects!"

"Now that is quite unfair Priya, I'm sure Vaishali works hard. And Ira's career prospects are far from bleak! She has had excellent grounding with her impeccable language skills, articulation, and exposure. I'm sure there are multiple career choices that will emerge after whatever degree she chooses. There is no need to mourn!" Popping a *pedha* into his mouth, handing one to the sulking Ira, Damodar breezed out of the room, patting Priyamvada's sleeve gently for her to follow. At the door, he turned back to address his mother with a smile,

"Congratulations to you *Aai*, for recognizing talent and seeing the girl through!" Left alone with her grandma, Ira finally burst into angry tears.

"I let you down *Ajji*. I'm sorry. And life is never fair!" In the labyrinth of Ira's illustrious extended family tree, was Dr. Anandi Joshi, India's first woman doctor who graduated from University of Pennsylvania in 1886 but died of tuberculosis at 22. It was Saguna's wish to see Ira as a doctor, mainly because she could not be one. Saguna placed her wrinkled palm on Ira's forehead, her lips set in a straight line, in what can only be described as a grim smile,

"Ira, you haven't let me down. I know you tried your best and you never know; you may one day get a doctorate and I may even be around long enough to see it. But that's not important, what your father said is right. You had an excellent education, the work ethic you have imbibed in this home and genes that show at least five generations of educated men and three generations of women before you, mean there will always be doors open for you. Despite the struggle of these demi-gods and goddesses in my study,

Rakhma and Laxmi did not have what your mother and I had – nurturing of the mind. And what is fair and unfair my dear, is far too complex to squeeze into a quick conversation. So never underplay or discount your privilege." Saguna's wise discourse that evening lasted two hours over sips of sweetened ginger tea and sojourns into the books of that library.

Chapter 7:

In the name of A STATUE and a MINARET

November 26, 2018.

Ira was in her apartment scouring the Indian TV channels for further news of Sameer and his saffron brigade. News reports on their bizarre pronouncements dripped with sarcasm, but the dramatic symbolism assured viewership. Ira was relieved to catch a glimpse of Sameer now and then, though it was difficult to believe that he was the child she had brought up.

As she flicked through news channels, there was elaborate coverage marking the tenth anniversary of 26/11, the midnight attacks orchestrated by the *Lashkar-e-Taiba*. She watched as a news channel re-told the story of the ten heavily armed men who sailed from Pakistan to Mumbai, unleashing carnage at five locations, guided by live mobile phone directions from their "handlers". The coverage featured "Baby Moshe", the heartening story of a two-year-old Jewish baby, who lost his parents in the attack. During the gunfire, Moshe was rescued by his Indian nanny Sandra Samuels at Chabad House, where Moshe's father was a Rabbi. She had found him wailing next to his parents' corpses. Sandra then travelled to Israel to look after Moshe in his grandparents' home. Ten years later, Moshe and Sandra had a warm multi-faith welcome in Mumbai. The coverage included a series of interviews with families of police and defence personnel, who lost their lives trying to save the hostages and religious leaders. Ira had just stepped into the kitchen to refill her plate with the grilled chicken and salad.

She stopped in her tracks. The voice was unmistakable.

"Two-year-old Moshe's cries of *Immie* during the service to mourn the victims of 26/11 had been reported as one of the most poignant moments of the tragedy. Today, as he returns to India, we Mumbaikars, across religious barriers, see him as the beacon of hope for the secular Mumbai we were proud of, and we intend to still live in..." Ira continued to stare at the speaker's face.

Heavier around the girth, a receding hairline, clad in a white linen shirt and dark blue jeans and speaking with the same intense green eyes...was Omar. He continued,

"Why did they pick Leopold café, the Taj and Oberoi? Because apart from Mumbaikars, there are international visitors here. Why CST rail station, because it is one of the busiest spots in Mumbai and maximum people could be killed! This is not just about one terror attack. Take the 2005 London bombings, a day after London was announced host of the Olympics. Once again, London experienced bombings in 2011. Despite this, the 2012 Olympics went off smoothly. The perpetrators of terror want to stall everything that unites human beings – sport, music, cricket, films. We won't let them. Their aim is to scuttle normalcy, curtail globalization, suppress the pride that comes with an urbanised flat world that offers evolved beings more interested in the future than in the past, to be able to do anything anywhere. We are proud Muslim, Hindu, Christian, Jews, Sikh, and Buddhist residents of this tinsel town, the *karma bhoomi* of so many professionals, the city that works relentlessly for a living, where survivors thrive. The fear of an attack will not stop us from living the lives we want to lead."

The anchor moved on to another speaker. Ira sank onto the sofa, her plate untouched. He spoke with the same ardour, the sincerity of their debating days, a heady mix of logical thought and poignant emotion that made it impossible for his audience to do anything else but sit up and listen. Like she had for years, she battled the flood of emotions, anger at the futile wait for Omar on the dark night before her wedding and disbelief at the news of his arrest.

A few evenings later, Ira tuned into a talk show on "Secularism and the evolution of Bollywood". The camera captured the urban Indian audience in a sleek modern studio done up in black and silver, and then turned to the panellists seated on bright blue stools. The camera zoomed onto Omar, today clad in white linen again and dark blue trousers. Omar began to speak,

"Often unintentionally funny and loud, mainstream Bollywood films of the 80s in their own entertaining way, propagated good old epistles - the triumph of good over evil, and that love always won over everything else. But nobody gave much thought to this. If there was a plastic pouch with turmeric infused popcorn, the clink of glass-bottles with sickly sweet fizzy drinks, and somebody to share this with, whatever went on screen was just fine! The formula films we devoured in the 70s and 80s featured questionable acting, hideous costumes and a series of contrived situations that led to lives being torn apart but assembled again. The crucial factor in these films was the "not so subtle" message it passed on – love reigned supreme, overcoming opposition from the impeding forces of caste, religion, and socio- economic differences." Omar went on to talk about the iconic 1977 film *"Amar Akbar Anthony"*, the story of three separated children, each raised by good samaritans of different faiths and showing up at a hospital years later to donate blood to their blind mother.

"Let's not get lost in stereotypes being endorsed. Let's not miss the strong messages in this film, that each of the love interests for the three lost and found brothers is a woman professional, the Muslim doctor wooed by the incorrigible *Qawwali* singing, green flashy jacket clad Muslim lad Akbar, the Hindu girl supporting her family for the Hindu Amar and the stereotypical Christian girl in a skirt for Anthony. The nation was entertained by this "unity in diversity" tale, nobody objected to anything," Omar raised both his palms. Shrugging, he continued, "For these were the happy times in Mumbai, before the horrific riots ripped its secular fabric...before Gods of all hues were dragged on to the streets and confused souls manipulated by Machiavellian minds destroyed the lines between faith, religion, and politics." Omar's voice was drenched in affection for the innocence of the times gone by, the nostalgia of the films they had enjoyed, and a tinge of regret for what had ceased to be.

Ira was interrupted by a call from Cahya, an interaction which filled her with embarrassment due to Sameer's deplorable behaviour, but a link she cherished. When Sameer introduced Cahya to the family at his graduation, his grandparents had been cold, whispering to each other *"aaplyatli naahi"* (she is not one of us). Ira had ignored them.

Later when they were by themselves, during one of the "make-believe" Bollywood spiels she and Sameer shared, Ira made a dramatic statement,

"One day I'll be like a Bollywood Mum and shed copious tears over a daughter-in-law snatching away my precious, pampered son from me!" Ira giggled and Sameer shook his head smiling,

"No Mum, the way you and Cahya seemed to be texting each other, I think you'll start a new trend of overly dramatic, sugary sweet mothers-in-law in Bollywood. Also, a correction. Cahya is not your daughter-in-law. I'm far from asking her to marry me. She needs to get her master's, I need to get my promotion, save up for the house."

But given his characteristic half-smile, Ira knew that Sameer was immensely pleased by how they were getting on. He had attributed his grandparents' hostility to their inability to have a social interaction with anyone who was not Maharashtrian and that too, preferably Maharashtrian Brahmin. This was especially true of Ratnaprabha, whose interaction in English was limited to a grocery store. Sameer had never heard of his grandparents being invited over to a non-Indian home. But Cahya, knowing how important his grandparents had been in Sameer's life, made an effort with them.

Who would have thought, today, three years later, that Cahya would be Ira's only link to Sameer? Ira quickly pressed the record button, eager to watch the talk show later, but even more eager to answer Cahya's call. Cahya sounded breathless,

"Sameer is in London. John told me he will be going to the St. Paul's office tomorrow to hand in his resignation. They have refused to extend his leave any further and insisted he come in person to hand over. I don't know if Sameer would agree, but John and I are planning to meet him for a drink at 7 pm at one of the Paternoster Square places." Her son had arrived in London and had not gotten in touch. It hurt deeply. Ira brushed away a tear. Immensely grateful to Cahya, she now needed to make a quick plan to meet Sameer.

"I was thinking, I should sit at the coffee shop at Paternoster Square. There is just one entrance to the office building and if anyone emerges from one of the two elevators, I would still be able to catch a glimpse of them if

I manage to park myself in a strategically located table. What do you think?" Ira was anxious that the plan should not involve any embarrassment for Sameer. She had always been extremely conscious of this, right since Sameer was little, an Indian boy trying to blend into his predominantly white boys' school. No adult would want a Mum floating around their office building. But having yearned to see her son for a year, Ira had no choice.

"Yes, I think that's a good plan. Can you be there a little before half five? John said Sameer's meeting with HR and his manager is at half four. It shouldn't take longer than that,"

Cahya concluded.

"And Cahya…" Ira hesitated. In the old days, Sameer would have chided Ira for being a dramatic Bollywood Mum for saying this.

"Yes?" Cahya waited.

"Thanks for being the daughter I never had. May you get all the happiness in the world you so deserve…" Ira's voice cracked slightly.

"Thank you, you take care of yourself," Cahya's voice was calm.

The next evening, Ira left work early, and took the tube to St. Paul's station. Feeling even more like a dramatic Bollywood Mum; she had spent the previous evening making Sameer's favourite sweets – *besan laddus*, balls of chickpea flour and butter. The plastic takeaway container wrapped in a discreet brown envelope tucked into her handbag, Ira fretted through her underground journey. She had decided to make one final attempt to break Sameer's obsession with the "purity of his Hindu Brahmin lineage".

Emerging at St. Paul's station, she traversed the short distance to Paternoster Square in minutes, pulling her coat closer against the crisp chilly December air, wading through office-goers and shoppers. Until the Christmas of 2016, they had celebrated the day with gifts under a tree in the living room and a traditional Christmas meal with vegetarian options. The earlier years had shop-bought ready meals, mince pies and Christmas pudding in glistening cellophane paper. In the Godse house, any non-vegetarian cooking was unthinkable, but Prabhakar had indulged little Sameer's wait for his stockings to fill up with Santa's goodies and the chocolate eggs for Easter.

After Ira and Sameer moved out, Ira started looking up recipes for a variety of cuisines and marking every festival with apt meals. Gradually,

Sameer took on cooking a full Christmas meal. She had always wanted her offspring to respect cultures and blend in. The Christmas of 2017 had been a nightmare with Sriram's demise, just a month prior. The Christmas of 2018 a few weeks away, would not even see Sameer at home. Ira looked away from the forced cheer of the reds and greens of retail Christmas and stepped into the warmth of the coffee shop at Paternoster Square. She was on schedule; at precisely 5.15 pm, she was seated at a tiny table by the window sipping her tea. For the next 25 minutes, every other man walking out of the opposite building appeared to be Sameer. Alternating between peering into her phone for a message from Cahya, in case there was a change of plan, and squinting at the window, Ira was poised to chuck her paper cup in the bin, pick up her handbag and sprint out of the coffeeshop before Sameer melted away into the crowd of early office-leavers. But Ira did not have to sprint, for Cahya and John had made things slightly easier. John and Sameer were outside the coffee shop.

"I'll get my Secret Santa shopping out of the way Sameer and see you back here in about an hour," John walked away. Sameer walked in, paid for his coffee and oatmeal cookie, and settled into a corner sofa at the inner end of the coffee shop. He opened his laptop. Ira had been seated at the window, her back to the serving till. Nervous, she walked up to Sameer and placed her gloved hand on his shoulder. Sameer looked up.

Before he could react, she sank into the empty chair, placing the brown envelope before him. "They are just a few *besan laddus* Sameer. They will last at least a month during this weather. I will not be a dramatic Bollywood Mum and scold you for not eating well or comment on how you have lost weight." Ira smiled, trying to thaw Sameer's icy glance. Sameer did not smile. Deeply ingrained into him was the value of never ever disrespecting food. He put the brown envelope into the laptop bag. Sameer knew his Mum had him cornered. In a public setting, he could not raise his voice. Ira also knew that there was nothing she could do if Sameer chose to walk away. She could not afford to embarrass him. She also knew that she had to exercise extreme self-restraint, and not allow herself to shed a tear.

Ira spent the next 30 minutes narrating the story of his half-Hindu, half-Muslim genes, of Omar, who was wrongly arrested like so many other Muslim youths in the streets of Mumbai for the bomb blasts of 1993, and how Omar was now a public figure upholding peace in Mumbai. Sameer listened in disbelief and rising anger. He raised his palm across his nose as if to slice through her narrative.

"That's enough Mum. I don't buy any of this. I am a Godse by birth, a pure-bred Aryan. My political career hinges on my lineage and of my illustrious ancestor Nathuram. Like the intellectual pacifists who have taken the punch out of Hinduism and let these terrorist Muslims rule over the world with their fear, don't make up stories to dilute my story. I'm off to India to fulfil the mission I was born for. Raghav Swami has appointed me as the head of the mission. He says I'm the inspirational leader for Hindu youth who need to come together against the terror forces. I'm not going to let this story, you are making up, come in the way. And before making up such a story, you should have at least had some respect for the memory of my late father, who gave up his life so I would have the realization of how important my mission is. *Saadhvi ji* told me Nathuram's second birth was the martyr Sriram Godse, his spirit wounded in Manchester by the terrorist forces, which I, the third Godse and blessed with the strength that my father lacked, must avenge."

"How could I possibly lie about this?" Ira was aghast.

"Well, look at the contradiction. If your story is to be believed, you've effectively been lying to me all my life! Why should I believe anything you've ever told me?" His green eyes flashing, Sameer picked up his laptop bag and, in a few seconds, was gone.

Ira did not ask who *Saadhvi* was, assuming this was yet another politician in religious garb capitalizing on Sameer's exuberant spirit. Drained by the effort of trying to crack through the smokescreen of the life her son was living and by the memories she had buried for so long, Ira dragged herself back to St. Paul's station, one of the many lonely souls on that London Street, trying to shield themselves from the Christmas milieu that ached with its attempt to make merry.

At home in her apartment, Ira finally decided to do what Claire had been asking her to for years, reach out to Omar. Claire had often questioned Ira about her standard answer to whatever Claire suggested, including signing up on a dating app –

"The in-laws wouldn't appreciate it."

Exasperated, Claire had pointed out that Sriram's parents were not even her in-laws, given the years that had passed since their separation.

"Fine they have been good to you, but you've been good to them, not even getting a speedy divorce because of their misplaced sense of society, which supposedly values marriage more than happiness!" Ira's other objection was that Sameer wouldn't appreciate it. Maybe that had ceased to matter now too.

But the most pressing of reasons was her worry, what if Sameer, having finally absorbed the truth, may accept it, question it and given that he was in India, may even say something about Omar on a public forum. Even worse, what if the political forces that had gripped Sameer and even robbed him of his inherent logical reasoning, picked up on the story and tried to harm Omar?

Ira had been reading about Omar since the news item a few weeks ago.

Apparently, Omar had a death threat from an Islamic fundamentalist group that did not appreciate his "moderate depiction of Islam". The news item said it was a small, amateurish group and Omar had dismissed the idea of police protection following the threat.

That night, Ira did what she had been tempted to, but never mustered the courage to do. She sent Omar a social media request with a message and her phone number.

The next morning, Ira awoke to a call from a +91 number.

"Ira?"

Chapter 8:

In the name of HISTORY

"Ira...this is Omar."

Without realising it, Ira held her breath. She instinctively moved to the window, holding the phone in her right hand, her left-hand twirling the edge of the white lace curtain.

In the early 90s, as their friendship evolved into armour and intimacy, Omar and Ira's long conversations donned the colour of passion. In those days, the landline in the Dixit home was placed in a corner of the living room by the window. The phone calls were strategically scheduled to work around the absences of key members of both Siddiqui and Dixit bustling households. Omar would do most of the talking, so it was unlikely for anyone passing by to know what was being said. But Omar had once told her that when she spoke to him, her face changed. A voracious reader, Omar recited excerpts of romantic prose and poetry at a languorous pace. Ira's eyes softened and as she blushed, her lips parted in a half-smile. Ira had got into the habit of turning to the window as she conversed with Omar, her face, at least, partially hidden by the curtain. Ever active and bustling about the house, Saguna had encountered Ira behind the curtain, looking into the distance with her half-smile. Immensely fond of Omar, Saguna had chosen to ignore the discovery.

Ira's voice quivered, "A, hello Omar..."

Unable to say anymore, unsure whether she should have reached out, she held back tears, the lace curtain tightly entwined around her fingers. Omar waited.

Desperate to break the silence, she fumbled,

"I watched your TV interview."

"Oh yes, they are doing a follow-up 26/11 episode on Friday. Maybe you could watch the re-run on Sunday afternoon, unless you have an emergency at the hospital," Omar continued as if it was just yesterday since they last spoke. The edge of the white lace curtain was balled up in Ira's sweaty left palm. Ira was glad it was not a video call. She did not need to ask Omar the obvious - How did he know she worked? How did he know she worked at a hospital? Like Omar, she did not get quoted in news articles and appear on talk shows, but she did have a skeletal social media presence. Omar continued,

"Ira, anybody who is a contact on your social media profile knows you are a doctor and work at this hospital. The fact that you are a doctor is no surprise." Ira did not ask Omar how he knew what she had been thinking. Omar had always fulfilled what she had articulated, every silly wish, a new movie in town, a new music album, a new book released. And all that she had left unsaid, he had sensed and done anyway...except for keeping the appointment on the eve of her wedding.

In disbelief that Omar would not keep a promise, Ira had wept herself to sleep that warm March night. Should she venture out to look for him? If he still lived in the Siddiqui bungalow down the street, she would have. Thrown out of his home, Omar had found refuge with various cousins in Mumbai's ghettos and at times with his maternal grandmother in Alibaug. With the *henna* on her hands and feet, and the green glass bangles interspersed with the heavy 24-carat gold ones from her mother, Ira had been warned not to step out of the house after the departure of the bangle seller, who had expertly and respectfully measured the wrist of each woman in the Dixit home, and pushed the right size of green glass bangles up each forearm – Pratibha *mavshi,* Priyamvada, Ratnaprabha, Rakhma *Kaku* the cleaner, everybody got their bangles, six, eight, ten, twelve in each hand as they preferred. Ira the bride, had 11 bangles in one hand and 12 in the other.

The previous evening, the *henna* artist had asked her to spell "Sriram", so that she could intersperse the letters into the intricate design on her palm for the bride and groom to locate during their moments of intimacy. This was among the customs borrowed from Bollywood, and the poor *henna* artist did not expect a telling off.

"Come on, don't be shy, tell me should I paint the letters of his name on both palms?" she winked at the other women. Given their irreverent penchant for anything Bollywood, Omar and Ira would have quite enjoyed this exercise of spotting the letters of Omar's name in the *henna* design.

"Maybe we should do this as a fun event at our anniversary," thought Ira, making a mental note to tell Omar about the over-keen *henna* lady. She had politely told the *henna* lady to keep the design simple and avoid the name, thank you.

With her jingling bangles and intricate henna design, the idea of Ira venturing out to look for Omar seemed preposterous.

A beautician had been deployed to arrive at the wedding venue at 6am to start Ira's makeup and drape her saree. Extremely fond of sarees and jewellery and having done a part-time beautician course (a skill which she never used except on herself), Priyamvada had booked the beautician's time after an elaborate discourse on the options involved. However, as the sun rose, with the bomb blasts having marred the city, neither the beautician nor the priest turned up. With the preparations done, the family had decided to go ahead with the wedding at any cost, at home with the few guests who were present. Saguna asked Priyamvada to delegate all other work and focus on Ira's make-up and hair. Two precocious teenage cousins from Nashik were deployed as Priyamvada's assistants. They flitted in and out of the room, fetching a bowl of ice cubes to cool her skin and some rose water to soothe her puffy eyes.

Her own hair clasped in a messy bun, Priyamvada brandished a comb in her right hand, clutched a portion of Ira's jet-black hair in her left palm and held a plastic hairpin between her clenched teeth. She skilfully covered Ira's dark circles with a tube of concealer and cakes of creamy foundation. The two worker bees continued to fetch objects she needed, scurrying in and out of the room, leaving the door ajar each time. Mid-way through painting an eyelid, Ira heard Rakhma's distinct voice.

"*Ajji*, that boy Omar has been arrested for his involvement in the blasts along with some others from Mahim. Abdul *Chacha*'s cousin lives in the same locality. He used to be such a good boy, talking to us so nicely, always touching your feet whenever he visited at festivals!" Saguna uttered under her breath, "Hey Ram!"

Led by her instinct that Omar was bad news after all, she said a silent prayer to her Gods for Ira's wedding to Sriram to take place in the next few hours. Saguna masked her reaction to this news, with a quick reprimand,

"Rakma, get your *rangoli* in order at the doorstep, instead of being the bearer of this burning city's gossip!"

The shutting of Ira's room door drowned the sound of Saguna's next instruction to Rakma. Stunned, Ira's eyes began to water. Priyamvada exclaimed it was the liquid eyeliner and scrambled to clear the mayhem on Ira's face with cotton wool and cleansing milk. The mayhem within her mind wreaked havoc for the next two decades.

She never knew what really happened and heard later that Omar had been released after weeks in prison. But by then, Ira was in London. She had never tried getting in touch and neither had he.

Today, years later, it seemed strange to be able to speak with the same ease and comfort, as if they had never been away.

Ira said, "Omar there is something important I want to tell you. When can we speak on video?"

"Ira, you have waited 26 years to reach out, why wait any longer? I'll call you on video in 10 minutes. Get yourself some tea and I'll get mine." Ira rushed to splash some warm water on her face, wipe off the kohl that had run down her cheeks, quickly ran a comb through her hair and dabbed on nude lipstick. She had no time to agonise over what to wear. She pulled on a baby pink V-neck top over a pair of jeans and stepped into the kitchen to set the kettle to boil. She had just thrown away the tea bag and was stirring sweetener into the teacup when the call came through. Stealing a last glance at herself in the glass window, and taking a deep breath, she touched the video button. For a few seconds, neither spoke.

Ira struggled to hold back tears. Omar wiped a non-existing speck of dust from the corner of his dark rimmed glasses. He hadn't been wearing glasses on the TV show, and these gave him a more academic look, Ira thought to herself. Omar broke the silence,

"I'd always imagined you like this Ira, gorgeous in your natural, unassuming, pristine way, of course wiser, quieter. But how do we bring the sparkle in those eyes, the half-smile back?"

Ira's lips parted in a sad smile. Weighed down by her conversation with Sameer, her face clouded again, and she said nervously,

"Omar thanks for calling back promptly. It's quite important I tell you this."

"Ira, Ira, wait. Why would you want to thank me for calling you back? If we want to start where we left off, I need to first apologise for letting you down, for not being outside your home that night. And after that, every time I wanted to call, I stopped myself, knowing that I had no right to disrupt the life you were leading. Of course, I would try to find out if you've been alright but being discreet as to not ruffle anything that may have been going right for you.

You have become a private person I can see. But I did hear about your husband's demise last year through the school circles. I'm so sorry you've been through so much. I don't know if you are working today, but I've just cancelled my commitments for this evening. I'm here if you need me. There is so much to ask and so much to tell but let me stop here. You needed to tell me something? Don't hold back, tell me what that is," Omar paused.

And then, over the next two hours, the flood of Ira's tears and the story of Sameer's life flowed. Ira recounted her panic at the discovery of her pregnancy, the Godse's acceptance of an early birth, Sameer's job and now his disappearance to India.

Astounded, Omar interrupted,

"Our son? My son!" He leaned over, his eyes lighting up and then glistening with tears.

"Ira, you had to bring him up all by yourself. How can I ever forgive myself for not being there? You must have been an exemplary parent…" Ira spoke briefly about Sriram's erratic behaviour, the terror attack, and his death.

"It was lonely, but I thought I'd done well on one thing in my life – bringing up Sameer. But I've failed terribly. He refuses to engage with me, and the fire that is burning within him since Sriram's death, fills me with fear. The single person, the sole reason I lived for all these years, is on a path of self-destruction Omar, and there is nothing I can do..." Ira rubbed her temples with her thumb and forefinger. Through their breezy, carefree childhood, there had been no predicament that they couldn't have overcome if they put both their heads together.

"Ira, you cannot blame yourself for the actions of a 25-year-old man. Tell me, what is this mission Sameer claims is more important than his family and his future?" Ira told him about the names Sameer mentioned, how it started with the London priest driven by commercial gain, a Raghav Swami and a *Saadhvi* who seemed to have assumed importance in the mission. Omar pursed his lips,

"Ira, this is the brigade who have donned saffron for political gain. These self-styled upholders of the Hindu faith are not interested in nationalism, Nathuram Godse's ideology or anyone else's. It is in vogue to unearth descendants of key historical figures and seek votes in their name. The secularists have claimed Gandhi as theirs, Shivaji's name is usurped by anyone fighting for anything and now Godse is on trend. Nathuram Godse's own family does not have any living relatives interested in politics, so Sameer is a great discovery.

This will pass Ira; they will lose steam soon. Every time they make inflammatory statements, they retract in a few days as nobody, not even the ruling party wants to associate itself with Gandhi's assassination. Don't worry, he will be back. I promise you..." Omar held out his palm.

"And Ira..." Omar hesitated.

"What is it, Omar? Ask me what you want. I've lost so much; I have nothing more to lose. I have told you what I have had to hide all these years. There is nothing more to hide," Ira held out her palms.

"Ira, does he look like me? Can I see a picture? I've missed his childhood; I've missed so much of him. Is he the Aman we had imagined?" Ira smiled,

"Yes Omar, he has your green eyes, determined chin and more than anything else, without ever having met you, he has your mannerisms. He has your linguistic gift, your articulation, your confidence. The erstwhile reticent Sameer now seems to have taken to social media or maybe someone else is managing his presence. I'll send you some of his childhood pictures soon. And yes, you remember Aman and Eshani!" Ira giggled at the memory.

In their picture-perfect dream family, teenage Omar and Ira were to have a son named Aman and a daughter named Eshani, both carefully selected names that would be acceptable to both Hindu and Muslim sensibilities.

Wandering around South Mumbai during their summer holidays, Ira and Omar had enjoyed yet another film *"Amar Akbar Anthony"* over turmeric popcorn at Regal Cinema in Colaba. It was a 1977 film re-released on its 15th anniversary. In splits over how ridiculous this one had been, they had ended up at the Mondegar café around the corner. Over tall glasses of cold coffee, they laughed at the convoluted coincidences in the plot, the three brothers, separated, then adopted by three blessed individuals who were the very embodiment of the stereotypes defined by each faith, the loud costumes, and the foot-tapping songs. The conversation had progressed to what Omar and Ira would call their children after they would marry one day.

"If we have two sons, let's call them Amar and Akbar. Amar to keep the Dixits happy and Akbar to appease the Siddiquis," Omar had guffawed. Also, Akbar is the stereotypical *Qawwali* guy in bright, shiny green shirts and his girlfriend is a doctor. So, if you still end up being a doctor of some sort, I can be the stereotypical *Qawwali* guy!" Omar thumped the table. After much banter, they had agreed on the two agnostic names, tucked away safely in a dream compartment that had remained shut forever.

On the call, they relived the gaiety of those years.

"Omar, I did try naming him Aman. It has a lovely meaning – peace. As you know, naming a child is the *Aatya's* (father's sister) prerogative. Unfortunately, Sriram's sister has been removed from our lives. That is another story to tell you later. Sriram was fine with the name, though like everything else about me, he said my choices were always "anglicised". Sriram's mother wouldn't stop pushing the envelope for various Hindu God names so difficult to pronounce and spell, certain to have been shortened to something meaningless. She reluctantly agreed to - Sameer. I was satisfied with the meaning – 'the breeze' in Sanskrit, 'the amicable friend' in Urdu.

Come to think of it, that is what Sameer has been to me, my confidante, my ally, through his precocious childhood and rapid maturity during his teenage years, except now…" His chin cupped in his palm, the cup of tea by his side, Omar lived through Ira's bitter-sweet sojourn.

"But you had him Ira, and still do. He is sure to return. Also…" Omar fumbled again,

"Also, Sameer seems to be devoted to the memory of your late husband and rightly so. Does he…does he know who his biological father is?" he held his breath, his trepidation mounting as he waited for Ira's answer.

Ira told him about her meeting with Sameer in the London café and the shocking allegations of her concocting stories to ruin his political career. Omar took in the deep furrows that appeared on Ira's forehead when she spoke about this hurtful incident.

"Ira, he's shocked, why wouldn't he be? I'm bewildered by your revelation, naturally he would be. Besides, he is in a trance, don't expect any logic to work. I have seen this with the indoctrinated Muslim boys. These religious influencers seem to work magic. Go eat something now Ira, before your head starts hurting. I'll call you tomorrow. Take care."

Omar disconnected the call. He remembered how she had once tried to observe Ramadan resulting in a splitting headache. So much had happened and so much changed since.

Chapter 9:

In the name of RACE

December 26, 2018, Boxing Day.

Leila and Ira were on a train from London to Bradford, via Leeds. The ever-efficient Patricia had sent Ira her tickets and told her Leila would meet her inside the train at King's Cross station. Ira had not met Leila since the visit to her office. But there had been a brief call from Leila directly, this time.

"Hi, this is Leila Maria." Ira noticed that she did not address her as either Ira or *Maami*. She had dropped the formal Mrs. Godse. Ira acknowledged that the call must have taken a lot of effort.

"Hello Leila, good to hear from you," said Ira warmly. Leila got straight to the point,

"Mum's not likely to be in London any time soon. I'm visiting her in Bradford post-Christmas. I asked her if you could join. Would you like to?" Ira held her breath, trying to suppress her excitement,

"I understand Swati *tai* may not be traveling. Thanks. When did you say it is convenient?"

"Boxing Day. I take the 9 am train so that I can get work done on the way. I'll get Patricia to book you a day return," Leila's voice was muffled.

"Oh yes, Boxing Day would be fine," Ira spoke hurriedly, hearing another announcement.

"I need to rush for my flight. Patricia will be in touch," Leila was gone. And now, Ira was seated on the train at King's Cross with her handbag on her lap, and another home-stitched printed cloth bag in the overhead compartment. She scanned the stream of travellers. These seats were reserved, so she was unlikely to experience what she often did aboard public transport in London. As she walked past the fast filling over ground trains, the window seats were the first ones to fill up, then the aisle seats, then the middle. This was natural. What was not, and never publicly acknowledged, was her observation that often, the only seats empty were those next to overweight and black people. When she noticed this the first time a few years ago that some people preferred to stand for an hour instead of sitting next to a black person, she had found it unbelievable and tried to dismiss it as a coincidence. After 25 years of train journeys gone by, there was only so much that could pass off as coincidence. Ira also knew the suspicions that the sight of a woman wearing a headscarf, or Asian man with a beard, dressed in a long *kurta* would evoke in Central London. Ira had never faced this herself. But the quiet, non-confrontational person that she had evolved into, she would never venture into Central London wearing Indian clothes. Dressed in formal British workwear, Ira was unlikely to face discrimination on London transport. In the NHS, there were ample instances, but none as severe as what she had seen her black colleagues or patients encounter. Ira continued to scan the travellers. There was no sign of Leila. She looked around nervously. What if Leila missed the train? She was too nervous to meet the intimidating Swati by herself. Approaching Leila had taken such effort.

Ira caught sight of the flying figure of Leila on the platform, squeezing her case onto the train, seconds before the automatic doors shut. Panting, she dragged the case, ignoring the shaking heads and sidelong glances. Ira stood up and waved. Leila smiled, breathing heavily and sank into the seat. Ira held across a bottle of water and a tiny steel box containing cardamom pods, and dainty, translucent cubes of crystallised sugar. In response to Leila's quizzical expression, Ira smiled,

"In Marathi, this type of sugar is called – *khadi sakhar*. As children, it was a solution to all our problems, from a bout of coughing to just a fun treat. We did not see the volume and variety of chocolate that you see, so even a sugar cube seemed like a treat. I keep some with me as a solution to my motion sickness, and for when I need a bit of an energy boost. I can see you've had a rushed morning…"

Leila picked a cardamom pod and popped it in her mouth, sighing, "What a morning! Packing the kids into the car with James with breakfasts eaten. Leon was whimpering about how he couldn't be with Mummy and Daddy at the same time. He threw a tantrum about the unfairness of having to choose between being on a train with me and the pantomime with Daddy. Then followed Lady Ella's sermon to him about how life is often not fair and how one should learn to "maximise the privileges we have." As you can see, she overhears too many of my phone conversations. It wouldn't stop there. Leon wanted Mummy, not Daddy, to explain to him what "maximise", and "privilege" mean. Ella then flung the allegation of "stupidity" and Leon refused to finish his cereal until I had explained the terms and put Ella in her place for being rude. As you can see, I nearly missed the train!"

Ira's eyes lit up at the mention of the two cherubic occupants of the family picture in Leila's office she had seen a month ago,

"How old are the children?" she asked, smiling at Leila's account of the morning.

"They will be four, with Leon going on a terrible three and Ella sagacious 16!" Leila rolled her eyes.

"Ella sounds like Sameer as a child, sponging up words with all his senses, what any of us ever said to him, what he overheard, from TV, stories, guessing words from pictures, shop signs from streets and voracious reading," Ira's wistful eyes looked outside the window to hide the tears that threatened to flow. It had been her first ever Christmas without Sameer yesterday.

Sameer's birthday, marking Sriram's first death anniversary, had gone past, a day of lingering pain. So had Christmas. He had not returned Ira's calls on both days. She had not bothered with a tree this year but for the death anniversary, she had visited the Godse house, sat through Ratnaprabha's prayers before his framed photograph, and left. Too weary to live through judgement, the Godses did not invite anyone for the first death anniversary prayers. They did have a few well-meaning friends from the Maharashtrian community who could have kept them company. But the Godses, always afraid, had kept unannounced home visitors at bay, earlier because of Sriram's unpredictable behaviour, later to hide the fact that Sriram and Ira were separated, and then, because of the suicide. No priest was invited to officiate the ceremony. During that brief conversation in the coffee shop, before Ira revealed the story of his birth, and when Ira had wished him a belated happy birthday, Sameer had mentioned he couldn't have possibly celebrated his father's year of passing away.

Ira had been staring outside the window, her eyes dulled. Leila was engrossed in typing, Leila had specified that this was her work time without the children, Ira closed her eyes. Just like she used to when she and Omar were together and for years later, the first image that wafted in, was of their last interaction. After that first call, he called the next day, and then a few days later, and then yesterday. In between these calls, were the messages. While Ira's life was private, Omar's views, his social media profiles, his appointment to various committees...seemed to be in public view. If all these years, she had chosen to find out more, get in touch, it would have been easy. But she didn't want to. As a 19-year-old mother of an illegitimate child in India, what could Ira have given Sameer? Instead, he had a father's surname, doting grandparents, and a life of privilege. Ira thought she had no right to shake his world. Besides, she was determined to give him the top-quality education and career opportunities that the UK offered. With Cahya in the picture, the little globule of a life of normalcy would be complete. Devoid of the intensity of her relationship with Omar and the euphoria of their dreams, Ira lived her life with no complaints. But the shock of Sameer's irrational indoctrination had left her with no choice but to scrape the abrasions of the wounds of their parting again. Omar's social media profile said single. Ira's still said, married. She just couldn't muster the energy to deal with more condolence messages from long-lost friends and contacts if she changed it to anything else. There was so much to ask, so much to say. Yet, the predominant theme of the conversation with Omar was Sameer and what could be done to bring him back. Ira was woken up by Leila lightly tapping her elbow,

"Some tea or coffee?"

Ira rubbed her eyes, "Yes please, coffee with milk, no sugar," she smiled politely at the attendant with the trolley. Leila had put away her laptop. She had tucked the sheaf of papers into the space between Ira and Leila as the coffee cups were placed on the trays. Ira sipped her coffee quietly knowing she was treading on thin ice, careful to not mention the volatile subject of the Godses. Tightly woven with this topic was the potentially combustible time bomb of race. Time-tested British small talk was out of the way. The weather had been discussed. Ira had minimal knowledge of sport. Ira opened the conversation with what she assumed would be an uncontroversial subject, "You have amazing energy Leila, to get so much done during travel."

"Well, the regular cases of defending the downtrodden for crimes uncommitted, a free advisory for those who suffered gross injustice during last year's Grenfell towers fire, a committee for the outrage generated by the Windrush scandal, my own doctorate dissertation due in 10 months, delightful but demanding children, school runs and juggling day-care timings. Also, my husband James, though wonderful, does expect appearances at utterly avoidable social events, like yesterday's family Christmas lunch for instance! That sums up what I have on my plate, so a train ride to finish off pending work is a blessing!" Leila sighed. Ira was relieved to see that her question had not offended Leila. In fact, she wondered if Leila's crisp interactions were due to her being overstretched and the need for personal space (something she gladly gave Sameer). "Personal space" was a concept that had been absent in the bustling Dixit household, always teeming with guests and servants, and in the more compact Godse house overpowered with demands of Ratnaprabha's rituals.

Leila continued, "My 40th is around the corner and it doesn't help energy levels! After two IVF cycles, finally these two arrived. We had underestimated the demands of childcare and no family around to help. Ira hesitated. Sensing that Leila seemed to be revealing so much, she said softly,

"If you and James think it is alright, and if Ella and Leon would like, you could drop them off to my apartment in Islington on a weekend, or I can come round any evening after 6pm and keep them engaged if you need to be working late…only if you think that is appropriate," Ira looked at Leila with trepidation. The offer left Leila bewildered,

"Why would anyone want to do that, disturb your peaceful existence with high energy, incessant chatter, and with Leon, if one is not careful, potential damage to property. But that is nice of you, thank you for the kind offer!" Leila was touched. Considering that no-one, neither James' parents, siblings, nor his extended family, all living in detached affluent homes around London had ever offered to pitch in, Leila and James had a tough time, juggling travel schedules, work commitments, a day-care facility that had strict opening and closing hours, rain, sun or snow; and a succession of part-time childminders who Leon's boisterous behaviour had driven away. Leila was confused by Ira's statement.

"Islington? I thought you and my Mum's parents live in Croydon?" Leila asked, her left eyebrow raised, curiously, a mannerism characteristic of her grandma Ratnaprabha. Ira brushed the thought aside and took a deep breath before answering,

"Sameer and I have lived in a two-bedroom Islington apartment, initially renting a studio, then a one-bedroom, then finally this one, which will be ours finally after the last mortgage is cleared. The Godse's house is in Croydon, you are right. Sameer and I have been visiting the grandparents every week and since he's gone away to India, I still do. Your grandparents have preferred to tell people we live in Islington as it is closer for me to get to hospital and Sameer to secondary school. Respecting their wishes, I never moved forward with divorce proceedings but your *Maama* Sriram and I separated years ago." Ira sighed. Leila looked at her incredulously,

"Why would you do that? Whatever I understood of the funeral proceedings, the priest said, widow" Ira sighed again and said in a tired voice,

"What Swati *tai* has told you is correct. Sriram never got over the trauma of losing her. I was 18 when we got married, 19 when Sameer was born. I spent my 20s studying for my A Levels, and then medicine. I had a few simple expectations from the marriage. They couldn't be fulfilled. That was still okay. I had seen my husband living in fear of his parents, work colleagues and society in general. When I realised the impact on Sameer, I finally took the much-criticised step of moving out of the Godse house."

Leila knew that Ira was just a few years older than her. She was not like the domestic violence survivors she had met through her Mum's work, women who came from poor families from the Indian subcontinent, with little or no education. The financial dependence meant they were suppressed by their in-laws and parents, making it very difficult for them to speak out and even more difficult for them to step out and try to make a living, especially when there were children involved. Time and again, Swati and her co-workers at the Women's Collective had tried to impress upon them that their acceptance of torture was casting indelible debilitating impressions on daughters valuing "family honour" more than self-respect and their own health. Even more dangerous, the sons would grow up entitled and arrogant, assuming it was perfectly acceptable to violate a wife's dignity.

Swati's struggle to rehabilitate them continued. Why did Ira, an independent woman, have to undergo the humiliating motions of being the "widow" at her uncle's funeral?

Leila had seen no reason to attend the funeral. The iron-willed Swati had been distraught at the news of her brother's death, and Leila had made time to accompany her. What Ira had told her, had made her reflect and look at Ira with respect.

Leila's experience in handling complex cases for people of various ethnicities, had honed her mind to "sense" versus just "see". Her adroitness was gradually sensing valuable nuances to her unilateral perception of her mother's family, so far conspicuously absent from her life.

Chapter 10:

In the name of HONOUR

Swati *Aapa* lived alone, in a tiny brick home, which also served as an office, at the end of one of the smaller lanes off a busy Bradford Street. The front door, painted bright blue, led into a small lounge with a silver box television set, a sofa-bed, and a lightwood four-seater breakfast table in the corner. On the mantelpiece, next to the table, was a collection of photographs, Leila in a short, sleeveless pink dress, cut low, two strings of heavy imitation pearls around her neck carrying a silver clutch studded with pearls, her hair in a stylish, flattering bun at the side of her head, a copy of the one of Leila and Swati at her 60th birthday, one with Leila in a flowing white dress and veil and James in a tuxedo and a fourth of a beaming Swati holding the new-born twins. The kitchen was a single platform with basic fittings and a small refrigerator. The "office" was a small study room, posters and flyers pasted on the walls, cluttered with stacks of leaflets, stationery and two desktop computers. The study led to the conservatory, which opened into a prim back-garden lined with benches and a separate backdoor.

Swati had welcomed Leila with a tight, warm embrace, a peck on her cheek, and the inevitable maternal concern about Leila's dark circles,

"You are working too hard, Leila. You'll ruin your health!"

"Guess where I get that from Mum!" Leila quipped, placing her shoes in the corner and striding straight into the kitchen to put the kettle on.

Swati had greeted Ira with a non-committal polite smile, showing her to the downstairs toilet to freshen up after the journey, and asking her to take a seat on the sofa while she joined Leila in the kitchen. As Ira sat down, she could hear the kettle boil and the two in animated conversation. Not wishing to eavesdrop, Ira engaged herself in looking at the photographs on the mantelpiece. Momentous, joyous occasions were marked here, all of which seemed to have occurred after Leila's growing up. Like the photographic history of the Godses seemed to have commenced only on their arrival in England in the 1960s, Swati's life seemed to have begun only in the early 90s. Leila's voice rose over the din of the kettle,

"Mum, go, sit down. Don't I know where things are? I know you must have worked late last night so that you don't have to work for the next two days that I'm here. Apart from smiling politely through the Christmas lunch with James' extended family, I've done little else yesterday. For you, festivals mean nothing. The women of this lane sense a problem and first run to their Swati *Aapa*. When will they learn to stand up for themselves?" Leila's loving reprimand received a befitting reply,

"It is the same women Leila, who made sure I didn't have to cook a meal for an entire fortnight after my eye-surgery last year. They may squabble over their fences at other times, but the punctuality of the rota system would put the London Underground to shame. Three hot meals a day would arrive at the doorstep, sometimes with a child, a husband or the women themselves,

"*Aapa*, try this, *Aapa,* don't worry it is all vegetarian!" Even when I stop working, God forbid, I cannot imagine living in your neighbourhood full of London professionals too busy to smile or find out their neighbours' names! Though it would be great to receive more advice from Lady Ella and keep up with the brat's energy!"

Having had the last word of Round 1 of the good-natured verbal tournament, Swati came out to the lounge to join Ira on the sofa. Ira got up and handed over the cloth bag she had brought along for her. For just a few seconds, Swati's gaze rested on the Indore saree border on the deep blue cotton bag. She paused. Brushing away a thought, she exclaimed,

"What is all this? You shouldn't have. Indian food is so expensive in London. I always tell Leila she should try the Pakistani shops here instead of those overrated places," Swati shook her head. Ira marvelled at how much this statement reminded her of Ratnaprabha's frugality, including the shake of the head. Ira said instead,

"Swati *Tai*, I made these myself, they are just packed in takeaway boxes. Coconut *barfi* and peas *karanjis*. I had heard from Sriram that you like these," Ira said hesitantly, careful to not mention her in-laws, though these were snacks her mother-in-law had taught her to make. Swati opened the box and popped a small piece of *barfi* into her mouth. She slowly sat herself down on the single chair by the sofa, her eyes shut. Ira would never forget the expression on the face that bore such a likeness to her husband. Leila had emerged from the kitchen and had quietly placed the tea-tray on the table. Swati opened her green eyes, covered in a film of tears, mourning the loss of a family she left over four decades ago, a brother who had always remembered what she liked but not had the courage to reach out to her and relishing the taste of a lost home.

Swati opened the second box and took a bite from the crunchy, boat shaped *karanji*, deep fried, but devoid of traces of oil, an explosion of the subtle flavours of the spiced green pea and coconut filling tucked into the wheat pastry. She offered the box to Leila. Tears streaming down her reddened cheeks, she held out her palm to Ira. Like they often do in Indian homes, care had been expressed through food, the significance of a favourite dish remembered and the effort that went into getting it right. Nothing was said but as Ira took the palm offered and sat down next to her, the kinship was complete.

Leila patted Swati's shoulder and offered a teacup. Attempting to snap out of her despondence, Swati said,

"Try the *muttor karanjis* Leila. They are like *samosas*, but not just the shape, even the filling is different. There also used to be a sweet version of these. And the coconut *barfi* too - I have not had this for years. I've never seen these in any of the Asian shops, I guess these must be exclusive to Maharashtra," and then to Ira,

"The women I work with often express gratitude with food. Besides, I'm not a very good cook. I interact with women mainly from Bangladesh and Pakistan, and they call me Swati *Aapa*. For over 40 years, there has been no interaction with anyone from Maharashtra. I believe you are from Mumbai? I haven't been, not since I was a teenager, and Leila has never been, never wants to," Swati's voice was soft, a stark contrast to the firm, sloganeering, woman of steel image that had been a source of admiration... She explained,

"I don't practice any religion, but my work takes me to women from Sikh and Hindu families, mainly from the North of India. Bradford did not have a single Hindu temple till this one was inaugurated with fanfare by the Queen ten years ago. I've never been inside. Over the years, we've had Sikh weddings in one of the many Gurdwaras here, and the Christian weddings in the churches. I get invited by the children who grew up healthy because their mothers finally walked out years ago. There are over 100 mosques in Bradford now, but women are not allowed inside. For Muslim weddings (and we get a lot of invites for those), we cover our heads with dupattas to honour the tradition and attend."

Ira had read about the work of the Women's Collectives across the UK. The most widely known among these was a landmark case which was made into a critically acclaimed Hindi movie titled *"Provoked"* in 2006, among the handful of films she had watched in the year gone by of living alone. It took the ghastly story to people who still carried a rose-tinted image of life for Indians in the UK. The movie had shocked Ira, given how little she had to do with other migrant families. Ira had been curious to know how accurate these depictions were.

"Swati *Tai*, the movie *"Provoked"* really moved me. Are things still like that?"

"Oh yes, *Provoked*, inspired by the Kiranjit Ahluwalia campaign in 1991, valiantly fought by the Southall Sisters," Swati nodded.

"Kiranjit grew up in Punjab, North India, where she said her fate was to get married and have children like the rest of the girls in her family. She went to Canada, to her sister, after her parents passed away, hoping to delay marriage, study and become independent. She endured intense, physical and mental abuse at the hands of her husband Deepak. One night, something in her snapped and the brutalities provoked her to set him on fire and she escaped.

Even the law, British law, which Kiranjit had believed is a modern law, would not understand her provocation, ruled that she should have "calmed down" after the argument about his affairs and simply dismissed her injuries including the burning of her face by a hot iron. Even him threatening her with a hot poker the same night was not considered enough reason. Trapped in her abusive violent marriage for years, in prison she felt free.

She learnt English, played badminton, and even co-authored a book, which was then made into the film.

"To feel free in prison, what an existence that must have been!" exclaimed Ira and asked,

"Right through those court hearings, the question raised was why did Kiranjit endure the violence for years, why did her extended family not come to her aid?"

"In the name of "cultural differences"! The courtroom had no women of colour then and was questioning what had really transpired. Five years after she got married, Kiranjit had been to India and complained to her brother and his family about the abuse. Following a profuse apology from Deepak and the promise to behave, Kiranjit was dispatched right back to the UK to live with him!" Swati threw up her hands in the air, poured herself a glass of water and continued,

"Today just one pub remains on this side of Bradford. The Muslims do not drink, but that does not stop them from beating their wives. Across religions, races and cultures, the advice from family who try to gaslight the pain of a woman scrambling to escape domestic abuse is the same,

"A child in the picture would cure everything. So get pregnant!"

"And that is why I was keen to study law. I could never complete my education, but Leila Madam here fights like a lioness in court and with her clipped British accent, telling them things from their own law books, mind you!" Swati's anger dissolved at her discernible pride at Leila's achievements. Leila deftly diverted the attention away, saying,

"Mum's right. I was in High School, at the cusp of career choices when the Kiranjit case was raging on. I had seen Mum and her associates struggle to raise funds to engage legal aid for women who had strong cases but nobody to represent them. Why would white lawyers be interested in unrelatable terms like "family honour"? Why would South Asian male lawyers represent them and risk criticism and pressure from their own community? And the women, their passports held back by the husbands, were primarily concerned about their children. In their trapped existence, the daunting legal route which came at a premium, was meant for others with privilege." Leila looked out of the window. She turned a palm at the tiny back garden beyond the room that was used as an office.

"I would come home from school and find these benches outside occupied by women in headscarves. A child on the lap, two playing in the garden, a fourth on its way, still nursing the wounds the husband had chosen to inflict on his pregnant wife. An extreme case of abuse may be followed by a visit to the local clinic supervised by the husband. These were trained to inform the doctor, through gestures, how they burnt an elbow while frying *puris* or accidentally collided against a glass door resulting in the angry bruise on the forehead." Leila raised her upturned palm at the sofa-bed and the small table,

"In the early days of Mum's work, I would be here having my cereal before school and Mum would motion me to be quiet. Escaping the wrath of her husband for the crime of putting less salt or too many chillies in his elaborate dinner, a woman had run away from home, clutching a suckling infant. They had arrived at the doorstep past midnight. Mum had taken them in, nursed the angry scars on her midriff and offered bread, butter, tea, and bananas. The baby in her arms, she had finally fallen asleep on the sofa-bed just as the sun was rising,"

Leila shook her head vigorously, "The worst part of this story is not those angry wounds. When I returned from school, the woman had left, not to seek a living, but taken away by a delegation of elders from the husband's family who assured her that her remorseful husband had been weeping all night, worried about her and that her other two children were refusing to eat without her. What would Mum have felt at that moment, especially when some incidents were followed by aspersions on her own character, her own destroyed family honour, and threats to her life for meddling in family matters." Leila rose and walked to the window. Ira was looking at Swati with reverence, thinking,

"How could parents not feel pride in such a daughter?" Arms crossed, Leila leaned against the window. It was the formidable Leila, London's courtrooms may have seen,

"Years later, when I studied legal history in the context of gender, I looked up cases like Kiranjit's, known in British textbooks as *R V Ahluwalia*, that have contributed to changing laws for domestic abuse victims in the UK. This one changed the legal definition of the word "provocation". The case of the reclassification of Kiranjit's crime from "murder" to "manslaughter"

Manjiri Gokhale Joshi

has been cited in future cases leading to acquittal including a Welsh 24-year-old Emma Humphreys, who killed her boyfriend in his 40s and the British Sarah Thornton who killed her husband. Prior to the recognition of "battered woman's syndrome", provocation was supposed to be a characteristic male response to an act of violence that had just occurred and led to a "temporary loss of control". Demonstrating lack of empathy for the change in "reasonable behaviour" that is a result of continuing cruelty, Thornton's life imprisonment sentence had been accompanied by courtroom advice on how she could have walked out of the house or gone upstairs instead of killing her husband who had been beating her black and blue for years! Gone upstairs indeed! Would a male judge understand a woman trapped in a violent relationship?" Leila's dark eyes were flashing. Ira had goosebumps. One more time, Ira felt as Saguna would have reiterated, "privileged".

Snapping her fingers, Leila started walking about the room, clearing the teacups, picking up cookie crumbs from the edge of the sofa. She looked at her Mum. Swati nodded and they both looked at Ira. "Enough of work talk. Ira *Maami*, stay the night, let's cancel your ticket and book you to return with me tomorrow. You still have so much to hear from us and for you to tell us so much more..." Leila had referred to Ira as Ira *Maami*. Swati gave her a broad smile. This one reminded Ira of Prabhakar's luminous response to young Sameer's good grades. Swati placed her palm on Ira's shoulder,

"I would love to hear about Sameer. He has turned out to be so handsome and I believe he has a girlfriend? And your journey of studying medicine as a young mother in the 90s. I so wanted to go to university after Leila started school, never could. Stay, Ira, we have so much to catch up on," Swati's smile was gracious. It was difficult to believe that it had been just a couple of hours since they met.

Ira smiled back,

"I'm tempted. It would be good to make a quick trip to the shops for a pair of clothes. I'm not a very fussy shopper. If I'm staying anyway, can I make two requests: The first, I'd like to make a day trip to Howarth tomorrow, the Bronte sisters' home. We studied "Wuthering Heights" and "Jane Eyre" in school. These were my images of England before I came here and never could see the England I had imagined - a world so different from the Bradford you have lived in. And second, let me cook you a simple Maharashtrian meal, something I've never been able to find in a restaurant across the UK during my 25 years here. Leila should be resting or finishing the piles of work accumulated and so should you Swati *Tai*. After the empty nest I've had for the past year, it will be really satisfying to cook for someone else." Swati and Leila responded with beaming smiles.

"If the *karanjis* and coconut *barfi* you brought are anything to go by, you are an outstanding cook. I was too much of a rebel to learn to cook elaborate Indian food and then later, so busy, the meals were just to get by. Let me show you where things are and if you need any more ingredients, we have a Bangladeshi shop around the corner," Swati led Ira into the tiny kitchen.

During Ira's carefree existence in Mumbai, the cook *Janaa bai* dominated the kitchen. Saguna was always busy with her social work and Priyamvada with her social life and short-term attempts to engage herself like the beautician's course and embroidery classes. Saguna and Priyamvada had shared a strained relationship. Saguna's firm opinion was that Priyamvada and the women she associated with, through her kitty parties and hobby classes, were wasting the freedom and access to education that the social reformers had fought so hard to achieve. Saguna was in fact extremely fond of Priyamvada's sister Pratibha Joag and rather looked forward to her visits from Pune.

Another path breaker with her work as a priestess, Saguna would enjoy listening to Pratibha's stories of how their explanations in Marathi and even English of what the rituals in Sanskrit really meant were gaining acceptance gradually. This was in stark contrast with male priests who often continued to ramble on at weddings ignored by guests least engaged with the ceremony. Saguna and Pratibha would often discuss the origin of verses, traditions, and customs and if Ira was at home, Saguna would ensure Ira was invited to join the conversation. It is these conversations that Ira recalled as the evening progressed…

Chapter 11:

In the name of RITUALS

The high-profile lawyer from London had been her Mum's daughter in Bradford, tenderly taking care of her, cleaning up after the meal, browsing through the kitchen cupboards to see if any groceries needed replenishing. Swati had thoroughly relished Ira's simple, tasty food, reminiscent of the parental home she had left behind years ago.

Ira had made *aamti* (traditional Maharashtrian lentil curry), plain white rice, *bharli vaangi* (aubergines stuffed with peanut powder, grated coconut, and spices) and soft fresh *phulkas* which she rolled out deftly. Swati made a mixed *koshimbir* (cucumber and carrot salad) to go along.

"Do you mind if I add a *jeera phodni* to your salad Swati *Tai*? It will complete the traditional meal," Ira asked. In the smallest of saucepans Ira could find in the kitchen, she heated a tablespoonful of *tup* (clarified butter), added a teaspoon of cumin seeds and then a few curry leaves. Then went in a little salt, sugar, and asafoetida powder. The whole sizzling mixture was poured onto the grated cucumber and carrots as seasoning and mixed along with a couple of tablespoonfuls of yoghurt. Leila was amused to see her mother chattering away in Marathi, discovering common ground with a woman she had known about but kept away from, for years. With the dinner polished off, the three of them had settled down in the living room to chat. On the centre table, Swati had placed three wide glass bowls covered with aluminium foil and a plate of golden-brown slices of pudding.

"Surprise for Leila!" she beamed. Leila sprung on them like a child, uncovering the bowls covered in fragrant rose water and nuts,

"Oh my God *Phirni*! That's got to be Nasmeen *Khaala*. And Jamaican sweet potato pudding too!" Leila dipped her spoon into her favourite desserts.

"Nasmeen heard you'll be visiting and sent these around with her grandson. She's too frail to walk across. Maybe you should drop in? And Mrs. Brown, bless her, ambled down the lane this morning and spent an hour recalling memories of Christmas days gone by." Ira was marvelling at these relationships. It was almost like living in Mumbai in the 1980s, neighbours coming around unannounced, sending food. This was so different from Ratnaprabha's paranoia about offending neighbours in Croydon and in the Islington flat, Ira would have barely been able to tell who lived in each apartment.

Before settling down to dessert, Swati had offered Ira a floral print *salwar kameez* to sleep in saying,

"Leila does not wear Indian clothes. Maybe you will not mind."

Ira thanked her and gratefully changed out of her knee-length skirt and sweater with woollen tights into the soft, linen well-worn flowing garments. As a college student in Mumbai, Ira had worn a variety of trendy clothes – Jeans, skirts, dresses, short kurtas, long, flowing kurtas with baggy bottoms, batik printed scarves and more. Ira also owned a collection of pure silk long kurtas embroidered with gold and silver trimmings, which she would wear for weddings and festivals in India. If she felt like it, she would accessorise the outfit with dangling earrings, sometimes a single pearl drop or small gold hoops.

Whether she would paint her forehead with an ornate design to go with the outfit or stick on a coloured *tikli* just above her eyebrows…well, it just depended on the occasion and the mood.

During one of her early encounters with the Maharashtrian community in London, Ira was wearing one of these deep green and silver outfits, a long-sleeved kurta that reached well below the knees, the side slits trimmed with orange rosebuds and pearls. Her Mumbai tailor had teamed the top with black flared trousers with ornate green and orange embroidery at the ankles. Ira recalled a well-meaning Sunita *Kaku* in London telling her, "Don't wear your Indian clothes around London unless it is Southall, Hounslow, or Wembley.

They will think you are Pakistani. Still to experience racism or even realise that an action or word had racist connotations, was Ira's naïve response,

"Why *Kaku*, how does it make a difference?" Sunita clicked her tongue, and said in a conspiratorial tone,

"You are new to England, Ira; you don't know what that means. If white people see you in a *salwar kameez* and *dupatta,* they will think you can't speak in English, you have produced nine children and because of yours, their own children have no spaces in London's state schools. The country is theirs, over time, we get permanent residency and then British citizenship by naturalization. Of course, we work intensely hard for this. Our Indian degrees are not valued, so we study hard and re-qualify, we diligently pay taxes, almost never ask for council benefits, our families usually have one or two children, who invariably go to universities, and I understand from your mother-in-law, you are studying for a degree too, that is good, you must. But all this is not enough, you need to blend in. No need to wear bright clothes, no need to express your individuality too much, keep your jewellery to minimal and only be seen in toned down western clothes. Besides, most people here do not know or care about the difference between Hindus and Muslims. If you must wear Indian clothes, wear them at our private Indian events," Sunita *Kaku* had walked away with the air of a sermon giver.

Ira had stood rooted to the ground, shaking her head at the divisiveness that she had not seen in Mumbai until the riots, but seemed commonly expressed in circles the Godses associated with. Over time, she had come to realise that Sunita *Kaku* was right. Only, in her sermon, she should have added Bradford to the list of Asian areas. When Ira and Swati made a quick trip to the city centre, Ira spotted women in black *burkhas* and headscarves, a vision she had rarely encountered in Mumbai. Not for nothing was this called Little Pakistan.

Bradford had often been in the news for the wrong reasons, communal riots, ghetto violence, one of the crime locations of the Rochdale child grooming scandal and the cases of Muslim youth indoctrination. But in Swati's lounge, partaking delectable *phirni* from a Muslim household, pudding from a Jamaican one, Ira felt honoured to witness a slice of Bradford, which the rest of the UK rarely got to see.

Leila sighed,

"This is such pampering. First Ira *Maami*'s *karanjis* at tea, the most delicious dinner, I had never imagined Maharashtrian food could be so tasty and now this! How do women do this, and you especially Ira *Maami*, to dish out such delicacies after a busy workday. Were you always such a super cook?"

"Oh no Leila. I was a typical teenager, always out of the house, if not in college, at a movie, eating out, meeting friends. And when I was at home, I was devouring books by English and American authors from our library. I was least interested in cooking and not really expected to do housework given our able cook. Even for Diwali, we used to have a separate local lady we had nicknamed *Chakli mavshi*, who used to come in and make the *faraal* items." Ira laughed sheepishly.

"Oh my, Princess Ira, cook and cleaner huh!" Leila and Swati looked at each other. The concept of house help was alien and a sign of affluence. Ira tried to defend herself,

"It's quite common in India to have at least part-time help daily. It is not as expensive and at least my grandmother went out of her way to look after the families of the domestic help we had. They were loving and loyal. So, when I arrived in the UK, and was expected to roll out *polis* and shape *modaks* in the Godse kitchen, oh my God, I felt so inept, so embarrassed. But over time, *Aai*, given her discipline, ensured I continued to be berated for my failed attempts till I perfected the dishes," Ira stopped abruptly, covering her mouth with her palm. She had unearthed the elephant in the room – and referred to Swati's mother as *"Aai"*. Dreading the end of their amicability, Ira raised her eyelids in apprehension.

The uncomfortable silence was ultimately broken by Swati,

"Apart from her cooking skills, my mother seems to have passed on the overpowering emotional mood characteristic of the Godse home - Fear. The way other people need air to survive, the Godses thrive on fear, fear of what their Maharashtrian friends will say and the fear of what the English neighbours will think of them. Their solution to overcome these fears is to conform. Each member of the Godse household must scuttle their thoughts, feelings, their dreams and fall in step, and become one of the worker ants trudging along the fear-driven path of homogeneity!" Swati's embittered voice rose. Ira's palms broke out in sweat, the trepidation of a showdown mounting.

"This was not going well after all," she surmised to herself sadly.

Swati's voice thundered,

"There is nothing to fear anymore. Why should you feel guilty? Fear made Sriram a shadow of himself and drove me away. Leila tells me you separated years ago, but you pandered to their whim of hiding this – once again, conforming to combat their fear of society. Leila told me that you still visit them every week and here you are, trying to get me to put behind my humiliation and appease them just because they now have no-one in their lives! I know you are not their emissary. They are far too proud to reach out to me. We welcome you in our lives. What they did though, was so wrong. The perpetrators of the fear got what they deserved!" Swati was wringing her hands in agitation. Leila took her palm,

"Mum, must we?"

Swati patted Leila's hand; her flashing green eyes bore into Ira. She spoke in a steady, determined voice,

"Yes, we must Leila. Ira is here out of goodwill, and she must know. You've heard in bits and pieces, and I stopped bemoaning the past years ago. But today, you must both hear me out."

For a better part of an hour, Swati narrated how there was great joy at her birth in a small village near Nashik in Maharashtra in 1958. She had a vague recollection of studying in a Marathi school in Nashik and how she did not speak a word of English till the Godses moved to the UK when she was nine. She described a multitude of nondescript Yorkshire locations where they lived in houses with no central heating and questionable plumbing.

"Mind you Ira, this was not London. In fact, so tough was everything, that my parents never really took us on holiday to see London. Our childhood spanned across Ilkley, Keighley, Skipton, Halifax, far out places where white English doctors were reluctant to go. Finally, we ended up in a tiny house in bustling Manchester. The demands on an NHS doctor were heavy, as they must be today and *Baba* was always busy at work, dealing with his own demons of racism he faced but never articulated.

I never really picked up the language fully and my grades were just about average. With my halting, heavily accented English, two oiled pigtails and the maroon *tikli* on my forehead, I stood out, the butt of jokes in school. The joy of my life was the little one who followed me around everywhere, for whom, whatever I said was always the last word – Sriram," Swati's expression softened at the memory of her cherubic baby brother in a blue T-shirt that would make his eyes assume a greenish blue tinge.

She continued, bringing to life the Ratnaprabha of the 60s.

"I remember a Lele *Kaku* fluent in English, going to work at her surgery in a saree, her red *tikli* firmly on her forehead, the black and gold beads of her *mangalsutra*, peeping through her white doctor's coat. Amidst such doctor couples, was *Aai*, the daughter of a poor village Brahmin. She had finished High school, was proficient in reciting Sanskrit verses and assisting her father in his priestly duties. Of course, becoming a priestess was unthinkable at that time, but she had extensive knowledge of the customs to be followed for each event in a Brahmin's life that used the services of a priest – a *Maunj* (thread ceremony), a wedding, a death and of course the various religious festivals through the year. As a child, *Aai* had never associated with anyone who was not a Maharashtrian Brahmin. As the upholder of the path to God in their village, the priest's family was revered by people of all castes. Other Brahmin families would invite the schoolgirl Ratnaprabha and her sisters for a free meal on festivals, a much-awaited treat, as her parents could rarely afford a feast. Ratnaprabha would dress up the little girls in their only relatively presentable *parkar polkas* and following her mother's advice, also offer to help the hostess in the kitchen out of goodwill. People of any other caste, especially the scheduled castes, were never allowed anywhere close to the small Sathe dwelling as it was located within the temple premises," At this, Swati paused, shaking her head in disapproval.

"Incredulously, this woman continued to practise untouchability in the UK three decades later!" Swati's voice dripped resentment and she lifted both her palms in the air,

"Like other Maharashtrians around us, they were obsessed with their children getting a university education. Neither Sriram nor I could fulfil those dreams."

Leila observed that her Mum was able to talk about the past without agitation and venture into understanding the position her grandparents came from. Swati and Ira seemed to share kinship on the cultural connotations of the narrative. Leila asked,

"What's this *Maunj*, Mum?"

"Sriram had his *Maunj* ceremony when he was eight, when we went to India during half-term, the last time I've been. It was a small affair, with just *Aai's* sisters and their children, no one from *Baba's* side. I was irritated with *Aai* for coercing me into wearing a heavy silk sari in that heat and sitting next to Sriram through the *homa* fire. My aunts kept saying how pretty I looked, how grown up. *Aai's* mother then quipped that it was time *Aai* started "looking out" for a groom for me as despite my plus point of being fair, I was rather chubby, and it would be difficult later! I was horrified, knowing that my parents had no marriage plans for me until I finished university. But this flak about my appearance was uncalled for, at least among people who looked like me. I got enough of it otherwise in England.

I had no relationship with these people, and hadn't interacted with them for a decade. I had shut my mind to India, desperately trying to emulate my English classmates. I had also found a way to avoid people during the trip. I pretended my Marathi was not that good. This was deception, as we only spoke in Marathi at home and Mum would also coerce Sriram and me into learning Sanskrit verses. We would bumble through the Sanskrit prayers with no clue of what we were reciting. Eager to get done with it, we never asked what the meaning was and *Aai* never bothered explaining. I don't remember much about the *Maunj* rituals, but there was something about a stick given to Sriram and a bunch of women feeding him sweets while he sat on *Aai's* lap and a whole lot of Sanskrit verses Sriram was told to repeat. I have no idea why any of this was done and I was not interested!"

"Sounds hideous!" Leila raised her eyebrows, shrugging. Swati was moving on when Ira interrupted,

"If you don't mind Swati *Tai*, can I explain to Leila what you described actually signifies?"

"*Maunj* is a ritual that signifies a child's entry into student life. In the ancient times, the ritual was meant for Brahmin girls and boys as education was meant for both. In the Hindu texts, there are references to women scholars proficient in subjects like mathematics among others who were called to teach Sita, the wife of the King Ram, centuries ago. But with the invasions, it became increasingly unsafe for girls to travel to the *gurukul* (home of the Guru), so girls' education stopped. Over time, the *Maunj* ceremony was restricted to young Brahmin boys. The stalk of wood given to the child signifies a weapon that he must use to protect himself from the wild animals who may attack during his forest path to the Gurukul. In the modern context, this symbolic stalk represents wielding the weapons of self-control and discipline to guard students against distractions like electronic gadgets that threaten to take their focus away from the path of knowledge," Ira smiled. Mildly interested so far, Leila leaned forward,

"Interesting! And what's this about an eight-year-old being fed by a bunch of women? Ella has been dismissing attempts to be fed for over a year though I think Leon wouldn't mind the sweets bit!" Leila grinned. Swati nodded, smiling broadly at her grandchildren's antics. Ira answered,

"Well, in ancient times, children were home-schooled by elders in the family. After the *Maunj*, they lived in the Gurukul for eight to ten years, until the time the Guru was confident, they had gained not just the knowledge of the scriptures, maths and science, but also life skills and a good value system. They returned as teenagers having had little contact with the family in the interim given the arduous journey by foot and no means of communication. Naturally, a mother, about to be left with an empty nest, wanted to pamper her child. So, this was officially the last time the child sat on the mother's lap and was fed his favourite food by the women of the house, each of whom in the joint family setup, who must have had a relationship with him and may have even contributed to his home-schooling.

In fact, Leila, this is so much like the matriculation ceremony that some universities have, establishing your enrolment and committing to carry through. After the education is over, there is a brief ceremony called the *Soad Maunj* which is often conducted just before the wedding ceremony, for the teenager was now officially allowed to transition to phase two of his lifespan – from bachelor to householder with responsibility for earning a living, looking after a wife and extended family."

"Wow!" Phase 2, that's cool. No girlfriends at university!"Leila giggled.

"Yes, there are four prescribed phases of life – bachelor, married person, a forest dweller who passes on responsibility to the next generation and the last *Sanyas* – who gives up all desires. Hinduism prescribes that one should accept each of these phases with grace and move on. The purpose of religion is to show people the ideal path to live, not just burden them with rituals that bind them in a false sense of duty. Let me stop here and let Swati *Tai* continue with her story. I've launched into a discourse like my grandma used to!" Ira laughed sheepishly.

Swati spoke, her voice agitated,

"Ira, this sounds reasonable, we were just never told any of it. All I remember is Sriram's heart wrenching wail when his head was tonsured. The aunts were floating about admiring each other's jewellery, oblivious to the fact that Sriram's eyes were not watering because of the heat but his mortification at going to school in England, just a week later.

Aai had been called into the kitchen to sort out something about the sumptuous meal that followed. I ran into the room hearing Sriram's whimpering. *Aai's* younger sister Sumati *mavshi* had summoned her two sons into the room, aged nine and twelve. Like Sriram, their heads had been tonsured with just a circular patch of black and a little mouse-tail of hair left behind at the back of their heads. Her arm around Sriram and holding her youngest by the elbow, she spoke to him in a soft, kind voice,

"Sriram, your cousins have got their *Maunj* done. In the olden days, like your *Ajoba*, Brahmins would never grow their hair once the *Maunj* was done but maintain it as is. That was the sign of being Brahmin and it would give you immense respect in society. In fact, in those days, when all Brahmin men and boys sported their hair like this, chopping off the mouse-tail that signified your higher caste or growing your hair would be considered an aberration, inviting ridicule. Things change with time, and it is ok. Just because something is different, does not mean it is wrong. Your father, your uncles also went through it, but they went to college, then offices, they didn't want to stand out, so they let their hair grow back. Your hair will grow back soon. There is nothing to be afraid of. Some boys at school may play silly pranks like tapping your head and running away, but just ignore them. Your *Maunj* is done. You are a big boy now." Trembling, Sriram had not absorbed any of this.

Her fair cheeks reddened again as Swati related how Sriram had sulked through the India visit. Back in England, he had refused to go to school, even after *Baba* got him a cap to cover his head.

"For the next two years, Sriram would wake up at night, breaking out in sweat at the thought of ridicule. I was aggressive, I made friends easily, but

I also made enemies. I got bullied for being an over smart, brown cookie. But Sriram was quiet, made no friends and people just ignored him." Swati's tone had assumed a menacing growl. Swati narrated how she had thrown a tantrum at the dining table, demanding what was the need to go to India and do this *Maunj* business. Instead of launching into her usual mumbo jumbo of upholding Brahmanical tradition, Ratnaprabha's ever upright spine had curved over as she had bent over the dining table, wiping her moist eyes with the edge of her sari.

"He is eight years old. He barely speaks. He is so behind at school. There are nights I spend, tossing about, worrying about his future. *Baba* says his birth weight was fine, he was born here, we gave him all the vaccines and I followed everything the midwife had asked me to. He rarely falls ill, almost never had stomach upsets or colds like you did. You took some time to adjust to the cold after the Nashik heat. But he's fine. There is nothing wrong with him and still, I wonder sometimes, he slips into a world of his own. Your *Ajoba* had told me getting the *Maunj* done will bring about positive change. Am I wrong to wish well for my child?" Ratnaprabha had looked at her husband, who was unconvinced by her logic but had played along with what had seemed a harmless ritual.

Ira had not known this story. Her heart went out to the traumatised child Swati had described. Seeing both Swati and Ira settling into the silence that regret brings, Leila got up,

"That was intense, and we have hours of stories to go... coffee, tea, *kaahwa*, wine, brandy anyone?

Chapter 12:

In the name of SURVIVAL

Leila went into the kitchen to boil water for the *kaahwa* tea of Kashmir they had agreed on. Wrapping her shawl tighter, Swati followed her mumbling,

"Laiba insists on sending me this freshly ground tea mixture. Saffron is so expensive. But she wouldn't listen! I'll show you where it is." As Swati and Leila returned with steaming cups of *kaahwa*, the mesmerising aroma of saffron wafting through, Ira dwelt on the irony. Ira told Leila about the unending skirmish over the line of control (LOC) which had forced an entire generation of Kashmiri Hindu pandits to flee their homes. The Kashmiri Muslims remained, generations denied the humdrum of violence-free existence that the rest of India and Pakistan enjoyed.

"The wound of Kashmir continues to fester, the lives of its residents boiling over in the toxic salmagundi of partisan terror. There are explosions and deaths that do not even merit more than a passing mention in newspapers. Such is the tragic condition of India's erstwhile tourist spot and once a favourite filming location," Ira shook her head. She paused and uttered hesitantly,

"I wonder was Nathuram Godse's heartfelt cry for a single, undivided India wrong after all? His wish to have future Godses immerse his preserved ashes into the Indus river now flowing in Pakistan...was unlikely to come true. But was it wrong to wish this at all? And here I am, sitting in a Hindu woman's living room situated in the heart of a Muslim ghetto, sipping *kaahwa* lovingly gifted by a Kashmiri Muslim woman who had grown up on the Pakistani side of Kashmir."

"Godse, Nathuram?" Leila raised her eyebrows quizzically. Swati tapped her fingers on her lap, grappling with where she may have heard the name before.

"That's a lengthy discussion Leila, some other time. Let us continue with *Tai*'s story," Ira took a sip. Settling onto the sofa-bed, Swati continued,

"My board exam results were nothing to write home about. But I really wanted to go to the High School social evening. I knew *Aai* would throw a fit, especially at the clothes. No white boy wanted to go with me. The last to be picked was Becky with her red spots and thick thighs showing from under a floral white and yellow dress. My Pakistani classmate with her headscarf did not want to go, her family would not allow it. But I wanted to. When I told *Baba* that even the teachers would be present, he said I should. *Aai* was determined to hold up the values of her semi-rural upbringing in the 1940s and *Baba* was intent on blending in with English culture so that we would progress.

The skirt I left home in, was well below the knees. At the venue, it was four inches above the knees, deftly tucked in at the waist. Nobody asked me to dance. I sat alone on the steps, tapping my feet to the music I was so fond of, sipping lager from a bottle. *Aai* would have been livid if she found out I drank."

"Would you like to dance, Miss?" It was Joseph.

Angry with the world, I gave him a sidelong sarcastic glance. Instead of walking away, he asked if it was ok if he sat down on the steps. I refused to make eye contact and sipped my drink,

"The steps don't belong to me. Nothing in this country or any country is mine. Do as you please!" Joseph sat down, ignoring my rant about the world. With a soft, sad smile, Swati narrated how he had chatted away, made her laugh, interrupting the conversation just once to get them both bottles of lager. With three bottles of lager inside her and basking under a flush of compliments, Swati accepted the palm held out for a dance and then the offer to be dropped home.

The next few months were the happiest in Swati's life, the ever-attentive Joseph always had something silly and funny to amuse her, a single rose stuck into a twisted paper cup, a joke scrawled at the back of a receipt, a bottle of beer with a funny cap, an ice-lolly wrapped in crazy paper...

Always good with his hands, Joseph had spent his summers helping with odd jobs – trimming someone's garden, assisting a local plumber acquaintance with fixing a boiler, fixing the broken bolts of an old kitchen cabinet, running an electric saw on an old wooden door grazing the carpet. Through the years, the meagre pounds he gathered from these little assignments, he put away carefully. High school done; Joseph found a job with a real estate company. Swati didn't want to go to university, school had been bad enough. She wanted to take on work in social care and pursue any courses as she needed them. The Godses wouldn't have any of this. Swati was not given a choice but to study science at university, whichever one would take her given her grades.

The Godse's social circle, limited to other Maharashtrians, always saw the sharing of children's glorious academic achievements. These children, who Swati refused to associate with, seemed to inevitably pursue careers in science or maths, usually medicine or engineering degrees. These "superstars" also then went on to find partners within the community from India or the US," Swati looked at Ira. Ira nodded, sensing the bitterness in Swati's voice. Things had been the same when Ira went to medical school in the 90s and much better on varied career choices when Sameer went to university. But the pressure of high academic achievement carried through.

Swati continued her story. She was letting her parents down on both fronts, career, and partner. She knew they would never approve of Joseph. Joseph had assured her unstinted support and the two hatched a plan. Over the next few weeks, Swati smuggled tightly rolled clothing into her rucksack and handed the parcels to Joseph. On D-day, Swati went out as usual in the morning and never returned. There had been nothing amiss in her behaviour. Her daily hug for nine-year-old Sriram just lasted a few seconds longer. Like so many families of that generation, the Godses did not have a "touch culture", even among family members. Once children grew up, they grew physically apart. Sriram did not like anyone hugging him either, except Swati.

At 8 pm, Swati called, knowing her mother must be incensed. She shouted, "Where are you, Swati? How many times have I told you to be home at the very latest by 7 pm? It is not safe for girls to be wandering about after dark."

"*Aai*, has *Baba* reached home?" Swati said in a soft, unsure voice. Even under ordinary circumstances, talking to her mother was a difficult proposition.

In the name of SURVIVAL 101

"Of course, he's here, Swati. It's 8 pm, get home!" She handed the receiver. The events of the next few hours left an indelible mark on Sriram. Swati narrated what Sriram had told her among their many phone conversations. Prabhakar's mellow voice trembled with disbelief; Ratnaprabha's ordinarily loud voice assumed deafening proportions. Nobody ate, nobody slept. Ratnaprabha's tirade continued against the destruction of family honour, dilution of their culture by western ideas and the worst, evil Black forces preying on their fair daughter.

Looking beyond the floral print curtains on her small window, Swati smiled as she spoke of how she and Joseph celebrated the evening with a few of his friends. "With my absent domestic skills, very little money, and the arduous task of setting up home in a rental studio, they were tough years. But things were to look up. Joseph had made a good impression on his boss. He had been promised a raise and his own little team to do up kitchens in a new estate under construction." Swati's face clouded again, her green eyes still fixated on the window,

"The much-awaited promotion never came, his boss moved on to another part of the business and the new boss had no use for Joseph. He had brought in his own kitchen fitter. That night, Joseph did not get home till 11 pm having gone out with his mates at work to drown his sorrows in the unfairness of it all." Ira noticed the back of Swati's dimpled creamy fair palm had gone whiter as she held the worn-out sofa in a tight grip. She described how, besides herself with worry, she had been hovering at the door when he kicked it open, swinging onto Swati's cheek barely missing her right eye. She swallowed, caught her breath, and glanced at Leila standing by the window, her arms crossed across her chest.

Ira poured a glass of water from the transparent jug in the corner and held it before Swati. Grateful, Swati took a sip, and continued,

"Soon after, I discovered I was pregnant. Joseph was overjoyed and immediately commenced the project of building his child a wood-crafted crib, painted white with green and yellow flowers." Swati's throat was dry as she spoke, the turbulence in her watery green eyes,

"I never recognised the signs, the patterns we see among abuse survivors – the affection, pampering on one day and ruthless violence the next. The triggers too seem to be similar, insecurity, possessiveness, suspicion of infidelity. Is it schizophrenia as it is used as a medical term? In some cases, maybe. But most often, it is an inherent sense of entitlement, the power that comes from controlling, abusing another vulnerable human being who is dependent on you. Like was the case with Joseph, it is the confidence you can get away with it, simply because you have seen that others have!

She took another sip of water,

"The pattern is – the battered woman running away, him coming back to plead remorse and take you back into the same cage of abuse. Like *Aai*, I would hide money in a plastic pouch deeply buried inside the jar of rice grains. *Aai's* reason was different – saving for a rainy day, *Baba* would never ever raise a finger on her or us. My reason was, hiding it from Joseph during his fits of rage, especially after a night of drinking with the boys in the local pub. I endured it for years – an incomplete education, never holding a job. My schoolmates would take on summer jobs, but *Aai* and *Baba* never allowed Sriram and me to do it, insisting we should both focus on getting better grades." At this point, Swati paused, staring into Leila's dark eyes, a protective gaze as if what she was about to relate, had occurred the day before.

"When he raised his fist on little Leila's throat, I was stunned. She had been the apple of his eye, especially as she looked so much like him. He would insist I doll up Leila in the prettiest of frocks, warm caps, mittens and booties and he would take her with him to Sunday church. Once I had finished my household chores, cleaning for the week, groceries shopping, I would join Joseph and Leila at his mother's home for Sunday lunch.

In *Aai's* pristine kitchen, the Gods resided in a corner, perched on their wooden shelf, with *Aai's* diligence on their daily showers, fresh flowers, *haldi, kunku*, the glistening brass oil lamp and a tiny bowl of sugar as daily *prasad* and homemade sweetmeats on special *pooja* days. Following the pristine *naivedya* custom of her priestly father's family, *Aai* would prepare the entire plate comprising the full vegetarian meal, neatly arranged on a steel plate. She was so particular, spoonful each of the dry vegetables on the right side of the plate, the chutney, pickle, salad on the left, a quartered slice of lemon in the centre, a tiny mould of rice in its perfect *mood* (rice mould) form, a spoonful of *varan* (plain lentil curry) on top, the sweet in a bowl on the right of the plate. With the full *naivedya* plate ready, which she always cooked to perfection but never tasted herself until she had offered it to the Gods, *Aai* would pour a little water onto her right palm, draw a little square with the water droplets in front of the Gods, place the plate on it. After that, her green glass bangles would jingle as her wrist moved around the plate three times, clockwise. She would fold her hands in a Namaste to thank the Gods for bestowing the privilege of this dainty food on her family.

This ritual over, the plate was always preserved for *Baba*. I was permitted the special *naivedya* plate when I was old enough to confirm that I would finish every morsel. As Sriram grew up, he would fight for that plate, and she would refuse to give it to him knowing that he would not eat the things he would not like. Food thrown away on a plate was never permissible, but food thrown away on a *naivedya* plate, was sacrilege, it would make the Gods angry she said, for being so ungrateful for the fine food we were blessed with," Swati was lost in her memories.

"This is as is at Godse house, or at least was, till Sriram was alive", Ira was tempted to say it aloud. But she did not want to interrupt Swati. After the journey she had traversed to get to Swati, she wanted to listen to all that she had wondered about over the years but never known. She parked the thought to bring up later and listened intently to Swati's narration.

"*Aai* only cooked her vegetarian meal after showering, the mention of eggs or meat unimaginable and wine in the fridge, certainly not!" continued Swati.

"In stark contrast was Mamma Maria's kitchen - squeaky clean, but the fridge laden with all conceivable portions of meats and Sunday lunch meant the wine flowing freely. Her means were limited. But the swirling love in her derelict church meant that in the name of the one she believed had sacrificed his life for sinners, she had to say Grace before the meal, feed the less fortunate and serve with abundance at the table. Maria's Lord appeared in her conversations, as a wise man ready with sound advice, his wrinkled palm resting on the top of the tightly woven braids. If someone overheard, they may have mistaken Mr. Lord to be a kindly uncle fond of his niece Maria," Swati smiled at Leila who was nodding appreciatively at the apt description of her grandmother. Ira exclaimed,

"My, that's a contrast!" Swati nodded and continued,

"In that kitchen, I was overpowered by the smell of sizzling bacon and fish on the chopping board. I was fascinated by Mamma Maria's extensive use of the oven though, a space *Aai* had always exclusively used to store extra pots and pans in her lifetime. When I first wanted to bake a cake for Sriram's birthday, it had been quite an exercise to remove all the pots and pans from the oven, wipe it clean from the inside and for the first time, switch on the unused gadget.

As Mamma Maria, Joseph and his brother Leo enjoyed their meals, Joseph lovingly feeding Leila tiny morsels of meat as he ate, I sat in a corner politely eating my boiled vegetables and roast potatoes. But this was the only family I had now, and I did not mind," Swati was smiling softly at the memory.

"Until that fateful day…"

Swati's face clouded; her eyes sought Leila, who stood upright at the window.

"When Joseph raised his fist at his toddler, something inside me snapped, afraid now, not just for my own well-being, but for my precious child." Her eyes welling up, Swati spoke of how she had grabbed the toddler, scurried out of her home to Mohsin's corner store requesting to make a phone call. She rang the police, her voice quivering. Clutching the mewling Leila to her chest, her palm clamping the child's lips, her own trembling feet barely able to sustain their weight, she described how she stood with her back against the brick wall of the store, grateful for the kindly Mohsin and his wife Ameena, who blocked her from the front view of the shop. Her last vision of Joseph was of him tearing across the street, past the shop window in an inebriated state, swinging a sledgehammer.

In the name of SURVIVAL   105

Chapter 13:

In the name of HEAVEN

Early next morning, Ira was woken up by her father's call. Since Saguna's demise, a call from India at odd hours always caused Ira to panic.

"*Baba*, is everything alright? *Aai* ok?" Ira sprang up on the makeshift mattress.

"We are both fine Ira, don't worry. Sameer..." Ira panicked even further,

"Sameer. Has he got in touch with you? Did you see him! Where? Is everything ok *Baba*," Ira's normally mellow voice had risen by several octaves.

"No Ira, he hasn't got in touch. But first calm down. He seems to be alright. The number you gave us is always unavailable. Priya and I have been trying to reach him at various times. I suspect he has blocked us. But we saw Sameer in an advertisement on a Hindi news channel last night. I've taken a photo of the advertisement and sent it to you. It's a little blurred. With the dramatic background music and animated graphics, it was quite confusing and difficult to capture. Also, no other TV channel is showing this yet." As Damodar spoke, Ira flicked open the image he had sent. There was Sameer looking away from the camera, his arms crossed against his chest, flanked by a man and a woman both in saffron robes smiling at the camera. The caption was splayed across in bright pink letters in a Bollywood style flamboyant font:

"*Recreation of freedom fighter Nathuram Godse's daring act on January 30.*" Holding her breath, Ira stared into the phone.

"Ira, are you ok? Say something!" Damodar was worried about the impact of this development, but he did want her to know that there had been news of Sameer.

"I'm ok *Baba*. I've seen the image," Ira spoke quickly, with mounting trepidation at what "recreation of the daring act" was supposed to mean.

"Ira, I will keep checking this news channel and subscribe to their website. I'll send you the link too. Is there anything else you think we should do?" Always the practical one compared to his wife, Damodar in his late 70s, had been trying to remain calm and direct his worry into constructive action. Ira was grateful.

"Thank you, *Baba*, I'll be ok, don't worry," Ira ended the call.

Ira forwarded the image to Omar. It was pending delivery. Ira was still staring at the image when Leila walked in with her laptop. Looking at Ira's troubled eyes, Leila asked,

"Is everything ok?" Ira nodded and shook her head, clutching the phone. Leila got up,

"You freshen up *Maami*, let me get the coffee going."

Over coffee, Ira described how a normal, high achieving university graduate was chucking it all for what he believes is to be his political career.

"He has been fascinated by public figures who receive adulation. But this indoctrination, this lunacy! What does a mother, petrified that her son may be involved in a conspiracy, an act of terror…what does she do?" Ira rubbed her temple.

Ira had not heard the key turning in the lock or seen Swati walking in through the front door, dressed in a long woollen Kashmiri kurta and a Scottish tartan woollen scarf tightly wound around her head. Swati had caught the last part of the exchange. She shed her gloves and sat down next to Ira. Leila stepped into the kitchen.

"Can you tell me exactly what's happened?" Swati asked, observing the anguish on Ira's face. Ira explained, Sameer's sudden interest in his roots, his insisting on the Godse connection, his spewing hate for Muslims after

In the name of HEAVEN

the Westminster and Manchester Arena attacks, the man at the London rally who seemed to have donned saffron, now grinning broadly next to Sameer in the picture on her phone. Leila walked in with the steaming cups, trying to come to grips with this gargantuan family tree, being unravelled since last night. She asked, incredulously,

"What is supposed to happen on January 30th? Mum, you never mentioned my genes had anything to do with Gandhi's assassin!" Leila plonked herself on the sofa-bed, her head still whirring with the volumes of information she'd had to process.

"I don't know anything about this. My parents never uttered his name. In fact, even for the thread ceremony, no Godses had been invited. It was just the Sathes from Mum's side. With my own tumultuous life, I couldn't care! But why this capable boy Sameer, with everything going for him, would want to, I cannot fathom…" Swati looked at Ira for an explanation. Ira took a deep breath,

"First your questions Leila. Nathuram Godse shot Mahatma Gandhi dead on 30th January 1948. So, this poster talks of recreating that event in some way in 2019. I don't know what their idea of recreation is, and it scares me to see Sameer involved with such people. On whether you are related to Nathuram Godse, as far as I know, no, there is no relation. Your grandfather has categorically told Sameer that and he has even warned Sameer not to try and forge a relationship where there isn't one. The Maharashtrian Brahmins are a close-knit and relatively small community. So much so, my grandma had told me that her mother's family and your grandmother's family (the Sathes) were related through a common ancestor - social reformer and Mumbai's first Indian Chief Justice Mahadev Ranade and his wife Ramaa *bai*. I've been fascinated by the work done by these two for a long time, especially in the areas of women's education, widow remarriage and nursing schools for women way back in the 1870s. They were so ahead of their times, diligently working towards enhancing the lot of Brahmin widows bogged down by tyrannical customs. Maybe, Swati *Tai*, you get your penchant for social causes from there and Leila, her legal inclination from there! Our relationship is supposed to be by marriage not by blood, so don't worry," Ira smiled for the first time this morning.

"Now that's another new one! I never bothered asking why *Baba* was never interested in his family. I'd just assumed *Aai* didn't get on with them. Taking a family to India every year was too expensive and unthinkable. Calling was so expensive. I remember *Aai* heartbroken after she read about her own father's death through a letter, days after. She only got to meet her mother years later," reminisced Swati, touching upon instances she had never let come to the fore.

Leila interrupted, "But tell me about this fanatic Nathuram Godse. Why is Sameer so fascinated and who are these people wearing saffron robes?"

Clasping her palms, Ira answered, "Nathuram Godse was a fascinating personality, well-read, disciplined, hard-working, single, and celibate by choice, the writer and publisher of two periodicals, articulate and certainly not a fanatic. He continued to value Gandhi's contribution to India's freedom and had in fact followed his philosophy. He had even dropped out of school, following Gandhi's clarion call to boycott western institutions of education. On that day in January, Nathuram raised his palms to Gandhi, greeting him in a Namaste. After bowing down to him in reverence, he pushed away the two women walking with him so that no-one else got hurt, and then shot at him. He stood his ground and surrendered."

"Really?" Leila had sat at the tiny table, her laptop before her. Ira continued,

"Leila, you would find it interesting that Nathuram refused a lawyer and chose to represent himself in court. He spoke in court for five hours, laying down a 21-point logical argument for his reasons for killing Gandhi. The transcript of his speech "May I please your honour" is available. Even this was a strategy Gandhi had often used, of seeking an audience in court and making such an effective speech that the listeners would be convinced that his action was right. If you read this transcript, you will be convinced of his resentment, especially of Gandhi allowing the partition of India that killed so many and continues to today. But whatever the argument, how can we condone killing Gandhi, or killing at all!" Ira paused and gulped down the glass of water Leila had placed before her. Leila and Swati nodded in agreement.

"Coming back to your father Swati *Tai*, what he never told you is the real reason why he chose to migrate to the UK. Your parents were married in 1954, just five years after Nathuram was hanged. It was a time when people with the surnames Godse, Apte, Karkare, Parchure…any of the co-accused, faced social ostracization. Irrespective of their political views or connection with the conspirators, people were reluctant to associate with them, by marriage, or even employ them. Your mother recently told us that her own father agreed to a Godse match only because he was so poor and held the responsibility of three other daughters. This is something she seems to have resented for years," Ira explained. Swati's lips tightened and she growled,

"*Aai* never told us any of this, even when I was old enough to understand! Fear, these Godses!" Ira nodded and continued,

"*Tai,* by the time you were born, the Godse surname was relegated to history." Ira explained how the case resurfaced in the 60s and the Godses brought Swati to the UK to cut off connections with the much-maligned surname. Swati nodded, thinking how she had lived with her parents for 20, high-strung years. Ira had captured nuances of their life, which she had not because of all her anger.

Still trying to piece together this jigsaw of family relationships against the backdrop of a conspiracy 80 years ago, Leila quipped,

"But this seems to be the story of Mum's family, dead and gone. Where does Sameer come into this and what is he doing in Indian politics now?"

Ira explained, "I'm no expert on Indian politics. When we grew up, carefree in Mumbai, religion and politics were the last thing on our minds. But we are now seeing political parties laying claim on historical figures as their own demi-Gods, to be worshipped, exclusively by them. India had a Congress government for over 60 years and laid exclusive claim to Gandhi. Ranade and the freedom fighter Bal Gangadhar Tilak from our Maharashtrian Brahmin community were Congress party co-founders. But the Congress did not claim these demi-Gods. In fact, Mr. Tilak's great grand-daughter-in-law is currently the Mayor of Pune. Mukta Tilak represents the ruling party, *Bharatiya Janata* Party (BJP), not the party of her illustrious ancestor."

Leila quickly searched the terms – BJP, Congress on her laptop.

"BJP – ruling party, right wing, hmm…" she murmured.

Ira elaborated, "Having claimed Gandhi as their own, any endorsement of a person who assassinated him, is seen as anti-Congress propaganda and piggy-back as anti-Muslim, an attempt to appease the extreme right wing. The nuance is lost. After finding no mention in the history books for decades, it has lately become quite fashionable to glorify Nathuram Godse.

But even today, Nathuram remains a controversial figure in India. Though anti-Congress, the BJP and even its right wing, the *Rashtriya Swayamsevak Sangh* (RSS), refuse to endorse Nathuram. Gandhi's demi-God status looms larger than life to allow this. But then, those who indulge in extreme right-wing politics, don saffron and claim to be the upholders of Hinduism that they cannot even care to comprehend, indulge in dramatic Nathuram Godse endorsement acts. From attempting to build statues and temples in his honour to launching a movement to sprinkle his ashes into the river that now flows through Pakistan...they make news."

Ira rose and began pacing up and down the small lounge, clasping and unclasping her hands. In an agitated tone, she directed the story towards her son,

"But what makes me truly worried, is that at least one of these saffron-clad politicians has been accused of a bomb blast attack a few years ago, still pending trial. He is enjoying the adulation, but how can Sameer ever kill?" Nervously rubbing her temples, Ira murmured, half to herself,

"I brought him up to ignore stray acts of racism growing up in a country which he always considered his. I insisted he examine the disturbed backgrounds of anyone who has committed a crime, before labelling them as evil. Despite stray references within the Godse house to the inherent *"itar jaati"* (other castes) and the obsession with "people like us", I taught him to reach out to human beings as human beings and not through the lens of race, caste, and religion. When he introduced us to Cahya, I was over the moon, I thought he had transcended artificial barriers around him, until... terror came home." Distraught, Ira related how Sameer, inflamed by the Manchester Arena trauma, had lashed out at "all Muslims unleashing terror on the world."

She paused, sipped water, and said looking at Swati,

"Swati *Tai*, I've been marveling at the love and gratitude showered on you in a notorious, primarily Muslim area of what unfortunately has been rated as the "worst place to live in the UK". You have accomplished what I cannot imagine doing. For every act of terror committed, there must be a parent weeping somewhere, berating themselves for not being able to stop a child from taking a life and destroying his own. Today, I'm petrified at being one of those mothers..."

Standing by the window, Swati gestured towards the closely packed homes,

"You are right Ira; I live in the heart of potential terror factories. Vicious riots, murders, rape, rackets involving grooming of minor white girls...tell me one bad thing that has not happened in Bradford over the years. The once "Wool capital" of the world and one of the UK's richest cities, is grappling to hold itself up today. Out of a population of over 500,000, approximately 100,000 are Muslim, a third of these from Pakistan occupied Kashmir. There are always more coming, as husbands of UK citizens, just turned 18. They have not integrated into English culture, barely know the language, there is no limit to the number of children in a home...there seems to be no way to get out of the trap of poverty, of being left behind."

Swati locked her palms behind her back, took a few short steps towards the kitchen, turned, and walked back, a mannerism that Ira had often seen in her father. She continued to speak rapidly,

"To that, you add the sceptre of religion, always hovering low over a generation, forces who tell them that they must hate, to kill, to gain an entry pass into the heaven they have imagined. I don't interfere with their religion. The women tell me they cover their heads, their faces due to informed decisions, choices they have made. If a headscarf ensures peace in a home, if a woman can bring up her children without the threat of being wounded, we must let live!"

Swati's eyes softened with the warmth of hope,

"From one such home, rose a bus driver and seamstress' son, one of eight children who took his oath on a Koran as the Mayor of London. Growing up on a council estate, doing odd jobs to help his law education and still helping extended family in Pakistan by sending them money. Barely 50 days after Sadiq Khan became Member of Parliament in 2005, the London bombings occurred. He did not appease his community but condemned the attack." Swati's smile at an outlier's achievements melted into a frown of disapproval. She counted on her fingers,

"One of the London bombing attackers, Sadiq's namesake, took his pregnant wife to the NHS clinic the previous day, availing of every facility provided by this country. This bomber's mother-in-law was invited to Buckingham Palace to meet the Queen to appreciate her work. What is this woman meant to do!" She turned on her heel, taking short strides, one of her palms raised,

"That Manchester Arena attacker was Libyan. Their nationalities are different. But there is no doubt about the religion of the terrorist. That is why, it is now incumbent on every Muslim to stand up and prove that they have nothing to do with this war on the world, waged in the name of a religion which is still theirs. There are others, who do not need to wear their religion on their sleeve but practice it in its true spirit. We need their tribe to flourish, pull back the boys straying on to the terror path and see reason. It is this silent majority that needs to show courage, speak up, stand up to the risk of being ostracised by their own brethren and say,

"A person can be wrong, and the acts of terror show that he has been wrong. But that does not mean an entire community is wrong!"

Chapter 14:

In the name of the COW and the PIG

December 28, 2018.

Omar had been traveling to a school in rural Gujarat when Ira sent him Sameer's picture. By the time the message was delivered and he called, she was on the train to London. They finally spoke the next morning.

Ira was seated at her tiny breakfast bench with her oats and fruit, dressed for work in a pair of black trousers, navy-blue shirt, and a cream and yellow scarf. Without being asked to, Omar had investigated the origins of the poster and without being told how she was feeling, he knew she must have agonised over the implications of this event. Before she could say anything, Omar spoke,

"Ira first thing don't assume there is going to be a terror attack or anything dangerous. You must have looked up *Saadhvi* who appears on the poster. She is one of the co-accused in plotting terror bomb attacks in a Muslim area of a small town in Maharashtra. But that was nearly 10 years ago. As things go, she's been acquitted in that case. I'm not saying she is innocent. I wouldn't know whether she is. Her motive is to seek publicity with stunts that border on the ridiculous and the hope that given her "fame" or "notoriety", she will be a household name and people will vote for her. That's all," Omar paused, stuck his fork in a slice of papaya on his plate and popped it into his mouth.

Unconvinced, Ira rubbed her temples again and said anxiously,

"But Omar, what is this reconstruction on Gandhi *ji*'s death anniversary? That could mean anything! And the way they have projected Sameer in the poster as if he is the mastermind of whatever they are doing, and these two - *Saadhvi* and Raghav, grinning into the camera, are his ardent followers. They brainwash him and now they pin his face on a poster. What if she plots something terrible again and he follows? I can't recognise my son anymore!" Ira raised her spoon in despair, struggling to finish breakfast, not wanting to be late for work.

"Ira, trust me, our son cannot kill. I will not let that happen. Whichever God you currently believe in, all the Gods have witnessed that you or I have never ever intentionally hurt anyone. You've been hurt, the most by me, but that was never ever the intent, and I will not tire of saying that. I've been hurt by others too, but more on that later, OK?" Gently, but firmly, Omar would not let Ira leave till he was certain her fears had been assuaged.

"Now, you go to work rest assured that nothing dangerous is being planned. Whatever it is, will be something symbolic and preposterous. This bunch will get the attention they are seeking. If they cross the limits of decency, they will be asked to apologise. They will consume a little more footage in the face of the apology or conveniently declare that they were "misquoted" by the media. In just a few weeks, all will go quiet again. I'm doing what needs to be done to keep tabs on this dubious TV channel and also trying to get first-hand information," Omar spoke calmly, with the assurance of having done his investigative work and accurately identified the subjects of his scrutiny project.

"But Omar, how can you be so sure?" Ira's voice rose in protest. She gulped her coffee and rinsed her bowl. Omar removed his glasses and placed them on the laptop table. His green eyes bore into her brown ones. In a steely voice, he said,

"Ira don't accuse me of bravado or claiming innocence on behalf of my son, who I have never met and who refuses to acknowledge my existence. I owe it to you, the boy you have raised well, and to me. I know I did not keep just one and unfortunately, the life-changing promise I made to you. Then, I was helpless. Today, a few phone calls can quell a riot, but can also cause mayhem if I so wish. If any of these wimps try to lift a finger on our son, they have me to reckon with."

Ira shivered at the icy tone. Blanching, she paused her frenzied preparations to leave and looked into Omar's eyes. Omar's tone softened and he grinned,

"It will be done Ira *ji*! Now, go save some more lives! By the way, that blue and yellow makes you look stunning. Bye." Not leaving Ira with any room to fret any further, Omar was gone.

"Our son,

how strange that felt…" she thought, her eyes mellowing as she gathered her coat to leave.

***

January 1, 2019. Claire, Ira, and a few of their friends had spent New Year's Eve together. The antiquity of this curious bunch, went as follows –

Jane and Claire had been in school together and reconnected after years. Paul and Jane had been married for 15 years. Ira had met Jane and Paul at Claire's 40th birthday drinks a few years ago in a typical English pub with wooden beams and deep maroon leather sofas. Gradually, the other guests left and these four remained listening to Claire's stories about previous birthdays. Zweil had sauntered into the pub. Weirdly, Paul and Zweil broke out in broad smiles – long lost university classmates. Claire had been too drunk to be asked and each of them had been buying a round of drinks anyway, so Paul had invited him over to the table to meet his wife and two friends. That Saturday night, the conversation had lingered till 2 am. They had discovered common interests – history and culture.

The five had met several times over the years in pubs across London. Through the melancholy November of 2018, Claire sent in several pointers to boisterous New Year's Eve venues. Zweil had pitched for a karaoke night. Ira had turned down all these suggestions. She had revelled in spirited celebrations as a teenager. But today, the thought of blaring music, overpriced food and embracing inebriated strangers to ring in the new year – seemed far from appealing. Ira suggested they meet at her home. Paul had responded with a smiley,

"Always ready for a curry!"

Zweil followed up with a green chillies' emoji.

Ira did not correct them but murmured as she prepped for the evening,

"Indians do not just eat Indian food. Not everything Indians ate was curry!"

It had been a quiet, enjoyable evening. Ira had ultimately served what her friends liked the most – chicken curry, rice, and meat *samosas*. Jane and Paul brought chocolate cake and Zweil carried a bottle of wine. Claire brought bottles of cider. As it inevitably did, the conversation veered towards culture. Claire had been raving about the *Sankranti* festival she attended with Ira – the snacks, the sweets, the carved silver sprinkler that sprayed fragrant rose water on her hair, the black and gold sarees... Declaring that she was hoping to wangle an invitation to more such happy festival experiences, Claire passed around her phone showing pictures of her dressed in Ira's Indian outfit. Jane was admiring the finery but couldn't imagine herself in such attire. Paul was looking into his own phone. Having been to Bangalore and Delhi on business trips, he was not fascinated by Indian clothes. Zweil, as usual, was curious to draw out artistic connections between his own South Africa and India.

"Oh Claire, you remember. It's been a year!" Ira had never bothered retrieving that memory.

"Of course, I do Ira. But we rushed to the movie soon after and never got around talking about it. What was that about your otherwise lovely hostess, not giving you the goodie bag she gave the other women? You said you'll explain?" Claire dipped her meat *samosa* into Ira's tangy tamarind chutney, looking at Ira quizzically. Paul had put away his phone. Jane was pouring her second drink.

Ira paused at the memory, wincing in pain, seething at the witless Kritika's behaviour. In social settings, she was often exasperated with public pronouncements from "in our culture" spouting Indians who claimed to represent the views of all Indians equating her country of origin with everything that was retrograde. Whenever one of these ignorant Indians brandished a custom that made little sense in 21st century England, she could sense being caged into stereotypes once again by the unsaid words of her English colleagues. She still met people carrying impressions of a land of elephants and snakes wandering through the streets, picked up taunts about "time-flexible" humans always turning up late for everything and where the custom of child marriage reigned supreme. Ira was amazed to still get a comment about how good her English was, 26 years after she had first landed at Heathrow. And the short attention spans rarely let any explanation through. But in this small group interested in exploring the nuances of culture, Ira felt safe against an onslaught of judgement.

"Claire, that's because we lost Sriram a few months prior. As our hostess did not know we had been separated but never divorced, technically I'm seen as a widow," Ira explained.

"Oh, you must have been in mourning. I understand, there may be some customs to follow during that period," Jane nodded.

"Not just that period. If I were to show up at the same festival this year, she wouldn't give me the goodie bag. Once a widow, always a widow," Ira tried.

"Are you telling me if I die, Jane will not get any return gifts at parties? Weird!" Paul popped a spiced peanut into his mouth.

Zweil nodded slowly and said in a sombre, philosophical tone,

"Widows must be taken care of in our culture. In my culture, if a man dies, his wife becomes his brother's responsibility. He has to marry her." Paul nearly spilt his drink exclaiming,

"What! I'm not marrying my brother's wife. I can barely make it through the annual ordeal of sitting at the Christmas lunch table with her!" Jane smiled at Ira, shook her head and bit into a *samosa*.

With a beatific smile, Zweil continued his philosophical exploration,

"Which tribe do you belong to?" This time, it was Ira's turn to sputter.

"Tribe? No, I'm not a tribal Zweil! I come from a Hindu, Brahmin family from the state of Maharashtra, the capital of which is Mumbai."

Zweil nodded again knowingly,

"Aha Brahmin, upper caste privilege".

Paul interrupted, "We've heard about the caste system before. But what's this about Ira not being given a goodie bag? I wouldn't marry my brother's wife, but why would we deprive her of a goodie bag, especially if everyone else is getting one? See, Claire just showed us a grinning picture of herself holding her goodie bag!" Paul made a monkey face at Claire's phone. Claire scowled at him but was keen to get the bottom of the behaviour of the lady whose hospitality she had enjoyed.

"Go on Ira, what was that?" Claire snuggled into the cushions on the deep blue Persian rug by the fireplace. Ira poured a glass of rose and then delved into her exposition of this practice.

"In a way Zweil is right. When a man died, the financial responsibility of his wife was borne by male relatives and in turn, the widows lived in extended families, taking care of household chores. This unfortunately happened after the ceasing of a golden era when women were educated. Education for women stopped after the invasions that raised concerns around safety. So, women in the 1800s were confined to homes with no right to inherit property. Instead of a share in the family property, women were given gold when they got married and at subsequent festivals and occasions. This was called *stree dhan* (woman's treasure) and nobody else was allowed to touch it.

Unfortunately, like religion continues to be misinterpreted today, it happened then. Though none of the scriptures prescribe this, widows were treated in the most atrocious manner, robbed of dignity. The forceful tonsuring of a head is the first step in dismantling someone's spirit. My grandma used to tell us about her own grandmother, widowed in her twenties, soon after her third daughter was born. The lady lived her life with her head and body covered in a maroon-red cotton saree called the *alwan* as an *ashrit* (dependent) in her brother's home. The rules for widows, especially from upper-class Brahmin families were adhered to by families, including the parents of these girls, in the name of religion with the threat that non-conformance was a sin with an assured place in hell. They were to sleep on a floor mat, cook for the rest of the family, but not allowed spicy, tangy food or anything that may titillate the senses. These rules were supposedly made because the honour, especially of the upper-class women needed to be protected. Tonsuring their heads, trying to get them to blend into the innards of a household by denying them the opportunity to appear in public even for family weddings and festivals, was supposedly to protect them from the "evil designs" of men and suppress their own "immoral desires".

"That's horrible! And what about a man who lost his wife? Did anyone not object?" Perturbed, Jane had stopped eating, and had pushed away her drink. Ira continued,

"Widowers were married off within weeks of the demise of a wife, sometimes twice but widows were not allowed to be married. In 1863, a social reformer Vishnupant Shastri established the widow remarriage organization in Pune and like several social reformers of that time in Maharashtra, set an example by marrying a widow Kusabai. They faced a lot of opposition from traditional families who accused them of corrupting religion."

The group had been listening in rapt silence. Jane whispered,

"What a macabre existence...."

Paul put his arm around her.

Ira continued, passing around the crisps and dips to lighten the atmosphere.

"But the great news is that all this changed years ago. Women in India are speeding ahead with their careers. Re-marriage is encouraged and in some laudable cases, arranged by the girls' own in-laws. My grandma used to wear only white, by choice. If she wanted to dress in sarees of any other colour (like some of her friends did even after being widowed) nobody would have stopped her. But there is no such norm anymore. Not just in England, but a widow in Maharashtra, at least the urban areas which I have exposure to, would be treated just the way a married or single lady would," Ira smiled.

Paul welcomed the lightened mood. He bit into a carrot baton, still clasping Jane's palm with his other hand. The lives of widows had left her despondent.

"Ira, get back to the goodie bag business please and then let's dispose of this topic for today!" Paul wagged his forefinger at Ira laughing.

"Oh yes, the goodie bag. In the era I described, women did not go out unless there was a festival created for the purpose. It gave their otherwise dull, housework-ridden lives an opportunity to air those lovely sarees and jewellery and socialise. Widows were not allowed into these events under the pretext that they may resent and yearn for the pleasures that married life brings. I did not see any such discrimination – my grandma used to invite all the women we knew, widowed, married, single, divorced, rare in society that time, and that too of all the communities Hindus, Muslims, Sikhs whoever lived in the neighbourhood, for our festivals. Some homes may have invited the widows, but not given them the goodie bags, essentially comprising objects like bangles, the *tikli* (red dot on the forehead), combs etc, which widows due to their ancient ill treatment would have no use for.

My grandma was extremely particular about what return gifts she would ask my mother to arrange for – notebooks, pencil sets, handkerchiefs, envelopes, or tiny household items like a steel container, which everybody could use. And every woman at our festival was given her goodie bag. Now coming to the goodie bag episode in this little ignorant woman's London home. She was a great hostess but had picked up only the peripherals of the festival, the finery, the pictures on social media, the food, and the opportunity to show off her home. I heard Claire holding court with that woman's neighbours that evening. Claire has understood Hinduism far better than this Hindu lady ever would. That is because Claire questions everything, if she is convinced that it is relevant in the current age and social scenario, she follows it.

"To Claire then!" Ira raised her glass giving Claire a warm smile. Everyone raised their glasses amidst peals of laughter as Claire beamed, bowed, and did a little dance for the glorious toast.

***

The rest of the group left soon after midnight. Claire had stayed over. It was 9.30 am and Claire had taken charge of Ira's tiny kitchen declaring that she would have dished out a full English breakfast, had it not been for Ira's weird norms on which animals she ate and which she didn't.

"So, in your books of edible animals, the hen, lamb and the fish get a tick mark. And what do you have against the poor cow and the pig!" Claire crooned as she split open an egg. Slicing tomatoes, Ira explained what Saguna had to her, years ago about the connection between food and religion.

"The word for religion in Sanskrit *Dharma* means duty. It has a set of guidelines to do the right thing for one's family and society. These guidelines on diet are the first introduction to the concept of the carbon footprint, I would say. Imagine, in the 1800s, when food could not have been packaged and transported, if your ancestors in Scotland had a set of guidelines to be vegetarian, what would they have eaten?"

"Hmm, maybe potatoes, bread…?" Claire split another egg on the pan.

"Exactly! People in Scotland, given the severe cold, did not have much choice. The most nutritious food available at the closest range was livestock and people ate it. The same way, the entire state of Maharashtra has moderate weather conducive to good yield of pulses, vegetables, rice, wheat, fruit… everything. And that is the case with several parts of India. So, the guidelines were to – eat local. This is especially so among entire villages in what is now informally called the "Cow belt region" in Northern and Central India where the main source of livelihood was milk and milk products. The guidelines were to not go around killing the gentle animals – the cows. Besides, given that milking the cows was a daily ritual, their keepers treated them like pets. The cows were given names, women would stay up at night by the pregnant cow's side and summon midwives while the cow gave birth. The calves were brought up as you would bring up a puppy. With this bond, there would be sensitivity around killing," Ira glanced at Claire, aware that she had touched a chord.

"Look at you and George. You almost cancelled because you could not find him kennel space. If it hadn't been for your Mum taking him, you couldn't imagine leaving him alone. It seems barbarous to hear about dogs being killed for human consumption in some other cultures. But we are perfectly fine consuming other animals!" Ira lifted her knife in the air. She glanced at Claire abandoning the scrambled eggs to text her Mum to see if George had eaten. Even after a decade, Claire would call him Puppy or Baby.

Looking up from her phone, Claire exclaimed, "Oh my God Ira! That's hideous…" George is missing me, but he's eaten. So, I get this 'cows as pets' bit now." She gave Ira's foot long pepper grinder a twist and gave the eggs a vigorous stir, nodding at Ira.

"So fine with the cows. What's wrong with pigs?"

Ira sighed. Putting out cutlery for the two of them, she spoke slowly,

"I don't know much about this one. Hindus do not have any specific sentiment about the pig. We have just considered it dirty because it rolls in the mud and even its own excrement. Till Peppa came and stormed the world of our children, we did not think of pigs much, not as sweet, pink characters at least. But Sameer had a Bangladeshi school friend called Afzal. One day, Sameer came home, demanding an explanation. Afzal had requested permission to stay out of the class, as a pig dissection was in progress. You know how Sameer used to be with his questions – born to debate and would not stop until I could come up with a convincing answer!

So, I tried to look up why the Muslims are not allowed to touch pigs and thus pork. It seems the Koran has a mention that followers should not consume blood or the meat of the swine unless no other food is available and that if it is the only lifesaving food one must have to survive. Scholars and anthropologists have written about pigs living in filth and health reasons like pigs sometimes bearing diseases like ringworms. One of the articles I found quite interesting was about how in the desert areas, owning a pig was seen more like a luxury as it did not produce milk and ate as much as a human being, so the guidelines said it must be avoided. See, everything Hindu, Muslim, or any other religion, comes back to the same thing – do the right thing for society! Anyway, enough of a morning discourse on animal killing now, let's get those scrambled eggs on to our plates!"

Ira and Claire sat down to enjoy their breakfast, Claire occupying the armchair in the living room and Ira cross-legged on the sofa. Claire switched on the news,

"Happy new year to the rest of England…let's see what's on the news!" Claire paused her mindless chatter to place the fork in her mouth.

Struck by the frenzy on screen, Ira put down her fork,

"As long as you keep bombing other countries, this sort of shit is going to keep happening!"' shouting out this sentence followed by cries of

"Allah, Allah", a 25-year-old man had indulged in random stabbing of people waiting for trains at the Manchester Victoria station platform on New Years' Eve.

Ira trembled, staring mutely at the images of the same Manchester Victoria station last year – which had marked the beginning of the end for Sriram.

Chapter 15:

In the name of REVENGE

Ira could not tear herself away from the TV screen, the measured euphemisms of the news anchor piercing through the vivid memory of Sriram being hit by shrapnel. The youngest fatality in the Manchester attack then had been an eight-year-old girl whose innocent eyes had flashed across TV screens then. Today's Manchester attack dragged back the millstones that had oppressed every attempt to seek a stolen moment of cheer, especially after the breezy banter of the previous evening.

"There have been 700 investigations into suspected terrorism in 2018 in Manchester, five terrorist attacks in the UK in 2017, including four in London and one in Manchester," the anchor rattled off statistics on an infographic juxtaposed against a map of Northern England. With a grim nod, the anchor looked back into the camera, concluding that the terrorism threat level was pegged at "Severe" which meant that another attack was likely. Ira had abandoned her breakfast plate. Claire poured out a glass of water. The movies, eating out, staying over, last night's gathering, had been Claire's attempts to bring Ira back.

"Oh my God Manchester! Where's my phone?" Ira sprang to her feet.

"It's alright Ira," Claire was startled. She had seen Ira in tears occasionally but never felt she may be clinically depressed or experiencing panic attacks. In fact, she had attended to her professional duties without break.

"Are you alright Ira? Your phone is in the kitchen." Claire got up to bring it for her. Ira ran into the kitchen and began frantically pacing the floor. The number she was dialling didn't seem to be going through. Claire was alarmed. She said gently,

"Who are you calling Ira?" Ira continued to press the redial button.

"Sriram's sister was to be in Manchester…" and then into the phone,

"*Tai*, I'm so relieved! Just heard about the stabbing. Thank God, I just don't have the energy to lose loved ones anymore," Ira blurted in a single breath, her voice cracking.

Claire sighed, sinking into the chair. They had a lot to catch up on. The Bradford trip seemed to have gone off well. Ira was speaking as if to a family member, not someone she had met six days ago. Claire motioned to Ira that she would step into the other room for Mum to hold up George's injured paw on video call and complete the exchange with her "four-legged soulmate". Ira nodded, smiled, and switched to Marathi.

"*Tai*…Is it ok if we do a video call?"

Swati was touched. In the interim years, till Leila grew up, there was no-one who would have bothered asking after her. Leila and James were caring, but as should be the case, they had their own lives. They were holidaying in a remote village near Madrid and had probably not heard the news of the attack yet. Ira switched to video.

Smiling in reassurance, Swati explained that there was no further development after what was on the news. The attacker brandishing a knife with a 12-inch blade had injured a couple and a policeman before being overpowered by the police and taken into custody. No fatalities, no more attackers. He was operating alone.

"They have not revealed his name, but he was from Cheetham Hill, quite close to where I'm staying with friends," Swati's face clouded. Ira spoke rapidly,

"*Tai*, I know how passionate you are about your work. Manchester was never on my radar. Sriram too had gone there last year, just because his office sent him to get a client's signature on documents. That's how he found himself at Manchester Victoria station. After that, any news of Manchester draws me to listen attentively, read further. And it's only bad news. The Manchester Arena attacker Salman Abedi, only 22 years old, made his bombs living in a bed and breakfast (B&B) accommodation offered by an unsuspecting Manchester resident. People pushing Abedi in the direction of his own death and killing

In the name of REVENGE 125

others, are still alive in Manchester prison! His brother is being tracked down. The parents never returned from Libya. His sister says he was taking revenge for Syria!" Ira threw up her palm in despair. Living by herself, she had taken to watching the news twice a day and more frequently on weekends. When something related to her current concerns came up, she sought more from online media. Today, she finally had found someone who would listen to the disturbing facts that had been niggling her. She continued to rant.

"A year later, in March 2018, Abedi's cousin Hamman Forjani, just 21, assaulted a pregnant woman. I followed the story. He had the gall to defend this action in the Manchester Crown Court with the prosecutor presenting that this boy now has "recognition" and "insight" into how his behaviour has affected the woman. The prosecutor described him as a pleasant young man not lacking in intelligence when not on drugs or drinking. He's been jailed for 28 months. Thankfully, the baby was born safe. It seems that Forjani is facing backlash in prison for being related to the Arena bomber, no surprise there.

What do you think he is going to do when he is free? From these actions arise the stereotypes, of all brown men, and now women, being indoctrinated who dare to wear non-western clothes, being viewed as potential terrorists. After what's happened, why should Londoners not be afraid?" Ira gulped down her glass of water and rested the phone against a bottle of marmalade. She tucked a strand of hair behind her ear and continued, still agitated,

"The worst is still the bunch of 10 paedophiles featured in the odious Rochdale grooming scandal a few years ago. Nine Muslim Asian men including a preacher Abdul Rauf and supposed respected members of society, conned underage white girls in a sex scandal, offering a child as a "sexual treat" for a 21-year-old. In court, one of them prayed for his God to come and give him another chance, another would rather confess than swear on the Koran.

The 67-year-old prime accused Shabir Ahmed told a child that "In my country, 11-year-old girls have sex" and in court, tried to play the race card accusing the jury of racism, invoking human rights laws to avoid deportation! What does one expect will happen? Soon after the documentary about this was screened on national television, there were unexplained murders of teenage Muslim boys. I heard you mentioning your visits to Salford, Manchester, Leeds, Rochdale, Birmingham and of course Bradford for your work, especially the dangerous areas within these towns. Leila has been trying to convince you to move to London and now I'm afraid for you Swati *Tai*. If one group seeks revenge against a previous attack, the cycle of terror will never end!" Ira finally, unclenched her fist, her palm in the air.

Swati, once angry with the world and still fighting, had let Ira vent. Ira's fear was that her son may be seeking revenge for attacks by Muslims that took Sriram. Swati continued to mourn too. But she was not about to let go of the people who had stood by her when her own family had not. Swati smiled at Ira,

"True. Every time terror strikes anywhere, the common thread of the warped interpretation of their religion seems to bind them. Who suffers, is the woman. In the Rochdale scandal, young white girls entrusted to the social care system were exploited by brown Muslim men. These crimes had nothing to do with religion. But all nine men flouted every religious norm to commit these crimes. When the question arose why only white girls and not brown girls were exploited, came the answer, that brown girls are strictly supervised in these areas as if it gave men the license to trap unsupervised girls!" Swati shook her head vigorously. She paused, nodding in acknowledgement at a steaming mug that a bangled hand placed before her. She took a sip and continued,

"Over the years, our women's movements have raised voices against the price women pay, campaigning against virginity testing for Asian women, female genital mutilation (FGM) and such horrors, conveniently committed in the name of a religion only men seem to own. I see the other side of terror Ira - wives and children hanging their heads in shame. Even as these men were convicted, they continued to hold their heads high in arrogance, claiming the girls were consenting adults, insinuating racial discrimination, throwing bombs, slicing people in the name of God's war and whatever else! You are right, they will finish their sentences and return to their suffering wives."

Swati related a hideous case of a man killing his own mother-in-law because she helped her daughter escape his clutches and encouraged her to go and live her life in Bradford with her true love.

"Mrs. Begum was an outlier and tried to save her daughter from ruin in the name of tradition, but lost her own life in the process..."

Swati paused, her palm circling the warmth of the teacup and looked at Ira kindly. Her sister-in-law had won her heart in a matter of days. She said softly,

"Ira, you are just a little older than Leila. I see selflessness in you, the ability to empathise, the ability to forgive. I have not forgiven my parents, but you have, despite them wittingly getting you married to a naïve, harmless human being clearly suffering from what you explained with your medical knowledge, must have been Asperger's Syndrome. I know my mother never accepted that I was simply not academically inclined. Her accepting that her son may have a medical condition is unimaginable. She would have accepted heart disease, cancer, but there was no way she would accept that her precious Sriram, with her genes, could be on the autism spectrum. If I had still been part of the family and if my opinion mattered, I would never have let this happen. I would have called the bride-to-be and given her an accurate description of Sriram's condition. I pushed my parents away from my mind for years, but how could I push Sriram away? Apart from all else, I also lived with the guilt of abandoning Sriram." Swati lifted her mauve paisley scarf to wipe a droplet on her cheek.

Ira had often berated herself for not being able to make the marriage work. Ira was taken by surprise at the acknowledgement. "Under the weather" is the furthest her in-laws had gone in acknowledging Sriram's condition. She exclaimed,

"*Tai*, please don't blame yourself for what happened to me! We know families mean well. The institution of marriage is so overrated that families are convinced that marriage is a cure for everything, including in the case of Sriram!"

Ira pursed her lips in a wry smile and unveiled another layer of the Asian fascination for the west. Swati was surprised to hear how even in the 90s, how common were instances of "foreign returned" (mainly the US and UK) Maharashtrian professionals returning to India for a fortnight, going through a whirlwind of "bride viewing" ceremonies over cups of tea and *pohe*, shortlisting a suitable bride, and returning to their country of work, with the wedding done. Ira pointed out that these girls were not from poor families.

"The urbanised Maharashtrians of the 90s were university graduates. They were making the choice to move to a life in the fascinating first world, they otherwise may not ever have been able to visit. These were arranged marriages pre-internet, social media and little was known about the groom.

Sometimes, this backfired. There were stray cases like that of a Maharashtrian boy living in the US with a white woman, but coming to India and getting married to an unsuspecting girl with dreams. But mostly, these worked and sometimes, like in my case...nobody would have known." Ira spoke about how she too had lived with the assumption that Sriram was just shy and over-sensitive. It was only much later, after literature about Asperger's Syndrome started coming through that the symptoms seemed to match perfectly. She suddenly remembered something she had been wanting to ask Swati about,

"*Tai*, it sounds silly but each of us has a secret place we visit in mind or body, when we feel low. It just makes life better..." Ira began.

"Ah yes, like chocolate muffins, or *phirni* and the coconut *barfi* you brought. It used to be my escape, pop one into my mouth from the little round steel tin in *Aai*'s fridge. I could never get that one again but found replacements as you can see! This secret escape makes us feel nicer and fatter!" Swati laughed heartily, tapping her rotund tummy.

"Hmm yes, for some it is food, others it could be a shopping binge, doing their hair or nails, some find recourse in music, greenery, seaside, sport or whatever else. These escape routes are needed only when life is far from perfect. Before I got married, life itself seemed like an unending holiday. Even then, I was fond of watching movies, however far-fetched the storyline, however outlandish the acting, the popcorn, and a cold drink in a darkened movie theatre, made everything good," Ira looked up at Swati's eyes searching for understanding.

"Ah yes, your Bollywood. Our Pakistani friends are dogmatic in their belief that there is just one God and that is Allah. But when it comes to Bollywood, everything is consumed with glee!" Swati chuckled at her experiences of women swinging to Bollywood songs in the privacy of their own homes when the men were away and displaying the latest Bollywood dressing styles under their *burkhas*.

"Yes, the three most popular stars are the Khans. Indian audiences don't care about the religion of a movie star. The Muslim movie stars of the 60s often took on Hindu names – the heartthrob of the nation Dilip Kumar born in pre-independence Pakistan, is Muhammad Yusuf Khan. But the stars post the 1980s use their real names. But I'm digressing, I wanted to ask you why Sriram had such a dislike for the cinema.

When I moved to England, among other things, I buried my love for movies. With housework, Sameer, my education, there never was time. Like all working mothers, I used to feel guilty about *Aai* looking after the baby. The last thing I wanted was to take away more of her time and go off for a movie. But it was Sriram's birthday, and I wanted to do something nice. As you know, he did not like social gatherings or explore new kinds of food. His idea of dinner was *Aai*'s standard *aamti bhaat,"* Ira looked at Swati. She nodded vigorously.

"*Aai*'s idea of a meal was *aamti bhaat*. That's what she fed him through his childhood. I used to go out and experiment with whatever food I could lay my hands on. But the fear of punishment from the Godse Gods instilled in me never really went away!" Swati shook her head. Ira continued with her story,

"Naïve and hopeful, I desperately wanted to make things work between us, draw him out of his shell. I also knew that most of us who grew up in India swiftly alternate among three languages – English, Hindi, and mother tongue. I had understood that Sriram did not speak Hindi at all. I was quite impressed with his Marathi though. But *Aai* and *Baba* taught Marathi to Sameer too, so now I understand. I had thought Sriram would enjoy an English movie. I pre-booked tickets. I had told Sriram we are going out to get something for Sameer and he had agreed. We reached the movie theatre. Sriram clammed up and left. I followed him home. He lay in bed in his street clothes curled up, his body shrinking within himself, as if he was defending himself from an onslaught. I never understood what that meant, but I never suggested going for a movie ever again." Ira had gone morose at the recollection.

"Ira, poor you, they never told you right? Why am I not surprised!" Swati raised both her palms and cocked her head to the side. Swati then told Ira about her multiple attempts to reach out to Sriram as he grew up. I used to call on the landline knowing Sriram never went out anywhere once he got home from school.

"The Godse home had a fixed time for everything – what time *Aai* would start with chopping the vegetables and kneading the dough for dinnertime *polis*, what time the pressure cooker would go up on the stove with the lentils and rice, just in time for *Baba* to arrive and be served a hot meal. I used to make the call knowing *Aai* would be busy in the kitchen. Sriram would answer, so pleased to talk to me. I would ask him about the bullies in school, give him input on how he should step around potential puddles of ridicule. He would so look forward to my calls. For him, everything had to be like clockwork, a few minutes of delay on my part would make him anxious. The fear that he would never hear from me again, would surface. I tried to keep time, speak about his life but never reveal the vagaries of mine."

Swati then narrated the story of Sriram's date. Ira had been told that Sriram had never had a girlfriend, never dated. That had explained why a good-looking boy from a reasonably well-to-do family, would agree to marry a girl his parents found.

"Oh, that's good, he went on a date!" Ira was surprised and happy for the awkward teenager that Sriram had been. She listened in rapt attention, mildly envious of the tender brother-sister bond. Ira had missed having a sibling. She did have cousins who lived in Pune and Nagpur who she would send *rakhis* by post to, and they would send her gifts on *bhau beej*. Maybe, she had sought and found everything in Omar. Or maybe because she had found everything in Omar, she had not sought other close friendships. Ira was lost in thought.

"Ira?" Swati nudged.

"Oh yes, Sriram's date, tell me more *Tai*," Ira smiled eagerly.

Swati told Ira about their shared excitement on Sriram's upcoming tryst with the lovely Julia. "Some of Sriram's classmates were not rude like the gang of bullies, but they didn't give Sriram a second glance, leave alone considering going on a date. Sriram had told Swati how Julia would smile at him kindly when no-one was looking, how she made space next to her on the school bench when almost everyone either actively blocked the space next to them or pretended to look away when Sriram walked past. Sriram had plucked a rose from their back garden and shyly presented it to Julia. She had accepted it with a smile and even agreed to go for a movie with him the following Saturday."

Swati recounted how they planned the rendezvous. Swati had given him precise instructions on what to wear, use a light deodorant, and carry enough from his pocket money to buy them something to eat and drink before the start of the movie.

On the designated Saturday, Julia and Sriram were seated in the movie theatre, a tub of popcorn between them and fizzy drinks in paper cups. As the titles concluded, five heads popped up behind their seats and the cackling voices reached a crescendo,

"Well done, Julia! You've won the bet…you managed to date the boy-child nobody ever could!" Startled, Julia turned, and the tub of popcorn blew into Sriram's face just as he had taken a sip of the drink. Coughing, his eyes smarting from the salt and the fizz up his nose, Sriram clambered out of the soiled seat and fled home.

Still reeling, Swati concluded another tragic tale in a sombre voice.

"He was curled up in bed for days, refusing to speak. When I called at our usual time, *Aai* answered. I hung up. Maybe she knew it was me or maybe not. I continued to call, at our usual time. Weeks later, he finally answered the phone. After much probing, he spoke about the morbid "bet" and his anger in bits and pieces."

Ira and Swati shared a moment of silence laden with regret. Ira had been holding her breath as yet another excruciating scab of the wound that was Sriram's memory, was prised open. Exhaling, she looked away from the phone, out of the window. The corner shop had opened for its first customer on the first day of 2019. Milk cartons and eggs were exchanging hands. The mundane ensured that life dragged on.

Shaking herself from her melancholy, Ira peered into her phone and smiled,

"When I saw you look at Leila, I was reminded of Sameer. Leila for you and Sameer for me is a culmination of all we have, overcoming sorrow, the acceptance of what we were not destined to have and the wistful prayer that their future would be fuelled by what we tried to do…a bright golden sun that refuses to set!" Swati's green eyes lit up in a joyous smile,

"Beautifully articulated Ira. Leila would find this cheesy. She is 40 going on millennial and they don't like to articulate emotion, at least not to a parent! But that describes exactly how I feel when I look at Leila. I am so touched you called, and I know you understand why I must stay on and fight for these women here. Keep me posted on what you hear about Sameer. Take care."

***

January 31, 2019

Omar had been right. The "reconstruction" event did not receive any publicity. Damodar and Omar had been separately tracking different news media. *Dhamaka* (meaning explosion), the same Hindi news channel which had shown the poster, continued to air updates. Omar later explained that this channel was also owned by the extreme right wing "socio-religious organization" floated by *Saadhvi's* brother-in-law.

But on January 31st, the event found its way into a mainstream news channel with politicians, media and citizens condemning the proceedings. Omar sent her the link to watch. Ira sat at her desk; eyes glued to the unfolding events on her laptop.

Two men held up an effigy of Gandhi. Swathed in saffron, the expansive frame of *Saadhvi* marched on to the screen and fired a gunshot at the effigy at short range. Fake blood oozed out of the effigy before it dropped to the ground. The saffron figure then turned towards the camera, the robes bellowing behind, the right hand pointing the gun skyward, the left hand in a victory sign. *Saadhvi's* incandescent smile exposed betel-stained teeth and she brayed into the microphone thrust before her,

"Jay Hind, Jay Sri Ram!"

This enactment elicited outrage. The speech spouted by *Saadhvi* on how the "true Hindu Godse of pure Brahmin blood needed to be emulated in seeking revenge on the Muslims causing terror", would have put both Godse and Gandhi to shame for the blatant use of their names for something neither of them stood for.

Shrieking into the microphone, *Saadhvi* exhorted the defenders of the Hindu faith to rise in action against the communities who blatantly murdered the holiest animal in India, the cow. These communities, she alluded, were not just emissaries of the neighbouring state created by Gandhi to pollute the Hindu land, who should have gone to Pakistan when a separate state was created for them, but pollutants at the fringes of Hindu society itself. And then, bowing deeply, she sang a eulogy to her honourable *Bhraatashri*, the invincible Raghav Swami who had mobilised an army of "cow defenders" armed with sticks and social media access to keep vigil on the possible sale and purchase of beef in the entire belt they controlled and call out these offenders.

Ira stared at the screen in disbelief. Had the "sovereign, socialist, *secular*, democratic, republic" she had grown up in, dropped the "secular" from its Constitution? Not just Muslims and Christians, but there were certain oppressed castes among the Hindus who consumed and traded in beef. So, were all these people to be hunted down and killed in the name of the cow? Gandhi was vegetarian and so was Godse. Gandhi propagated unity among the diverse populace. Acknowledging the historic caste-based oppression, he gave them a new name – *Harijan* (people of God). He wouldn't want their means of livelihood snatched away.

Following Sameer's trail, Ira had begun to read about Nathuram and had recently found this nugget - though a practising Hindu Brahmin, he did not believe in the caste system. He and his associates used to participate in multi-community public dinners with representation from all castes – certainly a radical occurrence in the 1940s. Ira had read that Nathuram's lament against Gandhi had been that the father of the nation, so accepted by all communities, including Nathuram himself, should have demonstrated the responsibility towards protecting the interests of all communities. Nathuram, in his statement, had accused Gandhi of being partial towards Muslims. In trying to keep Muslims happy, peaceful, and well-behaved, he had always called upon the Hindus to be sensible, not retaliate. His famous "fasts unto death" had always been for Hindus to not rise to provocation, never for Muslims to not attack. And the worst outcome of this had been the 600,000 lives lost during partition, women abducted and raped. Whatever their ideologies, neither Gandhi nor Nathuram would have endorsed the killing of humans in the name of the cow!

Ira shook her head, about to shut down her laptop. But as the "resurrection of the killing" story concluded, a debate on the "cow question" kicked off. A student activist in a dark blue chequered shirt surmised,

"Between 2010 and 2017, cow related violence injured 124 and killed 28 Indians, out of them 24 Muslim. Following a petition from the cow protection army, the Delhi High Court had ruled against a beef and pork festival in Jawaharlal Nehru University. He spoke of a "Cow Ministry" being announced in a North Indian state riding on the crest of populist election promises. A man from the cowherd community, who owned 25 cows himself, was elected. The activist smiled broadly into the camera, raising his hands to gesture "inverted commas".

"The "Ministry" was then converted into the "Cow Department" with the elected representative appearing in public dressed in traditional cowherd headgear and white robes proclaiming his allegiance to the protection of cows. As an afterthought, it came to the State's notice that the Indian Constitution does not permit States to create their own ministries," he threw up his palms in mock despair.

The screen showed an infographic with two statistics and a voiceover:

"Even as this cow department exercised its power over "keeping vigil over cow related criminals", 500 cows had perished in a government-owned shelter in the state during a flood. Soon after, 24 more cows died of poisoning." The news feature ended with the final piece of information that the Cow Minister/Department Head lost the next election.

As the anchor moved on to other news around the country, there was a ticker at the bottom of the screen. A national level leader in the ruling party had condemned the "resurrection of Gandhi's death" event on social media. The anchor presented more flashy snippets of the social media war that ensued. Finally, *Saadhvi* apologised accusing the media of "distorting the coverage" of the event.

Ira shut down her laptop. Though disgusted by the political, exhibitioner sludge that her religion had been reduced to, Ira had been relieved to see that Sameer did not seem to have any visible role in this drama. But then, where was Sameer?

Chapter 16:

In the name of DIVERSITY

March 2019

Ira's Friday visits to the Godses continued. She had got them a subscription to a bouquet of Marathi and Hindi TV channels. His grey eyebrows set in a curious frown, Prabhakar listened to the news anchors speaking a strange, anglicised version of Marathi, wearing business jackets. The lady newsreaders back in time on black and white television, had worn sarees and sported a prominent round *tikli* on their foreheads. On the current affairs shows that he now watched, the laptops strategically placed before the anchors bore the name of the show sponsor, brands ranging from spices to cement.

Ratnaprabha had settled into a new routine with back-to-back Marathi serials woven into her otherwise strict daily calendar. During the Friday dinners, she would criticise what she called the "advanced nature" of the women characters and how this would completely not do in her time. But she was quite engaged in the mythological shows being aired. Ira was pleased with herself for accomplishing this. Finally, apart from the dejection on the lack of news on Sameer, the mandatory lament on Sriram and the lackadaisical trial of the brother and co-accused of the Manchester attacker case, there were other topics of conversation.

After a simple dinner of *bharli vaangi*, *bhaakri* (flatbread) with fresh, homemade white butter and *thecha* (crushed chilli chutney with a dash of garlic and lemon), Ira and Ratnaprabha were clearing up before Ira was to leave.

"*Aai*, the *bharli vaangi* were excellent today. And after all these years, my *bhaakris* don't turn out to be as soft and thin as yours," Ira appreciated her mother-in-law cooking her favourite dishes on Fridays. Ratnaprabha's thin lips parted. After Sriram's passing away, a smile from her was rare.

"Patience Iravati, patience. The aubergines need to cook on a slow fire, the dough for the *bhaakri* needs to be kneaded till it is smooth as a pebble from a gushing river, no shortcuts. When you were pregnant and I asked you, what dish my grandchild was yearning to eat, I expected you to mention something sour and salty, for that's what pregnant women are supposed to feel like eating – tamarind, raw mango, lemon pickle. I thought you may ask for something sweet – *puran polis* (flatbread stuffed with sweetened chickpea flour). But you just asked for our simple, poor man's rural meal, something we used to make every day in the village as I grew up – *bhaakri*. My grandson-to-be wanted it, of course I would make it!" Ratnaprabha's stark green eyes, mellowed at the memory.

Ratnaprabha's wintry briskness was gradually thawing. Ira wished it wouldn't have taken such calamities for that to happen. She still fervently hoped that the super chef would once again have others, apart from Ira, to make special dishes for. Ratnaprabha had finished loading the dishwasher. Ira couldn't imagine being delegated that task in Godse house. When Ratnaprabha loaded the dishwasher, the utensils were almost squeaky-clean during pre-wash.

Ratnaprabha had turned towards the sink, wiping her hands on the kitchen cloth fashioned out of her saree, when she felt Ira's head resting on her shoulder, something she had never done before. Physical contact was far from welcome in the Godse household. Fatigued by all that had transpired and overcome by emotion at the mention of Sameer's birth, Ira had made that spontaneous gesture. To her surprise, her otherwise reticent mother-in-law patted her hair with her still-moist palm.

"*Aai*. If you get upset, I will understand. But I still want to request you for something." The irony of her only son's former wife visiting them even after her husband and her son had gone away, had not been lost on Ratnaprabha. She had always looked forward to Fridays, planned for them the entire week and now, Ira was all they had on the Fridays. The listlessness returned to her eyes, and she muttered,

In the name of DIVERSITY

"What can make me more upset, Ira? My anger has no teeth left."

Ira hesitated. Taking a deep breath, she said,

"*Aai*, I have not dared to mention this to you in 25 years, since the incident of my stupid mistake on the *Swastika rangoli* when I was pregnant. But so much has happened. We are dealing with life's blows with just the prayer and the effort to bring Sameer back to us. But he is not the only grandchild you have. Swati *Tai's* Leila will be 40 this year and you also have great-grandchildren, twins, a girl, and boy. Will you agree to meet them?"

Ratnaprabha froze. After years of tiptoeing around her moods, her wrath at breaking of the various religion-driven rules, Ira had become adept at reading her body language. She knew she had to get her story out and done with, before shock turned to blazing fury. Having finally mustered the courage, Ira blurted how she had visited Swati. She whipped out her phone and flashed a cheery picture of Ira flanked by Ella and Leon. Ratnaprabha did not lash out, nor smile, just clasped the back of the wooden chair till her fair fingers went whiter.

"Ratna, Ira…"

Prabhakar had made his way in, resting his walking stick, a tremor in his voice.

Ira sprung towards him,

"*Baba*, please sit down. Let me get the BP kit. Hope you've been taking your tablets," Ira drew out the dining chair for him while Ratnaprabha, overcoming her shock, quickly poured him a glass of water. Ira was rushing into the living room to get the blood pressure examination kit when Prabhakar stopped her.

"Ira, I'm fine. I take my medicines. Just lamenting our failure as parents," he moved his down-turned palm from side to side, indicating to his wife that he didn't need the glass.

Ratnaprabha had still not spoken, her cold countenance seemed to have hardened into an emotionless mask. The fleeting moment of warmth had disappeared. She hadn't done what she would surely have in earlier years – launched a tirade against the influences that had corrupted the caste her father had protected all his life.

Ira pulled a chair next to her father-in-law. Bending over, she said gently, "*Baba*, how could you have failed? It would have been impossible to raise Sameer without you. As you see on TV, the nationalism of the India you grew up in and the secularism of the India I grew up in has been taken over by opportunist politics in the name of religion. I am apprehensive too, but our value system will never permit Sameer to commit a crime. He will be back..." Ira spoke in a sincere, soft but firm tone.

Assured that there was not to be a tantrum and Prabhakar's health was fine, Ira gathered her things, adding that she would be back on Friday. At the door, she turned,

"*Baba,* you wanted your children to go to university. They didn't. At my convocation, at Sameer's, we saw the pride in your eyes. Leila has a master's in law, sits on committees of national importance and an upcoming doctorate. Swati *Tai* is revered by the women she courageously represents. She has surely done the Godses proud." Without waiting for a response, Ira stepped out into the cold London air, beginning to thaw before the much-awaited Easter break and the opportunity to see Ella and Leon again.

Ira's work week sped past, the Fridays at the Godses. On Saturdays, if she wasn't working, and Sundays, she woke to calls from Omar. She continued to text Sameer every two days. There never was a response. News about him filtered through via Cahya (he did occasionally respond to her messages). Ira's father kept a close eye on the dubious channels.

She had two new sources of joy, who had taken just 45 minutes to warm up to her, not questioning how she suddenly appeared. Generation-wise, she was in Nan's league. Age-wise, just a few years older than Mum.

"She couldn't be Mummy's sister for her hair was woolly black, her skin dark. Ira's hair was dark brown and straight, her skin fair but not as fair as their Daddy's family. Ella and Leon's hair was blonde and frizzy, their skin was olive, their eyes pale brown," such were Ella's astute observations. But to her or to Leon, none of this mattered. To them, she was Ira who stood outside their day-care centre when Mummy and Daddy were working, whose stories had them in such rapt attention that the vegetables vanished without a murmur.

In the name of DIVERSITY

Leila had been reluctant to let Ira have the children over, assuming that Ira had just been polite to offer. But Ella had walked up to Leila and said in her "grown-up voice",

"It's a winning proposition. The facts are evident..." Ella began her speech.

"What is prep poor station Mummy?" Leon interrupted, peering into the insides of the toy school bus he had managed to break open to explore. Leila suppressed her instinct to berate him for this dismantling. As per the school psychologist, this was supposed to be kinaesthetic learning and seemed to have kept him out of mischief for 30 minutes.

"Mummy, your undivided attention please!" Ella's "important person" voice was stern.

"Of course, darling, can you lay out the facts of the proposition so we can examine whether it qualifies as - winning?" Leila looked at Ira. Suppressing a smile, Ira pretended to admire the lace curtains. Leila looked solemnly into Ella's wide, brown eyes. Ella nodded in satisfaction at the situation being given propriety. She counted on her fingers,

"1. Leon has committed that he will not destroy anything in Ira's house.

2. I have committed that I will answer Leon's ignorant questions.

3. Ira has committed that she will tell us a new story, if we stick to these things and not fight." Ira looked at Ella incredulously. She remembered Sameer's prowess– English at school, Marathi with grandparents and the Hindi Ira had tried introducing to him. Ella spoke just one language and this focus was turning the child into a lexicon. Ira and Leila grinned. Leila held up both palms, exclaiming,

"Go on then!"

Ira nodded,

"Yes, I commit!", she raised her palm. Ella strode across to Leon, took his right palm saying,

"Leon, say I commit, so we can visit Ira, a new story, and double chocolate muffins. Come on quick!" Leon was too engrossed in the bus, he was now trying to reassemble, to bother asking what "commit" means. But, there was no way he would let Ella have a chocolate muffin by herself!

"Come meet" Leon raised the toy bus, its contents dangling.

Leila maintained her sombre expression,

"Winning proposition Ella!" Ella gathered their coats and extended her right hand,

"Thank you for having us, Ira. Look forward to seeing you next week." As Ella led Leon by the hand and out of the door, Ira and Leila broke into peals of laughter.

***

One evening a few months later, Leila came to take the children home. James was traveling.

"Come on in, have a bite. The children have just eaten – chicken nuggets and chocolate pudding as a reward for eating their vegetables and not trying to strangle each other. I couldn't refute Ella's argument on how no school tomorrow is a good case for device time," Ira smiled. Leila nodded gratefully. She slipped off her high-heeled black shoes, rubbed the sore toes wiggling against her black tights and walked across to the sofa.

"So, some chicken nuggets and then chocolate pudding?" Leila shook her head,

"I can't. I've given them up for Lent. I was going to open a can of soup at home. But a glass of water would be great. I'll go and say hello but trying to peel them away before the promised device time, would initiate criminal proceedings!" With a happy, tired smile, Leila deposited her laptop bag on the side-table and walked into what used to be Sameer's bedroom, now occupied by the two in their cartoon-print nightclothes, tucked in bed, their intense faces peering intently into a screen, where a bear was dancing to a song for a little boy with bushy black hair and clad in nothing but red underwear. Leon often fell asleep during the drive back home, so Ira had suggested that their back packs also include nightclothes.

"My darlings!", Leila put her arms around both. The two pairs of eyes did not move, Leon planted a kiss on Leila's cheek. Ella's dimpled palm patted her back with a crisp,

"Hello Mummy, hope you had a lovely day!"

Leila walked to the kitchen to join Ira with a spirited spring in her step,

"The court has been dismissed. Mummy is no competition for Jungle Book!" Leila was surprised to see Ira at the gas stove,

"I thought dinner was done. What are you cooking now? We'll leave soon."

Ira pointed to a bottle of Rose and two wine glasses. She poured the hot *phodni* mixture into a saucepan with yoghurt mixed with chickpea flour, sugar and salt and placed it on the stove to boil. She then slit open a packet of *papad* (poppadom) and placed them in the microwave. Leila looked at the bottle of wine gratefully.

"I could do with a drink, what a day! What are you cooking? Don't please!"

"This is the Indian version of *chicken soup for the soul*, our *dal khichadi*. I had made some for myself and had some left over, just warmed it up for you.

"Oh, I know that one. Nimrat Aunty used to send it across if one of us was ill. What's this white soup?" Leila handed a glass to Ira and took a sip of hers. Ira prepared her dinner plate – *dal khichadi* with a spoonful of *tup*, a bowl of creamy white *kadhi* with curry leaves floating on top and a spoonful of mango pickle. Realising how hungry she was, Leila ate with gusto.

"I cannot believe we are of the same age. You remind me of Mamma Maria, with your caring, accepting, forgiving spirit!" Leila shook her head, pouring herself and Ira the second glass of wine. She had relented to Ira's suggestion to stay over. The children kissed good night, Leila in borrowed pyjamas, the two had settled down by the fireplace.

Leila raised her glass to Ira and continued,

"To my new Maria! The church welcomed me as her granddaughter. The Pakistani communities embrace Mum as *Aapa*, but my skin attracts strange glances…until it is revealed I am the lawyer who can help their cause. Leila spoke about how Maria Joseph who, along with 500 odd settlers from Jamaica had arrived at England's Tilbury Dock as a 10-year-old on the Empire Windrush boat in 1948. Maria grew up nursing her father's illnesses caused by factory fumes and then found paid work as a nursing assistant.

"I'm telling you what Mamma Maria told me during our Sunday lunches, her version of England, so different from mine, yours and quite opposite of the one James describes. My grandfather Michael Clarke, who I never met, arrived on a similar ship from Barbados in 1959. They fell in love and married in 1961. Maria used to tell us about working late nights, Michael taking on arduous assignments, taking turns to look after the boys, of attending the Black church, initially just a bunch of devotees huddled in a neighbour's living room. Like good things that end too soon in the happy families that seem so rare, this one ended with Michael's death in a road accident."

Leila related how Maria had raised the boys in the Council home, ploughing on with her nursing job, never got a passport, never got to see her parents in Jamaica but how the church, neighbours, other black nurses became her extended family. And yet, Joseph's life took a path that she had ferociously obstructed. Ira listened in rapt attention as Leila recalled what Maria had explained to her after she was old enough - the sledgehammer incident was a result of Joseph being unlawfully dismissed from his job. Joseph had accompanied his friends to drown his sorrows in what started with a pint and rose to the ethereal cocktail of substances that went way beyond. After that fateful night, Joseph had never returned. Swati's police complaint wasn't the only one filed against him. The addiction led to a life dotted with prison sentences and ultimately un-investigated death in custody. Maria did not forgive Joseph, nor herself for being soft on him. She never forgave Swati for lodging that complaint. Things were never the same between them. Leila spoke about what her uncle Leo mentioned as she grew up,

"After Swati returned to Bradford after her futile visit to her parents, Maria sent across homemade bread and cake with Leo and the request to take Leila to church on Sunday."

"What does your uncle do?" Ira asked, marvelling at the relationships. Leila's face lit up.

"Oh, uncle Leo diligently kept his factory assistant job till he retired as supervisor. Aunt Helen was a fine person too, sending me gifts she used to knit herself, having worked as a seamstress before she and Leo got married. Ronald and his generation are where the problem started, always blaming the Council for everything, rarely if ever going to work and now his girlfriend has a fourth child on the way!" The mellow, nostalgic tone that Leila had adopted, rose in anger again,

"Therein you build the stereotypes. In the name of religion, the production of children continues. You produce more children, dip into Council funds to look after them, and other communities resent you. How come, this sudden awakening of Christianity does not extend to following any of the other tenets? The Bible describes laziness, swearing, cursing and not being responsible, as sins. The Sabbath is prescribed as the day of rest after six days of hard work. But Ronald does not work at all! He has a passport because his father saved up to let his son go on a school trip to Germany. With a passport facilitated by his school, Ronald is a legal UK citizen. Uncle Leo and Mamma Maria could never afford to go anywhere, even to visit family. The country Maria came from, was not even independent from British rule when they came to the UK."

"The Windrush," Ira exclaimed, amazed that what she had just read in the news, had such a connection. Clicking her tongue, Leila continued,

"Michael's passport, which Maria held on to as a precious memory, was issued in the name of the Queen of England. How were they to know that after over 50 years of paying taxes, they would be asked to produce documents to prove each year of their existence in Britain, be refused medical care and seek legal aid against being deported to countries they had left behind? So we have this Windrush scandal affecting over 50,000 elderly people of Caribbean origin," Leila paused as she transitioned from her tirade against the Windrush scandal to the fury over London's fire.

"In the other case, out of the 78 lives lost in Grenfell fire last year, are emerging abominable cases of institutional racism, sub-standard material being allowed as cladding in the building, lack of a central fire alarm system and more. Majority of the victims were of Black/Asian origin. What hurts the cause is the 22 false claimants asking for compensation for family members who didn't exist! These claims have been investigated and dismissed, but even one false claim, one wrong step weakens the fight…" With still so much to say but fatigued by her long day and the bottomless glass of wine, Leila stopped speaking.

Ira had been listening in silence, her eyes sad but serene. She had placed a glass of water and a bowl of cherries before Leila. She popped a cherry into her mouth.

"Were you always like this, calm, accommodating, able to ignore everything that is unfair Ira? How can you not be angry?" Ira spoke in a quiescent tone,

"Your paternal grandparents sailed to this country enduring extreme hardship, driven by what they believed was their "mother-country" inviting them to fill the jobs that needed doing, rebuilding all that had been lost in the second world war.

Your maternal grandfather flew in by choice to treat patients in rural England, a job that native English doctors were averse to. He was compensated very well for his effort.

I had the privilege of the UK's excellent education system. We are all still migrants, encountering stray cases of racism, largely by people who have not had the privilege of knowing that there is a world outside. There is no anger in me. My anger died on the first international flight of my life in 1993."

Chapter 17:

In the name of RELIGION

September 2, 2019

Ira was seated on a bench at her favourite Little Venice, a patch of paradise by the Grand Union Canal, right beside the buzz of Paddington. Ira's memories of this place were Sunday afternoon picnics with Sameer, after they moved to their tiny studio apartment in Islington. Ratnaprabha had thrown a tantrum, among her many arguments being why would a mother want to snatch from a little boy, a prim but green backyard, his own bunk bed, study desk and space and whisk him away to a rat-hole of a flat in London. Ratnaprabha was not wrong.

It was one of the sparse occasions that Ira had been assertive. She had long resigned herself to the fact that Sriram could easily slip into cold and, thus, hurtful behaviour. Whenever this happened, Ira raised a protective screen between Sameer and Sriram. She had learnt to do what Sriram's parents did very effectively. They told themselves that he was "under the weather" and left him alone, not even expecting basic courtesy. Without ever being told to, Sameer had learnt to do that as well. He played with Sriram when Sriram was in the mood. When he wasn't, he turned to his ever-willing grandparents and when Ira was at home – Ira.

One evening, when Ira got home, Sameer had locked himself in his room. Ira tried cajoling to extract what had gone wrong. She then pounded on the door furiously, pleading and scolding. She was met with silence. She then rushed down to the kitchen,

"*Aai*, what is wrong?" Ratnaprabha responded calmly,

"Nothing to worry Ira. After he comes back from school, I always give him one of his two favourite *laddus*– *rava* (semolina) or *besan* (chickpea flour) along with his milk. You know, I always make a tin full. Your father also likes a *laddu* with breakfast. But I've been so busy with the *haldi kunku* preparations, I didn't realise we had run out. Sameer came home from school, rushed to open the steel tin on the shelf and found it empty. I offered him a ginger cookie and a slice of the walnut cake you had brought yesterday. He stormed out saying his routine only has a *laddu* and has been sulking. Just like my father and grandfather – they would never compromise on the timing for the offerings to God, would fly into a rage if the Gods were not appeased with *naivedya*," Ratnaprabha shook her head at the ancient customs in a priest's home. She had not stopped grating the cucumbers for the *koshimbir* all this while, occasionally stirring the *aamti* (the lentil curry) for Sriram on the stove as she spoke.

"Don't worry, I'll get the dinner going and toss some *besan* into the pan. We'll have *besan laddus* for our little Prince in 20. Can you get me the tin from the shelf?"

"*Aai*, no. Make *laddus* at your convenience please. You've had erratic blood loss, back pain. If there is anyone who is under the weather, it is you. You need to rest, not pander to the routines set for everyone else's culinary cosseting." Of course, Ratnaprabha did not agree. After much enticement on promised treats over the weekend, Ira finally got Sameer to open the door. The two of them sat cross-legged on a lion print rug at the bottom of Sameer's coveted Spiderman bunk bed, Sameer sipping hot chocolate and munching on a slice of "walnut Santa". Ira had drawn an outline of a Santa Claus cap on the cake slice, cut away the extra bits, placed two raisins for eyes and painted a bright pink smiley out of strawberry jam. Sameer had forgotten about the *laddu* and was relating the occurrences of his school day and how he had returned hungry and angry after a boys' tussle on the school bus. Tousling Sameer's hair, Ira saw the ferocity in his eyes gradually dissolve into satiety that comes from a full stomach. She gazed at the birch tree outside the window. Ira had diagnosed, what should have been the most obvious - Sameer was imbibing maladjusted behaviours from Sriram. Out of transference of her love for the disappointing Sriram, Ratnaprabha was unwittingly encouraging her otherwise perfect grandchild's obdurate ways.

Ira made her decision, determined to bring up Sameer to be exposed to the plethora of cultures, foods, and habits that London offered and most of all, be easy about breaking any routine and embrace change. Locating an apartment, though her budget had stretched, was relatively easy, compared to the melodrama that ensued. Ratnaprabha's outbursts gave way to icy stillness directed at the party guilty of tearing away Sameer from his grandparents. Ira agreed to the Friday evenings and at least for the time being, Ira would not file for divorce.

Ira looked back at this rare assertiveness as one of the best things she had done for Sameer, especially in the later years, when she watched him and Cahya live life as Londoners, unconstrained by the barriers of food habits or cultural norms. As Sameer grew up, with his own weekend plans with friends, Ira developed a routine – of afternoons at one of the Little Venice cafes, sometimes seeing a friend, and often with a book, by herself on a bench by the waterside.

On that September afternoon in 2019, it was a Thursday, the festival of *Ganesh Chaturthi*, a public holiday in Mumbai. Ira had always booked leave on that day, to help install the statue at a place of pride in the living room, decorating the mini *pandal*, preparing the feast with the soft, steamed rice flour *modaks* stuffed with coconut and jaggery. Celebrations of the past had seen Sameer gleefully shouting out *"Ganpati Bappa morya"* after the prayers and elated at being allowed to do the veneration *aarti* as what Ratnaprabha told him "the man of the house" should do. When her own children were little, she had never allowed Swati to do the *aarti*. She was expected to help with the preparations and then hand over the *aarti* plate with the two oil lamps, pinch of uncooked rice, turmeric and *kunku* to Sriram to do the honours. This is what she had seen in a 1940s priest's home and saw no reason to change. The last *Ganpati* festival in 2016 had Cahya joining in. She stood at a distance during the *aarti*, paid her respects to the *Ganpati* idol by offering flowers, complimented Ratnaprabha on the excellent meal and even promised to return in the evening to help with the arrangements for guests who would be dropping in for a *darshan* (viewing) of the God.

The festival fell on the 25th of August in 2017 and had been a low-key affair with the household in despair dealing with Sriram's frequent nightmares. Within the next three months, Sriram was gone. For the first time in 60 years, the festival date of September 13 in 2018 went unmarked. This year, Prabhakar had convinced Ratnaprabha to get the *Ganpati* idol home, with the only argument that would work for her, that tradition demanded that once families started bringing a *Ganpati* idol home every year, they had to do it every year, pass down from father to son to grandson with the daughters-in-law expected to pick up the threads of performing the ritual in its prescribed form.

Ira had always done what was needed and imprinted upon Sameer that he should have no such expectations from his future wife. But this September of 2019, Ira had agreed with Prabhakar that the festival gave Ratnaprabha something to prepare for. Hopefully, during the 10 days the idol stayed in the Godse living room, she would find semblance of peace. So, Ira booked her leave, arrived at 7 am, helped with the arrangements, sang the lilting *aartis* that gave her peace too, had an early meal and left.

Here she was at Little Venice, gazing at the ducks who, like her, appeared to sail serenely along the canal and nobody could sense the furious paddling beneath. Ira's pensive reverie was broken by the ping of a notification. It was Omar,

"You must be at work. But call when you can, preferably, video. Some news." Holding on to her three possible routes to Sameer (Cahya, Omar, and *Baba*), Ira connected her earphones and made the video call. Omar exclaimed,

"Mesmerizing! Hold that look. A pensive but elegant stance against the water and the greenery. What's that – a narrowboat. I'll send you your picture. Where are you?" Ira's lips parted slightly at his ability to break her pensive mood. But she said briskly,

"I'm at Little Venice with historical significance to Lord Byron and Robert Browning. You can look up the connection later. And I'm not here to take pictures of myself or start you off on romantic poetry! Tell me the news about Sameer. Is everything ok?"

Omar grinned, basking in his old, highly enjoyable activity of showering her with blatant compliments and then sitting back to observe her blush, tucking away wisps of her hair behind her ears in embarrassment. He bellowed,

"Ira, if anything was wrong, would I spend precious moments admiring your timeless charm? Would I even bother with a message? If there was an emergency, would I not just call? At least at the ripe old age of 45, learn how to accept compliments. There is no need to respond to that. Listen to what we have found out." Ira gave up on trying to protest and eagerly clung on to every word. Omar had finally managed what he had been struggling with – plant a mole among the people Sameer had been associating with.

"We have a picture of him speaking at a meeting from yesterday. I'm sending that to you along with yours. Look at it, be assured he is fine." He paused, as Ira tapped her phone and stared. Clad in a white linen kurta and pale blue jeans, holding a cordless microphone, was Sameer. She smiled. Omar smiled back,

"He's fine Ira, ok?" She smiled through the tears of relief threatening to roll down.

"Now let's get on with the rest. I'm not a religious scholar or social activist. I'm just an ordinary teacher, trying to bring up my students with respect for another and the confidence to know that just because one is different, does not mean one is wrong. There are very few of us, from Muslim run educational institutions and some well-read practising Hindus, who come together as a *Mohalla* Committee. We work in communally sensitive areas of Mumbai to pre-empt possible violence. For instance, if *Ganpati* celebrations and *Muharam* fall on the same day, we sit together and give our input to both Muslim and Hindu youth to chart out routes for the processions or agree on timings for both celebrations." He tipped his thin-rimmed glasses and continued,

"If you talk to the children of people who lost lives in the 1992-93 riots, they will tell you, nobody in Mumbai wants a riot. Of course, there is polarisation that you will find difficult to fathom. Muslims do not find accommodation in Hindu dominated areas, on the pretext of non-vegetarian food being prohibited, especially by the *Jain* sect. The Muslims are asserting their bit, bringing home a goat to bleed as a precursor to *Eid*. So, we have highly conservative Muslim ghettos, where moderate Muslims don't want to bring up their children and ostentatious celebration of Hinduism on the streets. But anyway, more on this later. Trying to build bridges in Mumbai is easier, as at least the average family, Hindu and Muslim both, is still intent on education for children and jobs." Omar paused, looked out of the window and back at Ira.

"This polarization is even more intense in Northern India. This is where Sameer has been, mainly Gwalior and Meerut." Ira was intrigued by how the country of her birth had become unrecognisable with its intolerance. She asked,

"But Sameer? And the Godse connection?" Omar replied,

"Like Sameer told you, Pune and Mumbai are quiet on the subject. Support in Maharashtra is limited to the resurgence of a banned play on him receiving a spirited response and the annual gathering by his brother's family. But Sameer has been claimed by opportunists intent on packaging him as the educated, English-speaking, articulate descendent of the only man who dared to take on Gandhi, who the Congress party has claimed and will always hold on to as their own. The bunch that Sameer associates with, have several plans – ranging from constructing Nathuram temples and statues to launching a slew of healthcare products made of holy water from the river Ganga, cow dung and cow urine. Part of these preposterous plans is the cow-protection army set-up you witnessed during the January 30 drama and setting up private "Hindu courts" to dispense timely justice in the face of the inordinate delays of the formal Indian judicial system," Omar sighed revealing how one of the projects was to create a "Nathuram brand" Diwali gift hamper containing a bottle of shampoo, hair oil, soap, and toothpaste. Placing his phone on a tea-table, Omar crossed his arms, clicked his tongue,

"Given our penchant as a nation to pay lip service to history and the renaming of cities mispronounced by the British for centuries, the changeovers from Calcutta to Kolkata, Bombay to Mumbai, Poona to Pune, were accomplished over the decades. Mumbai has been cleansed of British names. The Victoria Terminus (VT) of our time goes by CST (Chhatrapati Shivaji Terminus). Like the Congress claimed the demi-God that was Gandhi, there are political parties clamouring for a share of Shivaji, with no inclination to imbibe his exemplary acts. Coming back to Godse, there is a long-standing proposal to rename Meerut district as Nathuram Godse Nagar. Let's see if that works out!"

Ira shook her head, still amazed that her son could be influenced by such ludicrous people. She asked innocently,

In the name of RELIGION

"So, nothing dangerous will take place Omar?" Omar picked his phrases carefully, conscious that Ira would wind herself further with worry,

"The more destructive plans include defacing or destroying Gandhi statues, organizing *havan* ceremonies to "cleanse the soil of Gandhi's filthy soul" and putting the imprint of Nathuram on these acts. These are fraught with danger as the sole purpose is to provoke a response from the other community." She asked,

"But Omar, what about that reconstruction horseplay? I was relieved Sameer was not a part of that. But why was his picture on the poster?" Omar laughed wryly,

"Oh apparently, Sameer had no idea that his photo had been used. They had found his picture, digitally modified it, added a turban on his head and popped it on a poster. Our source says that when Sameer discovered this, he objected to the breach of privacy. The junior bunch in the political lot wondered what the fuss was about. A picture on a poster is the most natural thing for aspiring Indian politicians, Hindu, and Muslim alike, they agree on this," Omar laughed. Ira nodded in comprehension, murmuring,

"Privacy, GDPR – dear Sameer having grown up in British environs… Go on Omar!"

"Ira, the *mohalla* we work in has hoardings with nine-year-old boys posing in sunglasses as future leaders. In any case, Sameer did not take this kindly and refused to don saffron to show solidarity. He argued that the Nathuram he had researched was a true Hindu, but always clad in an ordinary shirt and trousers. There you go!" Omar punched his fist, nodding in appreciation. Ira noticed Omar's pride in the argument proposed by the son he had not met. Shaking his head at the insanity of Sameer's current associates, Omar narrated how all this blew over and *Saadhvi* said, being a "true daughter of the soil", she would take matters in her own hands and wield the gun on Gandhi's effigy herself.

"She also took on the speech as we saw. I believe Sameer's Hindi is unlikely to compete with the authentic Sanskrit-infused Hindi they were speaking. So, Sameer was out of that farce but is readying for the big one coming up on November 15th."

Omar paused, looking at Ira sheepishly.

"Now what is it, Omar? This is quite a breakthrough! What is it you are hesitating to say?" Ira was impressed with the details Omar had been able to gather.

"Talking of breaching privacy, I'm guilty. It is not right, but I've gone ahead and done it, for your sake and honestly, for me too..." Omar looked at Ira nervously.

"Now what is it, Omar? Should I expect this to result in trouble?" Ira looked at him suspiciously, wondering what this could be.

"Oh no Ira, no trouble. I've managed to procure a private video recording of Sameer practising his speech on Nathuram for the grand *Maha-Sabha*, these people are planning to mark his 71st death anniversary. Adulation for Godse is picking up. They are expecting a massive crowd and national level TV coverage. My sources tell me that Sameer was asked to write the speech in English, it was translated into Hindi by someone else, the Hindi version written into English script for Sameer's benefit. Don't ask me how I managed to procure the recording. Like everything else we do to uphold peace, this is one more little crime that I hope will take us closer to bringing our son back. I'm transferring the file to you. You can watch it on your laptop later." Omar paused, still hesitating.

"Yes Omar?" Ira was fidgeting with her handbag, waiting to get home.

"I watched him speak, Ira."

Sensing the tremor in his voice, Ira paused her fidgeting and looked into Omar's eyes. With intense fervour, he exclaimed,

"He's nonpareil."

Ira held the gaze, nodding and barely heard Omar's whisper,

"Ira, Thank you."

With the faintest of tremors in his choked voice, Omar cut the phone line.

Chapter 18:

In the name of the DEMI-GODS

The next evening, Ira arrived at the Godse house with her laptop bag and a connector cable she had picked up on the way. As she had just visited them for the *Ganpati* installation the previous day, she had told them she wouldn't be coming in. On Friday afternoon, she called again to say she would be coming in anyway.

"We'll wait for you to perform the evening *aarti* then," Prabhakar was always pleased to have her company.

"No *Baba,* don't wait. I will be late from work, but I will come over," Ira promised.

That evening, Ira was pleased to see a semblance of Ratnaprabha back. She had planned the *prasad* items she would be making on all 10 days of her precious *Ganpati*'s visit to her home – *modak* on day 1 naturally, *besan laddu* on day 2, milk *pedhas* on day 3, coconut *karanjis* on day 4, *kheer* on day 5, *sheera* on day 6, *gulab jam* on day 7 and so on.

Ira was even more pleased to be introduced to Barkha, the new Turkish neighbour, her Italian husband Paolo and daughter Bella on their way out. Indian festivals were about warmth, food, family and sharing. It seemed odd to have just two people partaking of the delicacies that Ratnaprabha had laboured on. The family had moved in last week and had rung the doorbell to ask if they had a hammer they could borrow. One of their bathroom doors was stuck. Prabhakar had lent Paolo a toolkit and invited them to come in. As Ira stepped in, Paolo held out his hand. Barkha asked in halting English,

"What is your house number? This lane?"

"Oh no, I live in London," she clarified, introducing herself as Ira.

"Aha, relative visiting for the festival," Barkha broke into a friendly smile, nodding, as she gathered Bella in her arms to leave. This cheerful new family had no inkling of the morbid history of the Godse home and Ira chose to leave it just there. To her utmost surprise, it was Ratnaprabha's voice that rose from the kitchen door, in her halting English,

"Barkha, this is our daughter Ira."

The moment was interrupted by sleepy Bella's wail. The three of them left with Paolo carrying the Godse's toolkit under his arm and a steel plate with *thalipeeth* covered with another, for their breakfast and the promise to visit again.

That evening, after dinner comprising her favourite multigrain *thalipeeth* (usually considered a snack, but Ratnaprabha had broken the routine and made it for dinner) and homemade white butter, Ira struggled to connect her laptop to the Godse's old TV screen. Finally, with some plugging in and out of the cable she had brought along, it worked. Three of them held their breath as Sameer's familiar voice streamed across the living room.

"*Namaskaar*, I am Sameer Godse, grandson of Dr. Prabhakar Godse and Srimati Ratnaprabha Sathe, with Pune and Nashik roots, son of Sriram Godse and Dr. Iravati Dixit, born in Mumbai. I lay before you the authentic story of *Shri* Nathuram Godse." Clad in khaki trousers and a white shirt, Sameer's tall figure stood behind a solid, dark wooden chair, its back embellished with cream net design. Prabhakar leaned forward on his stick, his left palm pressing the armrest of the dark brown sofa. At the other end, sat Ratnaprabha, a corner of her pale-yellow cotton floral saree, twisted around her palm.

"He's lost weight. He won't be eating properly," Ratnaprabha muttered. Prabhakar gave her a sidelong glance and motioned to Ira that she should rewind the reel. Suitably admonished, she watched the recording in silence. Sameer's voice wafted across-

"Due to unidimensional projection and the downplaying of the contribution of all except Jawaharlal Nehru and Mohandas Gandhi, there are generations in the dark about facts regarding this grand nation's illustrious history. Because so little has been allowed to be said in public and nothing allowed to enter textbooks, there are myths about Nathuram.

Myth 1: Godse was a fanatic and killed Gandhi in a fit of anger

The only person who showed the courage to stand up to the larger-than-life Gandhi, has been dismissed as a fanatic, deranged individual who fired a fatal gunshot in a fit of frenzy.

It has been very convenient for this myth to be twisted further, so that the attempt to resurrect the memory of this thinker in theatrical form, was banned in 1997. But the play *"Mee Nathuram Godse Boltoy"* (This is Nathuram Godse speaking) is back in theatres. Apart from other sources, including direct interviews with Nathuram's family, the play draws from the most powerful legacy we have today, the authentic transcript of his defence presented in a five-hour session by Nathuram himself in the Ambala court in May 1948. Along with the copy of my speech today, printed in the party magazine, there are limited copies of Nathuram's defence titled "May I please your honour" at the party office. You will know that the man branded as a fanatic was an intelligent journalist, a selfless, brave human being, extremely well read, who put across his argument with logic, backed by research." Sameer paused, glancing at the sheet in his hand. Prabhakar nodded; Ratnaprabha's eyes had welled up and the storm in Ira's mind was brewing again. Sameer continued,

Myth 2: Godse killed Gandhi for supporting the untouchables

The caste system is misunderstood by the western world. We know that the origin was the *Varnas* (professions) based on which these divisions were made. I know from my great grandmother Saguna *bai* Dixit that the scriptures likened the four castes to four vital parts of the body – *Brahmin* (head), *Kshatriya* (arms), *Vaishya* (belly) and *Shudra* (feet). Can the body function without any of these? The division based on vocation became hard coded, as sons followed their father's line of work, education for women stopped and Brahmins cut off access to knowledge. *Shudras* and the casteless (untouchables) suffered the most and I'm sad to see that even after centuries, they continue to suffer today in so many parts of India. Have you, true Hindus ever thought why an advanced society like *Bharat*, continued to be plundered, attacked by invasions, and taken over by Great Britain, whose geographical landmass size equals to just one of India's largest states? The reason is evident, just open any history book or any Indian newspaper today – it is our refusal to come together as a unit, our obsession with the differences and the egos that would not allow us to view the larger good. I hope this will open our minds and help us reconnect as true Hindus:

1910 is Nathuram's birth year, the same year Adolf Hitler, dropped out of school. The same year when social reformer and Gandhi's mentor Gopal Krishna Gokhale, another *Chitpavan* Brahmin from the same community as us Godses, set up the Servants' Society of India in Mumbai with the mission to propagate education among all castes and classes.

The King Shivaji, the proudest *Kshatriya* we know had Dadaji Kondev and Ramdas among his teachers, both *Brahmins*. Today, when you send your child to school, go out to eat, to the movies, do you ask for the religion or caste of the providers of each? You avail of these because they offer the best music and best food. The way society was structured then, the best knowledge was with the *Brahmins* because they had access to it.

So why is there such an anti-*Brahmin* sentiment in the country? Why the demolition of the statues of Shivaji's teachers, why a row over the official headgear of Godse's Pune? A political party has objected to the *Puneri pagdi*, the silken cap worn by the *Brahmins*, social reformers and freedom fighters of that era demanding that Pune's official headgear should be the farmer's turban worn by Mahatma Jyotiba Phule, a member of the *Mali* (gardener) caste. Phule and his wife Savitri *bai* went on to do outstanding work for India. In the 1800s, the Phules set up three girls' schools in Pune's Brahmin Bhide *wada*, in the untouchable *Mahar wada* and in the home of a Muslim lady who offered shelter to the Phule couple after they were shunned by their own community for hobnobbing with the *Brahmins*.

The University of Pune is now named after the illustrious Savitri *bai* Phule, the Mumbai airport and railway terminus are named after Shivaji. We are here because the social reformers then set aside differences for common good, but among the Hindus, we continue to fight over symbols, headgear, statues, castes, and sub castes.

Nathuram did not believe in the caste system, freely joining in multi-caste meals. So, the second myth, that he killed Gandhi because he supported the Dalits, is wrong!" Sameer banged his fist on the table," Ira's heart swelled with pride.

Myth 3: Godse said - "Kill all Muslims"

71 years after the British left India, the monster of religion-based division permitted by Gandhi has grown in such a humongous, ugly manner, that it is unlikely that the Muslim nation created by the 55-crore donation from India would ever want to unite with its mother country. *Akhand Bharat* and Nathuram's fervent wish of his ashes being immersed in the *Sindhu* (Indus) river which now runs through Pakistan is likely to remain a pipedream. Less than six months after Gandhi gifted away Pakistan, the newly created nation had refused to let his ashes be immersed in the *Sindhu* river. What does that tell you?

Gandhi's memory lives on, usurped by those with no interest in understanding his ideology. Nathuram was hanged at the age of 39. All I ask is that his tainted memory be rectified, generations be taught about *Akhand Bharat* ideology, and accurate history be recognised instead of being crushed under the overpowering banyan like status accorded to Gandhi.

There have been other demi-Gods, with conflicting ideologies, but they overcame differences, submerged the self, and let the country rise above one's own interest. In the words of Bal Gangadhar Tilak, a co-founder of the Congress party, who Gandhi called the "Maker of Modern India",

"Religion and practical life are not different. The real spirit is to make the country your family instead of working only for your own. The step beyond is to serve humanity and the next step is to serve God." He was the same Tilak, who had given the clarion call to bring our religion, our prayer, onto the streets in the form of the idols of our favourite God - *Ganesh*. He initiated the annual *Ganesh* festival to be held in localities, the performance of educational and cultural performances, the singing of *Ganesh aartis*. When he called upon the public to invite God on to the street for 10 days every year, his purpose was very clear: Hindus, across caste divisions, would come together every evening for 10 days consecutive days and become the unifying force which would win India its freedom from the British. He was the same Tilak, a staunch Hindu, whose cause was represented in court by none other than Mohammed Ali Jinnah, first Prime Minister of Pakistan. By this logic,

Jinnah was a freedom fighter for India and Godse and all the Indian freedom fighters, fought for the freedom of Pakistan from the British, for till 1940, the idea of Pakistan had not taken birth.

Tilak had said that Shivaji's Maratha kind of governance practised successfully in the 17th century could not work in the 20th century and had proposed a federal government where every religion and caste would be an equal partner. Tilak tried to convince Gandhi to leave the idea of total non-violence "Total *Ahimsa*" and try to get self-rule *"Swarajya"*. Though Gandhi did not concur with Tilak on the means and was steadfast in his advocacy of *satyagraha*, he appreciated Tilak's services to the country. There have been other demi-Gods across India but with Tilak's passing, Gandhi became infallible. In Nathuram's words,

"Gandhi called himself a *Satyagrahi* and only he knew what a *Satyagrahi* was supposed to be" which ultimately led to the irreversible downfall of this nation.

I am not Nathuram. To understand what went through his mind before he fired the fatal shot at the person who was not just revered as the father of the nation, but ideologically a father figure to him, look at the images we have of Nathuram, read his transcript. His stricken face mourns the death of 600,000 victims of the communal riots that broke out due to the India-Pakistan partition and the heinous crimes against women during this period. Nathuram holds Gandhi responsible for relenting to the British decision of partition, a jagged line drawn through a nation within weeks by a Mr. Radcliffe who had never been to India by his own admission, who confessed later who cannot sleep at night, for the horrors haunt him too. You feel Nathuram's pain when you read that he admits to being conscious of being hated by a nation who would see his act as an unforgivable crime. He is about to throw away a good family life and respect as a journalist. But he says he is consumed by the mission to sacrifice all that he ever earned in his life and walk to his own death.

We need someone to eulogise, pray to, to emulate. The emulation is just in the aping of attire. If you believe that a vermillion mark on your forehead makes you a Hindu or a thread across the shoulder makes you a *Brahmin*, I don't blame you. Until barely a few months ago, I was guilty of the same. But I immersed myself in the gifts that our religion has given us – a sea of literature, practitioners, theorists and most of all, the freedom to interpret the Hinduism way of life in our own way.

The culture we are blessed with is far too rich and embedded in our hearts to be eroded by external onslaught. Like the mindless violence of Partition, the world continues to lose lives on the pretext of religion. Like we have tried to constrain our faith in an idol, our religious practice in a little box called the temple, let us not do that again with Nathuram. Statues are meant to commemorate, to help us concentrate our thoughts towards one, not to win points for being the tallest, fairest, or biggest, and certainly not to demolish or desecrate.

Did the demi-Gods want their own temples built? Their followers of course needed them, to be able to concentrate on their *lakshan* (external descriptors), while conveniently straying afar from their principles. Like we have done with Gandhi and others, we are about to confer demi-God status on Nathuram, who went at lengths to state that he was but a common citizen, a Hindu who believed that Hindus, being the majority religion of India, should have the right to have proportionate representation in all walks of life. The greatest injustice done to demi-Gods is that we expect them to be Gods, flawless in thought, belief, and action.

This is strange. For each of the Gods that I have grown up hearing stories of, is known to have publicly acknowledged a fault – Lord Shiva had his anger, Lord Rama is supposed to have been the ideal King but not necessarily the ideal husband as he banished his wife to the forest. We accept these flaws kindly. But we seek perfection in demi-Gods, exposing their vulnerability, giving their detractors the opportunity to widen the cracks in their armour and intensify the attack on their exposed flaws.

Gandhi's detractors have a field day pulling out his idiosyncrasies and his flaws in decision making. Like the rest of the nation, Nathuram sought perfection in the demi-God he once admired. He believed that given Gandhi's influence over the nation and with the departing British, he could have gridlocked partition, prevented the killings using his acclaimed fasting strategy or any other weapon in his armoury that always led him to succeed whenever he wished it to. If you read Nathuram's writings, you will see he was among the few people who understood Gandhi. For the rest of the populace, he remains an image on a bank note, the name of a street or a statue that is home to nesting pigeons.

By demanding temples and statues for Nathuram, we are trying to accord demi-God status to a man who explicitly said he was far from being one. Let us unveil a statue no doubt; but, not miss out the nuance of what Nathuram had to say."

The three of them had watched the reel in silence, soaking in every gesture, the sound of the voice of the one who had been the cynosure of their lives for 25 years. Ira had been enraptured by Sameer's demeanour. Now, the second time, she was beguiled by his ability for in-depth research, analysing facts and presenting them in an objective, but engaging fashion. His grey-green eyes brimming over with pride, Prabhakar nodded at Ira in approval. Transfixed, Ratnaprabha finally pried herself away. She made her way to the kitchen and placed a tiny steel bowl of sugar before her Gods, murmuring gratitude for keeping Sameer safe.

Chapter 19:

In the name of the SPIRIT

Saturday, October 5, 2019.

It was to be a busy weekend. Lunch with Claire, coffee with Cahya and then to Leila's. It was the children's birthday. Leila had insisted that Ira stay over for drinks after. The previous evening at the Godse house had been refreshing. After viewing Sameer's speech a month ago, the healing had begun.

The last evening had been a mini celebration. Ratnaprabha had made her husband's favourite *satori*, a sweet wheat pancake stuffed with cardamom flavoured semolina filling. The cause for celebration had been a letter. A British researcher had published a book on the contribution of Indian doctors to the NHS in the 1960s. The research was based on the case studies of 40 doctors and Prabhakar was among those featured. The book release was to be accompanied by a photo exhibition at a prestigious London venue.

Ira attributed this development to Prabhakar's diligence and Ratnaprabha's unflinching support. Ratnaprabha shook her head. Muttering her Sanskrit *shlokas* (prayers), she placed the *satori* in front of her mini temple, bowed in reverence and declared,

"Everything is better since we got Him home," she declared. Prabhakar smiled at Ira mischievously,

"Ratna *bai*, can I taste my *satori*, after *Ganpati* has eaten of course! *Tathastu* (So be it)!"

Saguna would have said that Ratnaprabha's unflinching faith led her to support her husband through adversity. Prabhakar saw God in his profession. Ira questioned neither. She folded her hands before the smiling elephant, who always ensured she returned his smile, enjoyed the luscious *satori*s with dollops of *tup* and went home with more than a reason to smile.

***

As he had, on every weekend over the last few months, Omar called, "Good morning, Miss!"

"Good morning, Sir!" Ira replied. It was an inside joke that children who went to Convent schools in India would be able to identify with. All lady teachers, irrespective of their marital status, were called "Miss" by the students and amusingly, by the other teachers. The male teachers (irrespective of the fact whether knighthood had been conferred upon them, as one of their Anglo-Indian teachers Miss Laurence in her posh British accent had pointed out sarcastically) were called "Sir". Miss Laurence had made this sardonic comment after two hilarious incidents.

They had a newly married Marathi language teacher Mrs. Katkar. This was the teacher's first job and her master's with distinction degree in Marathi had not prepared her for the nuances of working in a class full of insolent adolescents. When the class rose and greeted Mrs. Katkar in their customary sing song chorus,

"Good morning, Miss!" The indignant lady had turned around and admonished the class, holding up the gold and black beads of the *mangalsutra* around her neck,

"Can't you see, I'm Mrs!" The class had dissolved into peals of laughter.

The other incident involved Mr. Pawar, the Physical Education teacher. Mr. Pawar was a source of amusement for the over smart bunch always on the lookout for some good-natured fun. Mr. Pawar was blissfully unaware of the concept of knighthood. But he would stride across the school playground, blowing on a bright pink plastic whistle dangling on to a blue string around his neck, bellowing in his thick Marathi accent,

"*Lepht*, right, *Lepht*, right, chin up, *daaye mud*, childrens, call me Pawar Sir!"

Years later, Omar and Ira broke into peals of laughter again at these memories.

"But Ira, I called to tell you about something wonderful that happened. No, not to do with Sameer, with me," Omar could barely contain his euphoria. Ira sat down by the window, her chin resting on her palm, pitching in playfully,

"Can't wait to hear it, Siddiqui Sir!"

Omar related how in one of the Islamic schools he ran in Mumbai, some of the students came from an orphanage where he had been principal trustee.

"After the children finish their graduation, we try to help them with jobs and spread the word in the community to look for suitable partners. Two months ago, I had an unusual request. A Mr. and Mrs. Ghaisas from Vile Parle came to meet me, asking for one of our students Reshma's hand in marriage for their son Ashfaque. I was confused. The couple explained that they had found eight-year-old Ashfaque at Bombay Central station 21 years ago. The boy had lost his parents and was being looked after by his grandmother in Vapi, Gujarat. His grandmother passed away and his aunt began to ill-treat him. He had run away to Mumbai hiding from ticket checkers under seats and in washrooms during the three-hour journey."

Omar explained how when the Ghaisas' found him, they corresponded with his family. His aunt was least interested. They took him home, enrolled him into a Mumbai school. He grew up along with their own children.

"Wow, that's quite a story!" Ira exclaimed, charmed.

"Wait Ira, listen to this," eager to share what led to his euphoria, Omar interrupted,

"Ashfaque now works in a bank, has moved to a one-bedroom flat in Ambarnath and has started paying his own mortgage. He had seen our Reshma at a community event." Omar's eyes were gleaming. Ira gave him a thumbs up sign, drawn further into the story.

Omar paused, took a sip from a glass of cloudy lemon juice, and continued,

"Well, we have made certain non-negotiable rules in our institutions. We don't get into horoscopes, but insist on a blood test and basic medical examination for both parties. This was done for Reshma and Ashfaque and last Sunday, we had the *Nikah* ceremony in our school hall. We cannot afford anything grand but try to make it special. We decorate the school hall, serve a buffet dinner and the bride is given a pretty wedding outfit. People from the community donate towards the festivities. As you know, in a traditional *Nikah*, the bride and groom do not see each other, and the *Kazi* (priest) goes across to check with the bride if she agrees to the wedding and she replies *"Qubool"* (Agreed).

We have the *Kazi* conducting the ceremony with a *purdah* (veil) separating the bride and groom on stage and attendees are witness to the fact that the bride agreed."

"That's outstanding social reform Omar. You have managed to take everyone along, the radicals and the progressives. Like Justice Ranade of our Dadar's Ranade Road, maybe you will be the moderate of the 21st century," Ira had caught on to Omar's excitement.

"But wait Ira, the best part is yet to come," Omar was breathless.

"Last evening, in one of Dadar's typical wedding halls, the Ghaisas family hosted a wedding meal. Their relatives and friends had turned out in their typical Maharashtrian attire, with *pagdis* and turbans, some of the women wearing *nauvari* sarees. It could have been at any of your cousin's weddings Ira! Some of the relatives made speeches, talking about how Ashfaque had been such a part of their own festivals and ceremonies.

Mrs. Ghaisas called me on stage. She thanked me for agreeing to the single request she had when she came to ask for Reshma's hand – that Ashfaque be allowed to visit them for *raksha bandhan* and *bhau beej*, as their daughter had always considered him as a brother. Mr. Ghaisas spoke about how overwhelmed I had been by that request and had just told them that Ashfaque and Reshma would always be their children.

They invited Reshma's friends from our orphanage, the staff, cooks and cleaners turned out in their *Eid* finery. We ate at the long tables, served by the Maharashtrian staff. Mr. and Mrs. Ghaisas, Ashfaque and Reshma came to serve us the *jalebis*, believe me, the sweetest I have had." Omar put down his glasses and wiped his eyes. Ira laughed through her tears,

"What nobody else could do, one of your many daughters – young Reshma has done. She made you weep Omar!"

In the name of the SPIRIT

Heartened by Omar's story, looking at him wipe his glasses, Ira remembered.

"I need to leave Omar and need to locate my spare reading glasses. Our young man had a go at football in this little apartment, smashing whatever was on the side table. Leila was livid. Leon got an extended stint at the naughty corner; I was reprimanded for indulging them so much and Patricia had ordered a pair at the opticians before I knew what was happening!" Ira flung her arms wide, shrugging. Omar was not surprised. Having heard so much about the new entrants into Ira's life, he could predict their individual courses of action in any situation.

"However efficient Patricia is, she cannot shorten the wait for my glasses. Let me go now, I just can't remember where I kept the spare pair. Bye." Ira got up.

"Ira, can you please walk to the chest of drawers by the kitchen?" Omar said with authority.

"Whatever you are getting at, some other time please. I need to leave!" Ira was impatient.

"Ira, can you please open the second drawer from the bottom? You placed your spare glasses in there while we were speaking. As usual, you were fretting about something, you didn't realise you had done it!" Omar sighed.

"Omar, stop managing my life remotely!" Ira chortled, retrieving the small black case.

And then, Omar hesitated. Ira checked the contents of her handbag one final time and retrieved the house keys from their hook in the corner.

"Yes Omar? What is it? *Bolo!*" she exclaimed.

Omar looked intently into his phone and said gently,

"Ira one more time, when do you want to come to India? Or should I plan a trip to London?"

Ira's answer was still the same.

"We'll see Omar, I need to meet Claire in 20 minutes. Got to go."

***

Ira walked into Claire's favourite East London restaurant. Claire was seated at a corner table, giving her specifications to a Pakistani waiter struggling with her accent but impressed by her knowledge. Claire waved to Ira as the waiter departed with his order.

"*Masala chaas* on its way. I asked him to blot out the oil in the onion *bhajji* starter with tissue, a chilli garlic bullet *naan* for me, *tandoori roti* for you, chicken *korma*, go easy on the oil, go strong on the spices and mint *raita*." Claire ignored the roll of Ira's eyes and laughed,

"Do you remember the first time you came here with me? There was barely standing room at the door and people queuing up in the cold. But thanks to you, we got 5-star treatment!" Ira chuckled. She wasn't a fan of Indian food in London, especially at restaurants claiming to be Indian. She found the food too oily and tinged with food colour. But Claire insisted and she agreed. The waiter had been extremely gracious, checking in if they would like additional *rotis*, suggesting a chef's special lamb *kebab* starter and patiently explaining the new desserts on the menu, all this while people were waiting for them to free up a table. Ira had not understood the reason for this graciousness, but Claire was certain,

"Ira, he thinks you are real!" Claire had exclaimed. "What do you mean? All of us are real..." Ira had asked, chewing on her *roti*, puzzled.

"He knows you are Indian, the way you pronounce the words. Besides, your eyelids are not caked with brightly coloured eyeshadow, thick eyeliner and you don't say,

"Innit! instead of "Isn't it!" Claire pronounced breezily, wiggling her fork.

"Mean Claire!" Ira had laughed at the cheeky take on the East London stereotype.

"Talking about stereotypes, listen!" Claire updated Ira on the latest interaction thanks to her dating app.

"But Ira, when you walked into the restaurant, I could sense a spring in your step, after a long, long time, probably not since the day we celebrated Sameer getting into the university of his choice. Tell me all, including confessions, welcome to this House of Prayer!" Claire drew the holy cross in the air with her butter knife. Ira enlisted the reasons for her gaiety, Sameer's video, Prabhakar's felicitation, and this morning's story from Omar.

"You know Claire, the angst with which Omar spoke about how his community profusely thanked Ashfaque's adoptive parents for bringing him up as a Muslim...this was the norm when we grew up. Given Omar's articulation, musical inclination and sharp memory, he would lead the *aarti* renditions at our home with gusto," Ira's eyes grew tender. She picked on the onion *bhajji*, too engrossed to notice that it was dripping in oil. She spoke quietly,

"Claire, it is strange, Omar and Swati have grown up in different countries. She works among Muslims of Pakistani origin in Northern England. Omar works across Muslim and Hindu communities in Mumbai. Both said the same thing to me –

"We are amidst moderates who have chosen to be quiet, but we must keep trying. One among us, a certain Mohammed Mahmoud, Imam (Islamic religious leader) exhorted his community to not retaliate when a certain Osborne deliberately drove a van into worshippers outside Finsbury Mosque in London seeking revenge for the Manchester Arena bombings. The community listened. Those being indoctrinated are bound to see reason, one day," Ira was lost in her muse. But the pensive mood was tinged with hope. Claire cleared her throat,

"Hmm, this Omar sounds like a superstar. When can I meet him?"

"Oh, I haven't met him for 26 years, so not very soon. Sorry to disappoint you," Ira did not look up from her bowl of *malai kulfi*.

"Why not Ira, that's the point, why not. You two are like a languorous art movie. This is 2019, not 1993, get on with it," Claire registered her protest with a coordinated banging of her left fist on the table and clinking her dessert spoon on the bowl of carrot *halwa*.

"He's been asking whether I'll come to India, or he should come here. I have in-laws here, parents and Sameer there. I don't know how they'll react…" Ira dug into her handbag to settle the bill that arrived along with two mint pieces. Claire placed her palm on her wrist.

"It's my turn, remember Ira? Years ago, we agreed on two things. The first was your suggestion and I gave in. We will not pay for individual dishes or split any bill equally, which works for everyone else in England. We will meet each other the Indian way, share everything we order in a restaurant. One person pays so that it is a pact to meet again.

The second was my suggestion and you have followed it all these years. Whenever one of us is being stupid, emotional, irrational or doing anything that is likely to harm her, the other one will not bother being polite and will tell her exactly what she thinks, even if it sounds rude. You have done this multiple times and so have I. Though delayed, your decision to move out of the Godse house was the best for Sameer. You were to file for divorce when Manchester Arena happened, and you backtracked. I would have still gone ahead. You didn't and I understand." Ira had been nodding mutely. She placed the bill before Claire.

"All yours!" she smiled warmly. Claire picked up the piece of paper with a flourish,

"This is not about the bill alone! Let me not waste time in being polite and tell you that you are being utterly stupid. If any of the dating app options work for me, it will not be because my Mum likes my new boyfriend or my ex-husband or his Mum do! If anyone will have a say if it reaches a stage of anyone moving in, it may be George. George is my child and whether a boyfriend likes it or not, George lives where I live. The relationship you describe with Omar, the comfort, the ease, the care…sounds priceless. I know very few couples of the same sex or heterosexual, who share this kind of chemistry. So, get on with it!" Claire was satisfied with her sermon. She had swiped her card, popped a two-pound coin into the bowl and blessed the waiter with her beatific broad smile. Ira had been listening but did not respond. She rose to retrieve her jacket when Claire did something Ira was to remember forever.

"Wait Ira. It's from the most entertaining film we've ever watched. It's got a song at the Interlaken and Mount Titlis in Switzerland. The one where this girl Simran is held back by her staunch father to marry this axe wielding dude. And then, Simran's boyfriend is on a train waiting for her to join him," Claire rubbed her palms in glee. Ira smiled,

"Oh, you mean DDLJ, *Dilwale Dulhania leh Jaenge*." What about that now, I need to leave. Cahya will be waiting," She tucked her handbag under her arm. Claire squealed,

In the name of the SPIRIT 169

"Yes you got it! Remember the father in his booming voice tells his daughter to start living her life. And released from the parental bond, Simran gently lifts her gorgeous *ghagra* skirt and sprints across the train platform to grab her boyfriend's extended hand from the train door. Ooh what drama, what fun. Iconic! So, I've practised this for you,

"Jaa Simran... aha Ira, *jee le apni jindagi! (Go...*live your life!*)."*

Shaking her head in disbelief, thoroughly entertained and touched by the effort and sentiment, Ira gave her a warm hug and stepped out into the cool London breeze.

Chapter 20:

In the name of PEACE

The coffee with Cahya had been quick. Cahya had applied for a visitor visa. Her plan was to book herself on a "Buddhism pilgrimage tour" through a travel agent covering key locations in the North and Northeast of India. Ira offered that Cahya could stay with her parents in Mumbai if she would like, but Cahya intended to fly in and out of Delhi after visiting Sameer. This was just as well. Ira knew her parents would have welcomed Cahya warmly, but Priyamvada, given to ostentatiousness held in check by Saguna in the early years and Ira's disinterest in later years, would have enjoyed showing off Sameer's girlfriend. Though things were better, they were not great yet. Cahya was everyone's hope of bringing Sameer back. Ira handed Cahya a palm-sized parcel wrapped in soft, pale blue paper, held in place by a maroon, thick cotton string, saying,

"Belated Happy birthday Cahya. I know you like pastels and this is something you could wear anywhere in India." Smiling, Cahya politely unravelled the string and held up the lemon-yellow linen *kurta* and a pale blue vegetable dye scarf.

"It's lovely, you really shouldn't have..." Cahya thanked her profusely.

***

Ella and Leon's birthday party had been a riot. Competing with Leon's war cries was the bellowing of three boys and two girls from school, bouncing on the trampoline in the small back garden. The magician in the sky-blue suit with pink trimmings and red top hat drove in with his portable table, feathers, and cards, wrapped up his act in 45 minutes, collected his payment and sped off. Leila and James were left to deal with the raucous lot.

Ira and James had briefly met a few times before when he had come to pick up the children. He would thank her for her most kind offer to have them and mention that she should come over too. Ira was helping Leila get the chicken nuggets and potato smileys out of the oven. The pizzas had arrived, and James had finished slicing these into child-friendly portions. It was impossible to get the twins to agree on what cake they wanted. So, in their cartons sat a lovely violet book shaped cake with Ella scrawled across in creamy pink and an angry looking black hooded monster with Leon scrawled across his chest in blazing yellow letters.

On hearing yet another whoop from the garden followed by a shriek, Leila gave James a look. James was about to sprint into the garden when the doorbell rang. He looked at Leila, shrugged and took a U-turn.

"You manage the food. I'll check on the children," Ira stepped out onto the green. Leila nodded gratefully. Twenty minutes later, Leila stepped onto the patio and placed the two cakes on the portable, wooden garden table. James walked into the garden clapping his hands,

"Come on quick, Ella, Leon, wash your hands. Time to cut the cake!" The children had been seated in a circle around Ira perched on a garden stool engrossed in a "Complete the story" game. Ira was tempted to ask James to wait till the game concluded. But a glance at Leila gritting her teeth, James' polite smile and the elderly couple, told her otherwise.

"The Puppy said to the Kitten, " Wait! I need to polish off my dessert. Then clean my teeth. See you! Children, the Puppy has gone off to clean his teeth. While we wait for him to come back, let's cut the cake. Wash your hands before that, let's go!" Ira got up, clapping her hands. The children dispersed to wash their hands and eagerly crowd around the cakes.

"Hello, I'm George!" the gentleman extended his hand to Ira.

"Hello, Ira," she shook his hand.

"My wife, James' mother and though she doesn't look it, the children's grandmother Fiona," George's eyes twinkled. Fiona rolled her eyes at James and smiled politely at Ira, saying,

"You do have a way with children. I can't imagine having just Leon for an afternoon, leave alone Leon and Ella and certainly not this entire bunch. I heard hideous shrieks from the garden, but things seemed to have settled down since we got in. What do you charge? My daughter's got her son's birthday party coming up..." Fiona was looking into Ira's eyes, widened by the question, oblivious to her husband's efforts to correct her.

"I believe Ira is Leila's cousin," George corrected her.

"Leila's family? But she's..." the words that Fiona did not utter, were heard by the adults as they settled into the spaces still vacant despite the gigantic proverbial elephant in the room.

"Ira is close family. She was married to Mum's brother. He passed away two years ago; James must have mentioned it to you. Yes, she is Indian too," Leila answered all the questions her mother-in-law had wanted to but did not ask. Fiona's eyebrows arched. During the avoidable run-ins that Swati and Fiona had, she had recoiled at the working-class Yorkshire accent. She was still recovering from the morbidity of the scarf wearing women who had turned up at James' wedding years ago.

"Sorry, your English is so good. Which part of London are you from? I thought you were the magician. Your dress is lovely! Is it M&S?" Fiona was making this worse.

"I love children. I grew up in India, and moved to the UK after I was married," Ira maintained a neutral expression, sensing that an acerbic retort was on its way from Leila.

"Mum, Ira's a doctor with the NHS," it was James to the rescue. Leila flashed a syrupy smile,

"Yes Fiona, you are right. With Ella and Leon, she has been the magician!"

"This way please, let's cut the cake..." James had managed to round up the children and had his arm firmly around Leon in case he had other ideas.

The cake cut, the return gifts distributed, finally the last parent to pick up the last child was gone. James went upstairs to tuck the children in while Ira and Leila cleared up. Fiona and George had left soon after the cake was cut. George had a slice of pizza and Fiona orange juice. She said she had been off carbs since the last two weeks.

James handed Ira a glass of red wine and walked across to Leila with hers. With a peck on her cheek, James led Leila to sit down by the fireplace.

"I know it's not easy, Leila, never has been." He placed both palms on Leila's shoulders and rubbed her neck and the right side of her upper back.

"Better?" Leila nodded at him, her face gradually settling into a tender smile. James took a sip of the wine and explained,

"Hours of reading, committees, conferences, dissertation work and now a birthday party. My own travel is not helping Leila's neck pain. I've been thinking of taking on an easier job, at least something that involves less travel. Let's hope something works out. And of course, Ira, you've been a Godsend. Thank you!" James raised his glass to Ira.

"Any time! They are a delight. Sameer was quieter of course and I was still in my 20s with far more energy!" Ira smiled, walking across to the dark brown leather sofa.

"Ira, my apologies on Mum and thanks for being gracious. There is not much one can say in defence of overt or covert racist behaviour in 2019, especially in the middle of multicultural London. Mum just does not get it. Till we got married, Mum had never interacted with a person of colour except maybe at a till. As we speak, they are off to a black-tie dinner to celebrate someone's 50th wedding anniversary, where everyone will be white, they will discuss the weather and someone's European holiday with an English tourist company while consuming a standard three course English meal." James raised his glass, cocking his head.

Surprised to see James being so candid, Ira murmured politely,

"It's fine…" James continued,

"The phenomena of a flattening world, a typical London workplace that boasts of almost every nationality across the globe, seem to have just passed her by. But after all, she's Mum. So sorry," James pursed his lips, raising his glass at Ira. Seeing how deeply embarrassed he was, Ira tried to put him at ease with her perspective.

"James, privilege comes in different forms, and I see some parallels between white privilege and the Indian caste system. The discrimination by the upper castes has driven away Hindus to Islam, Christianity, and

Buddhism. In 1956, five hundred thousand "untouchables" converted to Buddhism along with their iconic leader Dr. Ambedkar. Today, most of his followers have never read any of his scholarly writings and are the first to take to violence. There is reverse discrimination due to caste-based reservations. I've experienced both sides but still feel fortunate due to inherent privilege," Ira maintained. Leila snapped,

"The privilege you talk about as a *Brahmin*, we have never enjoyed. Though legally, discrimination has no place, racial hierarchy rages on 50 years after Enoch Powell's Rivers of Blood speech warning the white British about the dangers of large-scale immigration. We, the black, are still the lowest, discriminated against by everyone including the browns we are bunched with. We are just supposed to blend, so we almost become white, but never do. To my position in the racial hierarchy, add my gender and the profession I chose, I will spend my life trying to blend and fight...it never ends."

James reached out to touch Leila's knee,

"Don't care about those who don't deserve your care. And those who care about you, don't need you to blend or to fight. You're about to make us even more proud – convocation in three weeks – Dr. Leila Maria Godse Clarke! In case that is too short a name, add my surname. It will give your racist mother-in-law something to gloat about - Dr Leila Maria Godse Clarke Moore, you are a thesis by yourself," James chucked a small silk cushion at her. She pulled a face at him and then sighed,

"Mum's coming. She said she couldn't make it for the birthdays and the convocation, so we picked convocation, considering it's only going to happen once." Ira asked,

"Leila, do you think you could wangle an additional entry ticket by any chance?"

"Oh, nice of you to want to come. Mum would love that too. I'll get Patricia to try and make it three. James will have to step out earlier though, to get the children from day-care. They are so strict on timing!" Leila growled but pleased to have full quorum for her big day.

Ira interrupted her again,

"Sorry to be a bother. Can you ask Patricia to book me as Dr. Godse and vegetarian? I'm fasting that day and would avoid meat. I should get going now. James, could you help? I still can't deal with people double parking," Ira stepped out.

***

October 27: At Leila's historic London University, it was not Ira, but Prabhakar who sat in the audience in a three-piece suit, not aired since his retirement day, his gnarled fingers resting on his cane, a seat away from his daughter. Between them, sat James, furiously taking pictures of Leila taking a bow in her resplendent gown. The flood of tears would not stop.

On a wooden bench at the university lawns opened for families that afternoon, was seated the diminutive frame of Ratnaprabha Godse in a deep green and pink silk saree, a garment that had not seen the outside of her wardrobe for years. Like always, around her neck were her black and gold beads, on her forehead, was a maroon *tikli*. The winter coat that she rarely used, hung loose from her shoulders. She waited nervously, clutching a round steel tin of coconut *barfi* she had made last night.

Ira walked up, Leon clinging on to her deep blue, knee-length dress with tiny pink flowers, Ella tugging at the soft chiffon fabric of her sleeves.

"Leon, Ella, this is your *Panji*. Your Mum's Mum's Mum. Say hello…" Leon pranced away, and Ira had to chase him back. Ella planted herself next to this new entrant in her life, ready with her flurry of questions,

"What's on your forehead? Can I have one? And a necklace too? How old are you?" An hour later, James led his newly doctorated wife, his mother-in-law and grandfather-in-law he just met, over to the bench. Ella was explaining to Leon in her grown-up voice,

"Leon, some people are old like Nan, there," pointing at Swati walking slowly.

"Others are very old, like this lady *Panji*, Nan's Mum. And there is also Nan's Dad, on his way. Ira said we are not to jump on to their laps or we may hurt them. *Panji* here has promised that she will bring me red dots like the one on her forehead and bangles. If you stop jumping, she may have something nice for you too. She has some sweets in this box that she says we must save for Nan because she likes them…"

James yelled, "Ice-cream anyone?"

Ira gave him the thumbs up sign.

James and Ira, the family reunion-plotting squad that they had turned into over the past few weeks, left the Godses and Clarkes to deal with awkward silences and high-strung emotion, leading the skipping Ella and Leon to the ice-cream van.

Chapter 21:

In the name of POLITICS

November 15, 2019.

Sameer was awoken by the persistent ping of phone notifications. He gazed at the orange glow outside the window, which against the English landscape seemed to hover on the horizon. But against this landscape, it seemed to soar, impatient to rise – quite akin to how Sameer was feeling today.

Two years since Sriram's death and a year since he moved to India after eight trips in 2018. Riding on the euphoria of the events to unfold in the next few hours, Sameer showered, and stepped on to the tarpaulin covered balcony. Gangadhar, the cook-cum-cleaner at the party guest house, had a steaming cup of coffee and a piece of buttered toast ready.

"Good morning, Sameer *babu!* There was a call from Raghav *Saheb*'s secretary. The car will be here for you in 30 minutes. Raghav *Saheb* will see you directly at the venue. His flight has not landed yet. The car will take you to join *Saadhvi ji*'s chariot and the procession will head towards the *Sabha* venue." Sameer thanked Gangadhar and tapped on the notifications on his phone. There was a birthday wish from his grandparents, which also said that Damodar had transferred his birthday gift money online for Sameer to buy something nice.

To add to the numerous messages from Ira, which he had read but never replied to, was another, this time a picture from one of his birthdays as a child flanked by Prabhakar and Ratnaprabha. She said his grandparents were sending him their love and missed him terribly. *Ajji* was making *besan laddus* for his birthday and was hoping he would be home soon to taste them. Neither Prabhakar nor Ratnaprabha was tech-savvy, and this message came to him via Ira's phone. There was nothing from Cahya. He had been responding to Cahya's messages occasionally, especially after one of her messages spoke about honouring the spirit of Nathuram. Sameer felt a pang of doubt, a tinge of regret. Had Cahya forgotten his birthday? Or maybe she was still to wake up, it was still quite early in the UK. Gangadhar came to clear his plate. He placed a stiff, thick, wide brown envelope on the coffee table.

"This arrived yesterday. I was told to give it to you this morning as it is your happy budday!"

Sameer thanked him. There was no sender's name, no courier or postal stamp. Curious, Sameer split open the envelope with the butter knife and shook its contents onto the coffee table. There was a collection of photographs. Perplexed, Sameer thumbed through them – a black and white picture of children in what appeared to be a skit, a set of class photographs, the kind they made the class teacher sit in the centre, the tall children stand at the back, the shorter ones sit in front, others kneel. The class photographs ranged from faded black and white ones of pre-schoolers to coloured ones of a high school class. There were other pictures of children singing on stage and one of a bunch of teenagers holding up a trophy.

Sameer picked up a relatively good quality framed picture of what appeared to be a wedding reception. He did not recognise the bridal couple, the bride's face covered by a red and gold veil, the groom's floral veil held aside to reveal his face. Wondering what this was about, Sameer was about to set aside the parcel thinking it was meant for someone else, when his eyes rested on two people at the very edge of the wedding party. The pretty lady in a bright orange and cream sari and a sleeveless blouse, her hair done in a chic high bun and bright tangerine lipstick, was unmistakably his grandmother Priyamvada. He peered at the man in a dark suit and mustache standing beside her. Sameer had never seen Damodar with a moustache or with hair. This man was his grandfather all right.

Next to them, dazzling in a purple and yellow saree was Mum. Sameer couldn't take his eyes off her. It was not just the saree, the jewellery, and the string of white flowers in her hair that made her so stunning. Though she was

In the name of POLITICS   179 usually in formal work clothes or jeans on weekends, he had seen pictures of Sriram and Ira's wedding. She couldn't have been much older at her own wedding than she was in this breath-taking picture. This wedding picture had captured a joyous sparkle in Ira's eyes, a carefree throw of her head and a coy, half smile...This was an arresting stance that Sameer had never ever seen in the mother who despite whatever happened, always had a smile for Sameer, a smile that had never reached her eyes. Shaken by the realization, Sameer wondered if the package may be from Damodar. But how did Damodar know he was here? Sameer spotted the sheaf of papers accompanying the pictures. A handwritten letter running into four pages,

"My dear Sameer..."

Sameer quickly flicked to the last page signed –

"Whether you choose to accept me or not – Your loving father, Omar." Incensed at the audacity, Sameer was about to crumple the two sheets. Gangadhar stepped into the balcony accompanied by *Saadhvi's* trusted lieutenants in saffron shirts and sunglasses bearing a cardboard box of syrupy orange *motichoor laddus* and a garland of marigold flowers.

"*Chalo* Sameer *bhai*. Let's leave. And before that Happy budday!" Bablu placed the garland around Sameer's neck, Dalip stuffed a *motichoor laddu* in his mouth, both gave him a bear hug. Munshi, subservient as ever and eternally hopeful that Sameer would be instrumental in getting him a job in London, rushed to pick up his laptop bag. Sameer hastily stuffed the envelope and its contents into his laptop bag and the party headed towards the car.

It was an hour before Sameer was able to meet *Saadhvi*. The car snaked through the traffic, blocked by supporters sporting saffron ribbons, arm bands, turbans and flags. A couple were selling cow-branded paraphernalia through car windows, several dancing to raunchy music blaring from the loudspeaker equipment carrying truck that trailed the chariot.

The "chariot" was a modified open motor vehicle with wooden cut-outs of white horses stuck on. *Saadhvi's* imposing frame was on a "throne" fastened in the centre of the vehicle flanked by lieutenants who took turns to clamber up onto the truck and garland her. *Saadhvi* waved to people who had lined up on the streets to watch and periodically threw the garlands around her neck at bystanders. Dalip and Bablu hoisted Sameer up to the throne.

Saadhvi bared her teeth in a broad grin. Her lieutenant helpfully held up a small plate with *kunku*. *Saadhvi* thrust her plump right thumb into the bright red powder and anointed Sameer, her thumb between his eyes and straight up his forehead.

Two lieutenants were holding on to the bust of Nathuram Godse covered in white muslin ready to be installed. A gust of wind blew away the muslin. *Saadhvi* clapped and yelped,

"*Koi hain!*" *(*Anybody there?*)* A spare saffron cloth was produced as cover. In the interim, Sameer had noticed the statue commissioned to a local sculptor. He turned to *Saadhvi*,

"Didi, I have looked up pictures and documents of Nathuram for my research. He was slightly built, with a thin, solemn face, close cropped hair, always dressed in a simple western style shirt. He never wore a turban, a shawl around his neck or anything like that. This sculpture shows a laughing chubby man with a turban, shawl and *rudraksha* beads around his neck. This is not his likeness at all?" Sameer's genuine query had *Saadhvi* livid. Her face blanched, her expansive chest heaved in rage. Maintaining her beatific grin for her target audience outside the truck, her jet-black eyes bored into Sameer's green ones,

"*Babua*, I granted you the privilege to call me *Didi*. Since I renounced the world and donned saffron, I have given up all relationships. You can even give up marital relations, but brother-sister bonds are forever. You must listen to everything your elder sister has to tell you, for *Didi* knows better. After 15 years in politics, I'm waiting for my day in the sun. Fine you gave some money to the party fund, it is *dakshina*, donation and for you NRIs, loose change anyway. You made trips to India, you quit your job and finally came here to serve the country. But compared to our sacrifice, this is nothing. Nathuram must look like what the people who will vote for us, want to see. In this region, we like well-fed leaders with a robust countenance. After all, he killed Gandhi. He should look like that! If he didn't wear all that true Hindus should wear, we will make him look like a Hindu. And young man, don't ask questions. It's not good for your political future," Not waiting for Sameer's response, *Saadhvi* threw a few garlands at the crowd. The chariot had reached the venue.

Saadhvi ascended the stage amidst the blowing of a conch shell traditionally used to mark a momentous occasion like the start or end of a war or a wedding. *Saadhvi* and Sameer sat on the gaudily decorated dais as her underlings made speeches in her honour with the fervent hope that she would drag them along eventually ascending the political ladder. They were running two hours late. Sameer should have finished speaking by now. But there was still no sign of Raghav. The messages coming through had said the flight had not landed, then the flight missed, taking the next flight and then, the messages had stopped coming.

"Was the self-styled big man with the claim of being very close to attaining *nirvana* and thus the saffron robes, perambulating in mid-air refusing to land?" Sameer smiled to himself; humour had left him long ago for intense fervour. It was Raghav's approaching him at that rally in Wembley stadium four years ago, Raghav's pursuit and mentoring that had brought Sameer this far. He had given up his career and savings but was about to make a speech of his lifetime on national television.

Sameer quickly checked his phone – still no birthday message from Cahya, thinking,

"Had he lost her too? Why was he so bothered by this today?" The speeches were done. The next filler was a local mimicry artist spouting famous Bollywood dialogues. He then started making strange sounds– a flight taking off, a train passing, the tapping of horses' hooves.

When others did not live up to expectations, *Saadhvi* took matters into her own hands and summoned the anchor in bright red lipstick and a glittering orange sequined sari. She bent low to stick her bejewelled ear to *Saadhvi's* whispering lips. Absorbing the instructions, the anchor reclaimed the microphone from the mimicry artist basking in unexpected glory.

After enlisting her college degrees and a eulogy to her priceless contribution to the world of cows, statues, and temples, she announced,

"Now, the one and only *Saadhvi ji*, the *daasi* (handmaid) of the Hindu nation, will bless us with her sweet words of wisdom and also introduce our budding leader, who will tell us in his own words, the memories of his illustrious ancestor, one and only Nathuram Godse *ji*," the anchor pointed to the forgotten statue in the corner covered in the now retrieved, slightly stained white muslin again.

Saadhvi ji repeated her achievements, called upon Gods, saints, rituals that she claimed were clamouring her, invading her dreams to let Hindus claim the land that rightfully belonged to them. After a solid 30 minutes of this, she turned to Sameer,

"And now my blessed Hindu brothers and sisters, let me introduce you to my dear *muh bola* (not in relation but in spirit) younger brother, the reincarnation of Shri Nathuram *ji* Godse himself – *Shri* Sameer Sriram Godse.

Saadhvi spent the next 10 minutes on the miracle of how today was Nathuram *ji's* death anniversary, how just today, two years ago, Sameer's own father was martyred in a cruel Islamic conspiracy and how today was Sameer's birthday.

"What more proof do we need that our Sameer is his reincarnation, sent by the heavens to save us, save India from the evil designs of the opposition, out to pollute the Hindu nation!" she bellowed! Our revered Guru, our own beloved Member of Parliament (MP) Raghav Swami was to be here today to unveil the pristine statue of Nathuram *ji*, lay the foundation stone of the temple we want to construct in his name, but Raghav *ji* has been held back by pressing matters in Delhi. As his obedient disciple, I will do the honours. Maybe by the grace of Lord Ram, he may even bless us with his presence or through video conference?"

She pointed to the 6 feet tall white screens erected on either side of the stage beaming her image. She nodded pointedly at her able audio-visual technician sitting right below the stage, headphones stuck on to the saffron scarf around his hair. He nodded in acknowledgement and shot her a double thumbs up. *Saadhvi* then extended her left hand in a flourish,

"Presenting to you, *Shri* Sameer Godse to speak on the life and times of his illustrious ancestor." Sameer walked up to the podium. Three underlings of *Saadhvi* trotted beside him ordered into sycophancy. Munshi stood in a corner, dutifully clutching Sameer's laptop bag. Sameer had waited for this moment for nearly two years, prepared the content for over a year, written the speech and practiced saying it in Hindi for nearly two months. To Sameer, the question whether Nathuram was related to him or not, was not relevant anymore. Sameer had imbibed the essence of Nathuram, his ideology. He spoke in succinct, measured terms, his Hindi almost free of his British accent, thanks to the earnest effort of the Hindi literature university professor who had helped him translate and practise his speech.

In the name of POLITICS   183

"*Namaskar!*" The crowd broke out in thunderous applause. Sameer began with the story of how Nathuram, born in 1910 was originally named Ramachandra. Given that infant mortality was so common during those times, he was the only living male child of his parents, following the death of brothers. Believing that this would help the child survive, they brought him up as a girl for the first few years of his life and he was made to wear a *nath* (nose ring). After his younger brother was born healthy, young Nathuram was allowed to dress like a boy again. But the name Nathuram (Ram who wore the nose ring) stuck. This was a crowd that even in 2019, valued baby boys more than girls, the gender ratio in this state still tilted in favour of boys despite the law against anti-sex-discrimination and convictions for any cases of female infanticide. The crowd lapped up the nose ring story, thirsting for more.

Sameer then led the crowd through Nathuram's own journey, how he dropped out of education following Mahatma Gandhi's clarion call to the country's youth to boycott western educational institutions, how he worked as a humble tailor.

"An avid reader, and knowledgeable about the world, Nathuram and his business partner Narayan Apte ran two newspapers. Apte married and had a son who died in infancy, but Nathuram had chosen to remain single. Among the 12 accused of the assassination, Apte and Godse were hanged on this day, at 9 am in Ambala. Nathuram's brother Gopal Godse, Parchure and Vishnu Karkare served life sentences. Their mentor, the revered Veer Savarkar was acquitted." Sameer spoke about the investigation, the witnesses – A Mumbai taxi driver who remembered ferrying Apte and Godse to Savarkar's Dadar home, maybe to seek his blessings. Another witness was an Air India flight attendant who recalled Apte asking for extra chocolate on the Mumbai Delhi flight. Sameer spoke about how the guns were procured from a region very close to the speech being made today. He painted a vivid picture of how Nathuram stood his ground after firing at Gandhi, did not try to run away and certainly did not try to harm anyone else in the crowd.

"My Hindu brethren, let us not instigate terrorism in the name of Nathuram. Terrorists plant bombs and fire indiscriminately in the name of revenge at innocents who were not the perpetrators of whatever act they are trying to avenge in the first place. Let me say it again – Nathuram Godse was NOT A TERRORIST."

So far, the audience was riveted, the plot was reading like a thriller movie, bits of the jigsaw were fitting in, the trivia was being appreciated. And then, Sameer went on to describe Nathuram's reasons for killing Gandhi. The crowd began to fidget. They had been fed that all Gandhis were bad, all Muslims were terrorists and everything Hindu had to be saffron and in their interest. This speech was getting too complicated. They had expected this young man to shout slogans denouncing Gandhi, perform an anti-Gandhi act like *Saadhvi*'s.

The expectation of fake-gun drama and Raghav's PR machinery had generated media interest and there were several TV journalists in attendance. The organisers sensed this was getting academic. One of the event organisers decided to bulldoze the *samosa* vendor to let him have one and helped himself to a cup of tea. Others followed suit. Sameer continued to wax eloquent on Gandhi's ill treatment of freedom fighter Subhash Chandra Bose, as the rumblings over tea and samosa permeated through the sea of humanity. Sameer was explaining how Nathuram had seen the assassination as the last resort, especially after his fast against the continuing communal riot started on January 14th of 1948. Some of the mobile phones started buzzing.

"TV, TV, Raghav Swami is on TV," somebody relayed the message to *Saadhvi*. She motioned to her trusted tech buster. Not bothered with asking Sameer to wrap up, the two screens flanking the stage switched from Sameer's speech to the live telecast of the news.

Saadhvi had expected Raghav to address the *samosa* wielding members of her constituency. The visuals on the giant screens left *Saadhvi* shell shocked. Raghav had defected to the opposition having been promised a ministerial berth following the next election, and undoubtedly, gestures of gratitude in cash and kind had reached Raghav's extended family in various parts of the state. No longer in saffron robes, Raghav was on TV dressed in a blue sherwani jacket, with a rosebud in his buttonhole extolling the virtues of India as a secular land with a place for citizens of all castes, and religions.

Saadhvi grabbed the microphone from Sameer and screamed hysterically,

"This is a conspiracy by the opposition. We will take revenge!" Spirited supporters tore away the fluttering cotton cloth from the barricades, uprooted the wooden pillars, clambered onto the stage, and poked the flex banner backdrop, puncturing the smiling countenance of Raghav who had ceased to be *Swami*. Others, less endowed with physical strength but greater perseverance, clawed at the punctured cloth. A gaping hole exposing the back of the stage now manifest where Raghav's face had been. Having shrieked herself hoarse, *Saadhvi* stormed out of the arena without a second glance at Sameer.

Munshi stood trembling in a corner, dutifully holding on to Sameer's laptop bag. Sameer approached him mutely. A few feet behind Munshi's puny frame, clad in a knee length yellow cotton *kurta* and pale blue jeans, stood Cahya.

The statue of Nathuram Godse stood forgotten in a corner, the white muslin cloth, now held in place by a piece of jute string, fluttering in the November breeze.

Sameer walked towards the statue mutely. He bowed, hands folded in a *namaskar*. Even as the scrimmage around him continued, his lips mouthed the words in silence,

"I was not able to convey your ideology and the dream of *Akhand Bharat* to these masses. I am sorry." Tucking away his rolled-up speech in the side pocket of his kurta, Sameer walked away.

Chapter 22:

In the name of DUTY

The Hindi news channels had been relaying the unfolding drama of the erstwhile right-wing Raghav's defection to a secular political party. Nobody seemed to be shocked. Cahya to Ira and Omar's source to Omar had conveyed what transpired at the rally. Cahya conveyed that Sameer had been devastated, disillusioned by the people who claimed to be driven by nationalism, cleverly confusing the electorate. Cahya had conveyed that Sameer was angry, not just with the people who had used him, but with himself, for being insensitive towards his family. He was too embarrassed to face his mother. But he had started replying to Ira's messages. And, he had agreed to accompany Cahya on her trail and also visit the Taj Mahal, before returning to the UK.

***

December 6th, 2019.

Twenty-seven years after a disputed temple site over 900 miles away from Mumbai had changed the course of their lives, Omar and Ira had planned a rendezvous again. It was not the Mumbai of their childhood, Ira's home - London or an exotic island. This was Auschwitz, Poland. Judaism was a religion they had barely encountered while growing up. Given India's dwindling Jewish population, it was no surprise that they had had no Jewish classmates. But there was Miss Ezekiel, teaching them "Writing and craft" ("as if these were subjects to be taught!") they used to snicker privately. In a strange mix of the posh anglicised accent because of her own education and broken Hindi and Marathi (as a life skill needed to haggle with vegetable vendors as a lower middle-class resident of Mumbai), Miss Ezekiel punctuated her sentences with references to the glories of Israel.

Once in class, Miss Ezekiel was exalting the virtues of her land, "In Mumbai, they are constructing buildings neck to neck. In Israel, they would not get planning permission. They would ask where the children would play!" Precocious Omar had countered this argument, in front of the class suppressing grins,

"Miss Ezekiel, considering that the population of Israel is barely equal to the ever-growing population of Andheri (one of Mumbai's suburbs) struggling to etch out a living, there really is no comparison, is there?" Omar punctuated his utterances with a gentle smile, making it impossible for anyone to not melt under his charming gaze.

The poor lady whose heart and part of her family resided in Israel, went quiet and moved on with her craft demonstration, once again relegating her wish to migrate to Israel to the weekly prayers she offered at the local Synagogue.

When Omar and Ira represented their school in debates, they had been invited to Miss Ezekiel's tiny one-bedroom home for a discussion on her perspective on the Israel-Palestine question. The living room of that tiny abode could have belonged to a family that practised any religion or atheists! The spinster Miss Ezekiel and her octogenarian father hid their feelings well, especially with respect to Omar who shared the religion that had proved to be their bane. Miss Ezekiel served plum cake from the local bakery to her students and waxed eloquent on the terror unleashed by Saddam Hussain, with no bitterness towards any of the religions that coexisted in Mumbai. As they researched Jewish history, Omar and Ira had woven dreams of visiting these places together one day. The dream destinations included London and Scotland (where so many of their favourite authors were born), but also included Venice, Israel, and Poland.

So, when in 2019, Omar suggested Warsaw, Ira was not surprised. During Sameer's years of studying history in school, they would watch documentaries together. Ira had ended up reading and watching so much more about the six million Jews liquidated by Hitler and his Nazi party. But none of the documentaries and reading had prepared her for the experiences of that December morning.

It was Omar who planned and arranged, and Ira followed. That had been the nature of their relationship. Krakow was closer to the two concentration camp sites, but Omar had booked them in a hotel in Warsaw and a car to drive them to Auschwitz and Birkenau.

The concentration camp premises were clean, neat, antiseptic, with even a modest cafeteria for tourists. The guide Esther led them through the entrance arch that ironically proclaimed in German "*Arbeit macht frei*" (Work sets one free) where the Jewish people were brought on trains supposedly to work and when they couldn't, to die. Esther narrated how the first "batch" of the gas chamber victims tossed and turned in the locked chambers for two days before the administrators of the poison got the proportion of the Zyklon B poisonous gas right that would result in faster death.

With a shudder, Ira marvelled at the remains of the villa at the edge of the camp, so close that the strawberries in the garden were often covered with the dust floating in from the gas chambers. The commandant of the camps such as these lived luxuriously with a wife and children, in the company of household staff-cooks, gardeners, nannies, seamstresses, some of whom were prisoners. They decorated these homes with artefacts confiscated from the prisoners sent to death. These children had lived, oblivious to the atrocities next door. During trials that followed, the fathers of these children had maintained that they had no idea people were being killed, they were only following orders to transport Jewish people on trains!

Frazzled by the proximity of this "normal family space" with the massacre ground, Ira and Omar followed Esther pointing to the place where one of Auschwitz's commanders Rudolf Hoess was executed by hanging in April of 1947 witnessed by 100 people.

"I have read those executions were public affairs?" Omar asked.

"The anger was so deep, that the public started believing that the perpetrators of these crimes deserved to be hanged before their eyes. Documents discovered later stated that when Arthur Greiser was executed in 1946, nearly 15,000 people watched, including children. Religious communities and intellectuals expressed concern about the "picnic-line atmosphere with ice-cream sellers and viewers fighting over a piece of the rope as a souvenir. These public events were stopped in early 1947 and Hoess' execution was done here." Esther recounted.

Esther led the way to the other side of the site, Ira fell into step. Omar walked alongside Ira taking notes in his small notebook covered in blue vegetable dyed cloth.

"You know Esther, I cannot help but notice how so many events which affected so many lives occurred during this period – 1942 to 1949. In Hinduism, we have a concept called *saade saati* (7 and half years). It is said that when individuals are undergoing a bad period in their lives, it ends after seven and half years. World War 2, the holocaust, the horrors of partition of India and so much more…the world's populace appears to have bled itself to death and left behind survivors to find ways to heal," Ira spoke in a sombre, philosophical tone. Esther turned to Ira,

"I know what you mean. I lost my uncle, my father's brother in this camp. We do not have a grave for him, nowhere to lay flowers. My duty as a guide here, somehow, is a desire to correct that, to help the rest of us remember and still heal."

They followed Esther to the ice-cold sleeping chambers, the holes for toilets, the dark, musty "punishment" cells, the documented cases of "medical experiments" on the walls. At the thought of Hans Asperger, Ira shuddered. If Sriram had been born 20 years earlier in another part of Europe, he too would have been categorised as an 'autistic psychopath', a burden on the family and thus shunned to Vienna's *Am Spiegelgrund* "euthanasia clinic." She had expressed her angst over Sriram's hidden diagnosis to Omar. As they passed the photographs of people with deformities pasted on the walls, she looked at Omar with anguished, watery eyes. Ira pointed at the wall chart,

"Look Omar, they decided who will be sent to die, based on the colour of their skin, hair, eyes and the despicable, disputable "Aryan race test of 12 body features" to examine whether the person whose fate was being decided was "Aryan enough". They decided that a person with a disability was a burden on society and was sent to die in Vienna as part of the Aktion T4 programme by gassing, starvation and the death misrepresented as pneumonia. What had come over the world in the 1940s!" Omar nodded and gently touched the elbow of her woollen jacket, steering her towards Esther.

In the next section, when he saw the glassed-in wall behind which was preserved as a silent reminder - black, deep brown curls, strands of hair and children's shoes, Omar too could not hold back tears. Too weary to take pictures like some of the other tourists and overwhelmed by the scent of the suffering soil, they thanked Esther profusely.

"I hope to bring my history students from India here one day and listen to your experiences, Esther. Till the economics of that work out, our school would be privileged to host you if you are ever in India," Omar handed a plain white card to Esther and noted down her email address in his blue notebook.

"Tea Ira?" It was not a question but a statement. He placed his palm on the back of Ira's winter jacket and led her towards the cafeteria. It was Omar making swift decisions, conscious that the last two hours must have resulted in throbbing pain in Ira's temples.

At the bare wooden table, they sipped their tea in silence. Ira spoke slowly,

"Being here is so much worse than what we've read. This is what hate can do! This is what our Mumbai could have been after the riots. I read about the Ayodhya judgement and plans to build the temple. But your Mohalla committees, your work with Muslim and Hindu youth, have quelled communal storms. Hats off to your teams Omar!"

Omar shook his head,

"The Mumbai you knew, is history. Unlike our schools that openly propagated the Christian missionary agenda, modern schools cannot risk offending any parent who may harbour religious intolerance. We read the Bible, sang hymns but never dreamt of converting to Christianity. In fact, my late father did not know what really happened in school. He was just happy school made me fluent in English so I could overcome his language shortcoming and help with the business. That was his dream, until the day I was disowned. Over the last few months, you, like you always have, unravelled most of your 27-year-journey to me. Given this incredible Cahya and your parenting, our precious Sameer will be back with you - the woman who gave him everything. But there is a lot I haven't told you. In fact, I've written to Sameer, but I still haven't told you."

Ira nearly choked on her tea, a few droplets spilling over, staring at Omar astounded,

"You've managed to write to him and not tell me! What is it?" Omar gave her a sad smile. The tips of his fingers gently brushed against Ira's palm, handing her a tissue. His eyes bore no anger, just deep hurt as he finally revealed the story behind how life spun out of control.

Ira was transported to the scene of Razia, Omar's sister's wedding on the 5th of December of 1992. This was a grand affair held on the terrace of one of South Mumbai's oldest 5-star hotels. For the Maharashtrian Brahmin community, a wedding meant pure silk sarees, pure 24-carat gold jewellery, waking up early to "catch the *Muhurta* (astrologically calculated auspicious time), religious ceremonies conducted in Sanskrit and a tasty but simple vegetarian lunch served on long rows of tables in a sparsely decorated "marriage hall".

In fact, the buffet dinner served at some of the Maharashtrian wedding receptions was a hint of relative ostentatiousness brought in by the mixing of communities in the late 80s. Ira recalled accompanying her parents as a child to a wedding reception in Dadar's Vanita Samaj hall where one had to wish the bridal couple on stage, be served a single slab of ice-cream in a quarter plate and go back home to have your own dinner. If the bride's family (yes, the bride's parents sponsored all of this) was affluent, the reception may have also encompassed a "limited dish" (a small silver paper foil plate with a sole samosa, an inch wide piece of sweet coconut or *besan barfi* and potato crisps). After all these experiences, Razia's grand *Nikah* and reception at a prestigious venue was a novelty to look forward to.

For the first time since they started school, it had been over five weeks since Omar and Ira had met, not since Omar had come home for Diwali, presented the wedding card to Damodar as the head of the family, warmly insisting that all of them attend. Understandably, as the bride's only brother, Omar had been extremely busy with the preparations. Even the phone calls had been infrequent, but Omar had found time for a conversation about Ira's all important and eager question on which saree she should wear. After much banter and silliness about whether her saree should match his sherwani (just like the star couple did in the last terrible movie they had watched together), they settled the question.

"Can we please save matching outfits for our own wedding? Right now, let's go with your mother's deep purple *paithani* with the golden yellow border. Go Ira *ji*, go make yourself look gorgeous like you always do!" Omar had pronounced and replaced the handset while rushing off to greet the messengers from the groom's side. There was the throbbing agony of recent events in the Siddiqui household, but this was not the time to tell Ira, until the wedding was over.

On that Saturday evening, Ira had stood in front of the mirror as her mother deftly folded the pleats of her deep purple saree and fastened the *padar* with a strong "baby safety pin" with a violet plastic hood. Blushing at the thought of Omar seeing her in this magnificent attire, Ira took a deep breath as the pleats were tucked into the waist of the satin petticoat skirt. The golden yellow blouse had sleeves that reached the elbow and a hint of a puff at the shoulders, a 60s style that had returned in the 90s. Her dark brown hair was held up in a tight knot at the back of her head. Ira had asked Abdul *chacha* to get a fresh jasmine flower *gajraa* to entwine into this knot. Omar loved the fragrance of jasmine more than any other. Whether to paint a purple *tikli* on her forehead or not, was to be considered. At a Maharashtrian wedding, turning up without a *tikli* would draw criticism among the cackling aunts. But this was a Muslim wedding and Omar's cousins, who had an inkling of their relationship, were sure to be observing and whispering among themselves about Ira.

At the plush venue lined with baskets of tuberoses, drenched in *attar* fragrance, Ira and her parents made their way to greet the couple. Much to their shock, on stage, posing for pictures next to the newly-weds along with Omar's father, was not Omar's mother but another woman in a sequined deep green *salwar* suit, a gold and red glittering dupatta over her head.

Omar's mother, dressed in a demure cream and gold saree, stood down below at a distance. Sakinabi softly touched the top of Ira's head saying,

"Go ahead *beti*, wish them. You are looking like a sliver of moonlight on the night of *Eid*. May Allah bless you!" Ira thanked Sakinabi for the lovely compliment. Stunned by the sight on stage and the bride's mother in obscurity, Ira turned to her parents. The Dixits nodded at Mrs. Siddiqui. She returned their grim, polite looks with a wan smile and a warm *adaab* (upward palm in greeting).

In the name of DUTY

Ira's eyes sought out Omar, attending to Razia's every need before she was to be passed on to a family in which everyone else's need would take over. If there was anger at what seemed to have happened in the few weeks that Ira and Omar had not met, it was masked by the glitter of the wedding. Omar greeted the Dixits with a cheerful,

"Hello, *Namaste*". Playing the gracious host, he asked his cousin Zainab to ensure that they were escorted to the women's section for dinner. With the men and women being served separately, he asked another cousin Abbas, to accompany Mr. Dixit to dinner.

The mandatory picture with the couple was taken by a professional photographer. There were radiant smiles all around, especially Ira's as she had felt Omar's admiring eyes following the gentle lifting of her wrist jingling with purple and yellow bangles to wish Razia *Aapa*. Even in that public setting, Ira's ruby nails had fluttered around the jasmine *gajraa*, tucking a wisp of hair that had strayed. Her glance had sought Omar and had caught what she had wanted to see – the look of appreciative approval. Basking in that momentary sensual gaze, cocking her head slightly, Ira turned to face the camera, her lips parted in a half-smile.

As Ira followed Zainab down the steps of the dais, she turned to Omar, seeking to assuage the turmoil that Omar would have gone through to see his father married to another woman, at Sakinabi's pain, insult, and the question – why? Omar stared back and in the piercing look that he gave Ira, he said "LATER".

The "Later" came today – after 27 years.

"It's a long, long story Ira. We should be heading back to Warsaw," Omar chucked their paper cups in the bin and waited at the exit for Ira to retrieve her coat. The drive proceeded in relative silence. Their friendly Polish driver Pieter made polite conversation, having assumed that they had been together for years. In this part of the world and in 2019, the watertight rules of marital status, legal bonds and most of all, their diverse religious backgrounds had ceased to matter.

Chapter 23:

In the name of a DOUBLE HELIX

They stopped at a services station café between Oswiecim (Polish name of Auschwitz) and Warsaw. Omar brought a tray of two bean wraps, a salad and orange juice. Omar had insisted they stop. Ira, quiet through the journey with a throbbing headache, gratefully took a bite. Noticing the green marking on the wrap, she asked,

"When did you start relishing vegetables Omar?" She smiled at the memory of both polishing off butter chicken at their favourite Bandra restaurant and the midnight feast at Mohammad Ali Road during Ramadan with their friends.

"I've been vegetarian for a few years," Omar smiled, picking on his salad.

"You, vegetarian, why? Health?" Ira exclaimed.

"Long story Ira and we have a lifetime to talk. To summarise, we have the unending skirmish over Muslims selling beef for their livelihood and the Hindus turning violent over the protection of their holy animals – cows. The Muslims have a problem with the pigs. Besides, there is the question of *halal*, the method that Muslims should use to slaughter. Here, the Jewish people have the concept of Kosher," Omar raised his fork in despair,

"Life, Ira, is too short to stress about food. In my area of work, I break bread with community leaders and staunch followers of each religion. I don't want to offend anyone. So, I just cut to the chase. Nobody seems to mind me slicing through a chubby green cucumber. Until someone invents a religion in which cucumbers have lives and holy spirits, I won't go hungry…" Omar laughed his infectious laugh.

"So, it's a good excuse to not fast during Ramzan then!" Ira giggled.

"I fast during Ramzan. You know I always loved your *Ajji's sabudana khichadi*. I enjoy that during the *Mahashivratri* fast. I also observe the Jewish Yom Kippur and give up something during Lent. A little restraint is good!" Omar chuckled, rubbing his tummy.

"Ira, you remember my bewilderment at *Ajji's* study? With the ghosts of these illustrious ancestors floating about in the historic home, your future as a doctor was cast in stone," Omar was looking at Ira intently, still hesitating to speak out.

"Yes", Ira smiled at the memory of a discourse with Saguna about Gopal Agarkar's campaign against untouchability, and supporting widow remarriage.

The sullen teenage Omar had rued that he did not have an illustrious family tree. He was going to start his own, he would say, with an endearing swing of his head, "with a battalion of progeny he would nurture with India's nth woman doctor- Ira. India's first woman doctor had died without producing any." Ira had blushed. Like it was the most natural thing to happen, Omar picked up the thought where she left off,

"You did become India's nth doctor Ira, so that box is ticked. I hope Sameer will want children. But a battalion of progeny for India's nth doctor seems…don't you think a bit unwise?" Omar chortled mischievously. Ira's cheeks turned a rosy pink.

Taking a deep breath, Omar was urging himself to finally speak out.

"I've been procrastinating on my story, I know. On a serious note, you deserve to know where I truly came from. Let me start where we left off—

Why did my father marry a second time? And what was the real reason that I, the erstwhile heir to all that wealth and the apple of his eye, was thrown out on the streets overnight?"

Restraining the tempest beneath a measured tone, he finally revealed his story – how the paranoid Mushtaque had always been suspicious of Omar's unusually pale skin and green eyes. He had wondered if the timid Sakinabi had found the gall to cheat on him. Sakinabi's mother Mehrunissa had announced at his birth that the baby looked just like her own grandfather, an Afghani Pathan. Nobody had seen Mehrunissa's father, let alone grandfather. But a fair, male child was welcome in India any time.

Omar revealed how, years later, Mushtaque's suspicion was fuelled by his scheming sister Farzana under the pressure exerted by her husband Taufiq Shaikh. Hailing from small town Junnar, Taufiq, Farzana and their three sons lived in a one-bedroom apartment in the outskirts of Mumbai's burgeoning Muslim ghetto Mumbra. Taufiq's own small business of hospital supplies had been suffering. The passage of gifts in cash and kind for the sake of his sister's marriage and upkeep of the children from the Siddiqui to the Shaikh household was common.

The business downturn had nothing to do with market demand, but Taufiq's own mismanagement, inertia and borrowing for consignments which never seemed to reach their destination. A solution to end his financial woes could have been for Taufiq himself to marry a second time (unlikely that a family would agree to a match given his reputation). The more feasible option then, was to milk the cow that he had already married – the sister of Mushtaque, whose business never saw a downturn. Their woes had been compounded by the arrival of Taufiq's sister Mumtaz and her daughter Fiza from Junnar, into their cramped home. Mumtaz lamented that Fiza had crossed the "marriageable age" due a dark complexion, uneven teeth, glasses, and Fiza's father's inept attempts to find her a match.

Taufiq hatched a plan, which if everything went right, would clinch him a direct line to Mushtaque's coffers. On a rainy afternoon in the August of 1992, Taufiq and Farzana took the suburban train to Dadar, laden with cheap gifts and Mushtaque's favourite beetroot chicken curry. Mushtaque indulged Farzana's wish to admire the new chandelier installed in his sitting room, where he entertained business associates and certainly no women were allowed. Away from the ears of Sakinabi, Farzana re-planted the seed of suspicion in Mushtaque's already doubting, possessive brain. Taufiq proffered a solution – paternity testing facilities, discreet, reliable, and managed by Taufiq. Mushtaque agreed. The stars were shining in Taufiq's favour. Weeks later, a shivering Omar was rushed to hospital. Diagnosed with malaria, with strong medication and pampering by his mother and sisters, Omar was sent home in a few days. Meanwhile, Taufiq got what he needed— a blood sample and a swab of the inside of Omar's cheek. During Omar's delirious state, nobody questioned which of the hospital staff was taking away what and why. Back to the grind, Omar would set off in the morning, distributing the green and gold footlong wedding cards, each sitting in its minaret shaped gold envelope, along with a box of sweets to his father's business associates and few influential acquaintances.

Omar was out on one such errand, when Taufiq came home with the paternity test results. It had been established beyond doubt that there was no biological relation between Mushtaque and Omar. All hell broke loose. Mushtaque ordered that Sakinabi be sent off to her mother's in Alibaug. He never wanted to see her or Omar again.

Farzana tightened the noose, in the name of what she called "family honour". She pleaded with her brother to "see reason". The groom's family were to visit for the pre-nuptial rituals. Who would perform the duties of a mother? Of course, Farzana would be honoured to offer her services, but how long could she park herself in her brother's home, it wouldn't look good – she clicked her tongue.

In a matter of two hours, the proposal of 29-year-old Fiza's marriage to 45-year-old Mushtaque was offered and accepted. Fiza was never asked. Sakinabi's desperate plea that she had never ever imagined cheating on her husband, held no water. If Sakinabi had any education, if she knew what DNA was, how testing worked and the story of Omar's birth, it would have been a different life. Sakinabi was grateful to be allowed to stay in her own home, her tear-stained palms clutching on to Omar's forearms, pleading with him not to say a word to his father, for the sake of his sister's wedding.

Fiza and Mushtaque were married off by a *Kazi* at the Mahim *Dargah* with Farzana and Taufiq in attendance on November 12. The bride stepped into the mansion, Sakinabi and the servants toiled over the feast, the sisters were expected to serve the newlyweds. Mushtaque made just one compromise for the sake of family honour. He waited for his daughter's wedding reception to conclude before banishing Omar from his home on December 6, the day worshippers rose to reclaim their temple site in faraway Ayodhya.

Ira had been listening, her gloved palm covering her open mouth, aghast.

"Omar, why didn't you ever tell me this, even during those few fleeting meetings till my wedding in March? Why did you have to bear this alone?"

Stricken, she instinctively placed her gloved palms on his fist curled around the coffee cup. Omar's glassy eyes stayed glued to the table-top, re-living the day,

"There was shame, Ira. Shame all the time. The honour of my mother was at stake. The story that was given out was that I was thrown out because I objected to my father's second marriage. This seemed to work well for all concerned for the remaining three daughters would eventually have to be married too. The religious tenets, Aunt Farzana proclaimed, did not question another wife entering a man's home while the first one was alive. In fact, the law for Muslims in India still permits four wives. But the religious tenets and societal norms certainly do not permit a woman's illegitimate child. So then on, till date, I'm known as the estranged son of Mushtaque Siddiqui whose first wife wilted into the servants' area of the household till her death. Fiza did produce an heir— Zakir, born with his mother's dark skin and limpid, night black eyes to match Mushtaque's, but afflicted with a serious learning disability." Omar looked up at the ceiling and then at Ira, placing his upturned palms on the table. She acknowledged his thought silently, marvelling at the ways of whichever divine super force was at play.

Omar continued, staring into the gray Polish sky outside the glass window,

"At Mehrunissa's request, my *Mamu* (Sakinabi's cousin) took me into their crumbling two-room flat atop a cycle shop in Mahim, teeming with generations. I feel grateful that I at least had a home for a while." Omar's voice assumed a sombre tenor,

"I'm not going to tell you what happened after I was arrested. I'm not going to say what happened in prison when they tried to extract a confession. I will not talk about nights at a train station bench, a job as a delivery boy, a receptionist, in a call centre, all of which ultimately paid for my education. I know it will hurt you too much." Ira started sobbing softly. Omar got up, walked to the till, and returned with cups of tea and tissues.

"I hope you don't need these as we are getting to the exciting bit of the story, but just in case, we're prepared." Omar had dried his own eyes and the pallid, sad smile was back.

Chapter 24:

In the name of HOLY TEXTS

"One of the reasons I was kept in prison for long was that I was unable to give a satisfactory explanation for what I was doing in Alibaug on February 4, when the consignment of explosives arrived by the sea-route from Pakistan and key players in the March 12 bomb blasts conspiracy met. The truth – that I had gone to see my grandmother was not enough. After weeks of torture, no evidence emerged, there was nothing that could have. A Muslim, from a ghetto seen near the blast sites was a good enough reason to be locked up. Finally, along with a few others who had been rounded up under "suspicious circumstances", I was let out. You were in London by then. I did not want to ruin your second chance of happiness. There was little I had to offer to you then. But even when I slept in a loft above a buffalo shed and used a grimy public washroom, I felt privileged. For my father had given me what the others in the ghettos did not have— a top-quality school education, access to literature, impeccable English, and confidence, which can get people a job in India even today," Omar looked up at the ceiling thanking a supernatural force that he had stopped trying to name. "Privileged." Ira smiled at him and nodded wondering, is that what had brought them together again, obstinate optimism? Omar continued,

"Who my biological father is, I do not know. I tried to find out and the trail led me to where I wanted to stop. When I visited *Naani*, she told me what she should have revealed much earlier, at least to her innocent daughter and saved her a lifetime of humiliation."

Omar related how in the monsoon of 1974, the sickly Sakinabi gave birth to her fifth daughter in a small Alibaug nursing home assisted by a midwife. Hours later, a baby boy wrapped in just a worn gray shawl, had been discovered on the synagogue steps by Mehrunissa's neighbour Yamu as she walked home from the fish market. With no other human being in sight, Yamu had rushed to the dwelling closest to the synagogue. She had found Mehrunissa outside her modest home, bolting the door to leave for the hospital, wailing angrily,

"Allah, just one, just one son for my Sakina would have saved her marriage. Aren't we looking after four of your unwanted gifts in the hope of that one?"

Tilting her just emptied cane basket, Yamu rushed across to Mehrunissa with the news, "*Aapa, jaldi*, come with me..." The breathless Yamu's voice rose as she described the creamy skin and sea-green eyes of the abandoned wailing child. Mehrunissa's eyes widened. Struck by a brainwave, her plaint to Allah transformed into a eulogy of gratitude. She unlocked the metal bolt and virtually pushed Yamu indoors. From an aluminium tin under the single cot, she extracted four Rs 100/- notes and thrust them into Yamu's palm.

"Go home Yamu, not a word about this. I will take care of the baby. Go."

Startled and confused, Yamu opened her mouth to protest,

"But *Aapa*...whose...what will happen?"

Mehrunissa unwound the black *taaviz* with a tiny pure gold sliver on her arm, placed it on Yamu's palm and drove her out of the door with a warning to shut her gob, or else!

Within minutes, Mehrunissa was at the synagogue steps, carrying a chequered, once inky blue bedsheet softened by years of washing. Ascertaining that no-one was in sight, she stealthily picked up the mewling infant, wrapped him in the cotton sheet, held him tightly to her chest and walked across to the hospital next door, striding confidently into the stark room with peeling green paint allocated to Sakina. Flicking away the bedsheet, she placed him in the metallic cradle hanging by a stand next to the delirious Sakinabi's bedside. Without flinching, she picked up the frail baby girl tucked in beside her weakened daughter, wrapped her in the same bedsheet and carted her out to the Synagogue steps."

Omar paused, snapped his fingers, and gave Ira a sad smile,

Just like that!"

"Omar!" Ira exclaimed incredulously. For someone she thought she had known all her life, she had known nothing. Still coming to terms with the theatrical tale, she asked, curious,

"Did you ever get to know who your biological parents are?" Sombre, Omar nodded,

"Years later, I found out about the one who gave birth to me. She was a poor Jewish girl from Alibaug's Bene Israel community, the victim of brutal rape by an intoxicated tourist at the Alibaug beach. She died in childbirth and the identity of the rapist was unknown – he was said to have been of German or Austrian origin.

Ira gasped, covering her lips with both palms.

Omar continued in an even, vapid tone,

"The truth is, even I don't know where I really came from. My biological green-eyed father who lusted after my hazel-eyed mother obviously had no thought of me. In his warped brain-washed ideology, like the perpetrators of heinous crimes across the world, she and her supposed ilk were not good enough to live in this world, but her body was good enough to abuse. My mother, the wretched woman, bless her soul, did not live to see me.

My adoptive grandmother, in her limited wisdom of procuring a male child for her own daughter who would have otherwise been disowned, took me away - to live. Sakinabi's unfortunate dark skinned, skinny baby girl was left behind, to live or to die, beside the synagogue steps where Hebrew prayers were being sung in a Marathi accent thicker than your Brahmanical ancestors."

Omar described how these startling revelations were made under duress. On his insistence, Mehrunissa called Sakinabi and confessed. Sakinabi listened, helpless, blaming her fate. Despite her frail health, Mehrunissa travelled to Mumbai and tried explaining in person. But Mushtaque was not interested in any more of Mehrunissa's fanciful tales. Her green-eyed

Pathan ancestor yarn had licensed Omar's luxurious existence for 18 years. This time, Mehrunissa's truth was dismissed as yet another concoction on the part of the spirited old lady struggling to save her daughter's marriage. Nobody cared to run a maternity test on Sakinabi that could have easily proved that she had no biological relation with Omar either.

Omar shook his head in regret.

"Out of prison, I was far too occupied grappling with just surviving, feeding myself, working odd jobs to complete my degree at any cost. A search for lineage was a luxury, I could not afford and a psychological disturbance, I did not want. I continued to live as Omar *bhai*, a Muslim for the community which supported me, Omar *bhau* for the Hindu community who gave me their love as Mumbai began to heal again. Much later, when I was studying for my master's degree, I tried to explore what I could have been, had I grown up in the Jewish community and this is what I found." Omar dipped into the wide pocket of his winter coat and handed a clipping from a news magazine to Ira.

She began to read out aloud, he walked across and sat down next to her.

"The Arabic speaking Baghdadi Jewish Community are supposed to have moved to India in the 18th century. Among the most famous from this community is the exceptional businessman and philanthropist David Sassoon (once the treasurer of Baghdad) who moved to India in 1833, the year slavery was abolished in Great Britain. He did not speak English but was given British citizenship in 1853. One of his sons, Albert, became a Baron and married into the Rothchild family."

Like they had done for years, even when they studied for their board exams, they sat on a bench and read out alternate paragraphs. Ira tilted her chin towards Omar. He read the next,

"This is the same David Sassoon of Mumbai's Sassoon Docks and Masina Hospital, which was the family mansion he donated, Pune's Sassoon Hospital and one of largest synagogues in Asia, the Ohel David synagogue also called *Lal Deul* (Red temple) by Pune's Marathi population," He put the paper aside and said,

"This is the Iranian string of the Jewish in India. My biological mother was called Amita Sagaonkar and came from the Bene Israel Jewish family.

Amita means infinite in Sanskrit and truth in Hebrew. The Bene Israel community maintain they are descendants of the seven men and seven women who survived the wreckage of ships that arrived from Europe thousands of years ago. They have integrated into the villages they landed in adopting Hindu attire, the *nauvari* sarees of your ancestors, the food - *puran polis* and *karanjis* for the Jewish Yom Kippur festival and even the surnames. So, people who settled into Naigaon village became Naigaonkar, those into Sagaon became Sagaonkar and so on," Omar explained, weaving his personal story with the information in the news feature. He read on,

"Alibaug is named after a Jewish landlord-Ali. The Bene Israel Indians pray in Hebrew, have the Star of David outside their homes, and celebrate Rosh Hashanah and Purim. Several early settlers adopted the profession of oil pressing and would not work on Saturdays. This earned them the name *Shaniwar teli* (Saturday oil pressers in Marathi).

From approximately 30,000 Jewish people in 1948, only about 5,000 remain in India, the rest having moved to Israel. Approximately 80,000 Jews of Indian origin keep their unique traditions alive in Israel," he paused, turning to Ira. She read on,

"The Israeli towns of Dimona and Ashdod have been dubbed "Little India" and it's common to hear Marathi and Hindi in some homes. Dimona's central municipal library even has a special section of Indian-language books." Intrigued, Ira looked at Omar, and asked,

"Marathi in Israel! How?" Omar explained how Israel's law of return gives every Jewish person the right to be in Israel and gain citizenship. He had heard that in Israel too, apparently there is discrimination between white and dark-skinned Jewish people.

"The Bene Israelis looked Indian and had to fight for acceptance as "Real Jew status" till the 1960s. My mother Amita was among the unfortunate who felt more at home in India than Israel and had returned to live in Alibaug... and then die," Omar stopped.

Ira began to understand why Omar had chosen Auschwitz to meet. Ira prodded him gently,

"You tried to find out about your biological father?" Omar looked away. She placed her palm on his, nodding encouragingly. This was gnawing into the recesses of Omar's mind. Omar looked into Ira's eyes beckoning him to accede. He took a deep breath and spoke in an icy, cold voice, his tormented eyes, flashing,

"Like we saw, post Gandhi's assassination, there were several maligned surnames, not just Godse but also Apte the other co-accused of the conspiracy. Similarly, there are some much maligned German surnames post 1945 that had the power to invoke the horrors of Nazi Germany - Himmler, Goering, Goethe, Hitler and Hoess among others. Like Sriram's father wants to let the sleeping ghosts of the Godse connection lie, so be it with mine. Beyond what I have stumbled upon, I don't want to dig any further. Nobody from my mother's side bothered to look for me, there was no police complaint, no infant reported missing. They had shunned her for the sin she carried and my father, whoever he was, escaped. What happened to the skinny dark baby, Sakinabi and Mushtaque's fifth daughter unfortunately, nobody knows and like it is with little girls often in parts of the world today, nobody cares.

As an 18-year-old accused of the Mumbai blasts, if I had tried to inquire, I would have got nothing. As a 40-year-old leading educational trusts, I got somewhere with my investigation. I got as far as my biological father's passport." Omar's body seemed to droop. Resting his elbows on the table, he held his head in his hands. Ira walked over to his side of the bench and placed her palms on his shoulders, resting her cheek against his peppered crown of hair.

"Whenever you are ready Omar. You have borne this by yourself for far too long…" she whispered into his ear. She strode across to the vending machine and brought back two paper cups of warm water.

Omar was blowing his reddened nose into a tissue. He took a sip and spoke aloud, an utterance more onerous than any other,

"He was…"

Omar paused again. Ira held her gaze, nodding,

"… a Friedrich Heller, born in Berlin. Whether he wooed Amita due to her religion or good looks, got into a relationship and then abandoned her or saw her as just a vulnerable slip of a girl he took advantage of, may be in a state of inebriation, I don't know." Omar slumped into his chair, his palms limp on the tabletop.

Ira moved the green plastic trays to the edge of the table. She leaned across and placed her upturned palms under his. For a minute which seemed so much longer, they sat in the stark chilly café in silence, the back of Ira's hands warmed by Omar's tears.

Omar looked up at Ira's warm brown eyes with a free view of his teary green ones, a sight the heightened masculinity of the erstwhile proud teenager would have never ever permitted. Her fingertips gently stroked his palms as she held his gaze. His speech was garbled, Omar was choking on his words, whimpering,

"Whose son am I? A lineage of ruthless criminals…have I passed on these genes to the Sameer you raised with such virtue? Am I not the son of the wretched poor victim too?"

Ira rubbed her thumb against his moist palm. She picked up a tissue, gently dabbed his glistening wet cheekbones and whispered,

"It doesn't matter who they were. You are Omar – the one who has only done good all his life. We are sure Sameer too will do no wrong. You are the only Omar I have known all my life and after an eon that encompassed so much, you are the Omar I want to know. Where he came from causes you agony. It does not matter to me – it never did."

Omar gave Ira a long hard stare. Ira, otherwise given to blushing and looking away when he did that, held the gaze, stroked his face, and said,

"My Omar, the only one I have known, OK?"

With a hint of the smile she kindled, he lifted Ira's hand with both of his and planted a delicate downy kiss on her wrist.

"My Ira, the only one I have known, OK."

Having regained the spirit of his mission, Omar assumed his brisk "in control" tone,

"Right Ira, the prisoners of the holocaust were officially freed in 1945. But the prisons of the wronged still exist in pockets, making radical Jewish men condemn their women to a life as "baby machines" to replace the six million lost in the holocaust. Descendants of the maligned German surnames are grappling with the guilt of their ancestors' deeds. Most have chosen to live in obscurity, changing their maligned surnames or found respite in denial. A German brother-sister pair have taken the extreme step of sterilising themselves to cut off their lineage as penance for a crime that they did not commit.

I have chosen not to pursue the investigation any further. I'm Sagaonkar from my mother's side, a Heller from my father's. Sagaon is the village where the horse's hooves are supposed to exist, a unique site revered by the Jewish, Muslims and the Christians. My dream is that one day, you, me, Sameer and Cahya would visit. One day, when it ceases to matter who we are and why our eyes, skin and hair are the way they are.

Ira nodded in comprehension. Her palms had been nesting snugly in Omar's. She lifted them and softly kissed the back of his hand.

"Is that why we are here, Omar?" Omar stroked the inside of her palm with his thumb and continued to speak briskly,

"There is a small gathering of these people tomorrow in Warsaw and I have signed us up. To be able to appreciate the profound emotional upheaval that must have gone into a 94-year-old German man's mind to apologise after decades of denial and the courage that the granddaughter of a Nazi perpetrator who she loved very much, must have gathered to confront descendants of the holocaust, we had to first visit Auschwitz here today." Omar held out a pamphlet. It said:

One-by-one, a non-profit co-founded by Dr. Martina Emme that brings together descendants of Holocaust survivors, Nazi perpetrators, and bystanders.

To educate students and the community about the Holocaust, to honour its victims and survivors, to cultivate tolerance, and to promote awareness of modern-day genocide in support of the world's promise of "Never Again."

Putting away the pamphlet in the pocket of his winter coat, Omar said,

"I wrote all of this to Sameer. The letter was hand delivered to him along with a package - my most precious possession." Ira looked at him, puzzled. Omar nodded,

"When I was thrown out, I was allowed to take nothing. After I was released from prison, I met Rubina outside the Mahim dargah. Petrified of our father, she had never dared to reach out. She told me that before they

In the name of HOLY TEXTS

destroyed all my things, Rubina had managed to sneak into my old room and retrieve what she knew I valued the most. I had no place of my own and on my request, Rubina held on to these for a few more years, till I finally had a hostel room to live in." Ira looked at him curiously,

"Precious possession?"

Omar got up, chucked their cups into the bin and asked Ira to follow him.

"I made copies for you. They are in the car. Let's go." In the car, Ira thumbed through copies of the priceless photos of their shared childhood which she had not seen for several years. She had never seen the picture of all of them at Razia's wedding. She then opened the letter.

"My dear Sameer

Please do not tear this letter. I do not expect a reply and I do not expect you to alter your views. The voice of reason, especially when it is gentle, cannot stand in combat with the powerful communal forces that have you in their clutches.

Until a year ago, I did not know I had a child. Like your mother has been aching to see the son who refuses to speak to her, I have agonised over losing a son even before I get to know him. Marshalling all the resources and the goodwill that has come my way after my tumultuous youth, I have shadowed every day of your eventful journey through the last year, from afar, without your knowledge.

I have been deeply disturbed to see you being used by politicians who are not interested in understanding the essence of Hinduism. In the religious community of Islam that I grew up in, which I know today, is not my religion by biology, I have witnessed several ambitious young men like you, being used and discarded in the name of promises of 72 virgins waiting for them in Jannat (heaven). This is a ridiculous claim, incorrectly and conveniently attributed to the holy text. The confusion is between similar sounding words "Houri (virgin in Arabic)" and "Hur (white raisins of crystal clarity in the Syrian language)". Brought up in the progressive, egalitarian environment you have been and as a Hindu, this demeaning projection of women in the prevalent practice of Islamic indoctrination of youth will see you repulsed, take you one more step closer to strengthening the growing Islamophobia in the world today.

Look at the story of Ajmal Kasab, one of the 10 indoctrinated Pakistani youth who was sent to Mumbai in 2008 armed with ammunition and the order to brazenly

kill Hindus, Christians, the Jews and spare the Muslims so that this Jihad would give him a fast ticket to the promised Jannat. The world that witnessed this horror live on TV channels has no sympathy for him. But what do you say about a boy pulled out of rural Pakistani obscurity with the promise to catapult him to notoriety, who continued to defend his actions in the name of Jihad? Kasab's frenzied allegiance to his handlers continued until he was shown the putrid corpses of his nine accomplices neither claimed by Pakistan nor their handlers. Is this the Jannat (heaven) he was promised?

Despite our differences, Hindu, Muslim, Christian and the Jewish communities in Mumbai, the police, and the political parties united to ensure peace – Mumbai's Muslim Council ordered that the nine gunmen killed, should not be buried in the city.

I have been yearning to tell you this because this is exactly what your handlers have promised to do, pull you out of a promising, but anonymous, existence of a London professional and catapult you to national fame.

How long will you let yourself be used by political forces who have no interest in your religion, or history? The robes of saffron they don, and the greens, blacks and whites' others do, have been watered down to garbs that provoke. They will use you and discard you, just like the garbs they will shed when it stops suiting them.

Do you want to go down in history as one who executed commands, orders issued to him that are wrong, immoral, against the spirit and grain of humanity?

The fire that warms can also consume us; it is not the fault of the fire." How close to the fire do you want to be?

There are coincidences and ironic situations no doubt, but do we assign "cosmic design" to all of these? Here are two more coincidences of significance:

One of India's earliest freedom fighters, the iconic Queen Rani of Jhansi's adopted son Damodar Rao was born on November 15th too. This was, in fact, reported in the travelogues of the historian Vishnubhat Godse, no relation to Nathuram Godse. Would you then dedicate your life to his unfinished duties too?

Here is another. The Magen Aboth Synagogue (Hebrew for Defender of brothers), on the steps of which I was abandoned as a baby in Alibaug was established in the same year as the year Nathuram Godse was born.

Designs are assigned by those who want to twist history and philosophy in the name of whatever suits them.

When you see injustice, a need to retaliate, the choice is always between
- *Going for a demonstration/joining the fight*

  or
- *Studying further/earning your living.*

Ira's family chose education. My blessed Muslim father (he disowned me, but he is the only one I have known, sent me to one of the best schools in Mumbai for which I am grateful.) He sent me to a school that gave me perspective, understood another point of view, instead of the madrasas my sisters were sent to, where they were told to know no better and where boys today are being taught that the only way to love God is to hate everyone else!

My plea to you is to see reason and to break the cycle of revenge. I fail to understand the controversies that are generated with conflicting numbers on how many people were killed.

How many were killed in the Holocaust, how many during the Indo-Pak partition, in Afghanistan, in 9/11 and more. Even this year, in 2019, Prince Philip on a trip to India along with the Queen of England, questions the numbers killed in the 1919 Jallianwala Bagh massacre generating a controversy. How can we continue to dwell on numbers? Is every number not a child of a parent who mourned their death?

If it had not been for a Mumbai riot, perpetuated over an ongoing dispute over a minaret and statue, your mother and I would have never been separated. You need to know that unlike me, who was conceived because of the most heinous crime of rape, you were conceived out of your parents' intense love, though unrequited for so many years. You were born because we wanted you, maybe not so soon in the flush of our intense passion of youth, but as the symbol of our unadulterated and enduring love and for the lifetime we wanted with each other.

The true practitioners of the religion you are chasing are your mother and–Cahya. The girl wears no holy garbs but is the very embodiment of what the Hindu scriptures have defined as the ideal partner. The respect and care she has accorded to your mother while you have been away, is commendable. Against the backdrop of the fragile relationships that we see around us, this young lady has stood by you. What I gather from your mother is that you have a bond that connects at all four levels in a relationship - the emotional, intellectual, physical, and spiritual. The last especially, is very difficult to find. Finding all four in a single human being in a lifetime is near impossible. From someone who found it and lost it, I implore you son, do not let this precious love of your life go."

My own horrific lineage speaks of "eliminating people without the Aryan traits." The crimes of 1945 cannot be corrected in 2019. But these are some attempts by the German leadership and ordinary citizens to acknowledge that the holocaust was a crime that must not be repeated and...to break the cycle of revenge.

In the year 2000, German President Johannes Rau addressed the Knesset, asking for forgiveness in the name of the German people.

In 2008, to mark the 60th anniversary of the founding of Israel, Angela Merkel became the first German chancellor to speak before the Israeli parliament. Israeli Prime Minister Ehud Olmert characterized Merkel as a great friend of Israel."

In 2011, the Israel Chamber Orchestra broke a seven-decade taboo by playing a work by Hitler's favourite composer, Richard Wagner in Germany.

Let us just use these examples, to make a beginning.

Today, we are part of the silent majority, the bystanders of crimes being committed in the name of religion and race. How will we face our descendants if this is repeated? Let us instead, confront, acknowledge, weep together, forgive and ensure "Never again".

(Whatever you choose to accept me as in your life or not)

Your loving father

Omar

Chapter 25:

In the name of LOVE again

Back at the Warsaw hotel, Omar did what he did best, counter despondence with his incorrigible sense of humour.

"Now Ira *ji*, I have two things set out for the evening. I've booked an early dinner at a vegetarian restaurant and got two tickets for a movie."

"Vegetarian restaurant in Warsaw! I'm ok with chicken and fish. Of course, you are now following the pacifist form of religion that demands you to be vegetarian. And movie, here! What will you come up with next Omar, which one is it?" Ira quipped.

"Ira *ji*, I've set all this up. So now you play your part, we have wept enough. Go, freshen up, life is too short to weep any further, wear something that makes you feel gorgeous like you always do and let's not be late!" Omar turned to walk away.

"Omar, maroon or blue?" Ira stopped to ask.

"When I saw you on screen, when you left for Ella-Leon's birthday party in that maroon dress..." Omar stared pointedly at Ira.

"And that picture in the deep blue dress at Leila's convocation..." Omar held his gaze.

"You know what I mean don't you?" Omar crossed his arms over his chest, looking deep into her eyes. Ira lowered her eyes, her lips parted in a half smile,

"Maybe not, maybe your eternal favourite white then!" she tossed her head and much to the bemusement of Omar, skipped away.

Ira emerged in a flowing white knee-length chiffon dress, her freshly washed hair still slightly damp, tiny pearl drops glistening on her earlobes.

Omar stepped back and sighed loudly, his eyes twinkling,

"Pristine!"

At the restaurant serving Mediterranean and Jewish food, Ira and Omar were ushered to a round table placed against an L-shaped dark leather sofa. A thick-set chocolate brown candle, carved with floral motifs cast its glow on the colourful spread of vegetables, dips, and breads. A bottle of Prosecco nestled in a sculpted wooden ice bucket. Ira glanced appreciatively at the leaping flames of the wood fire, an occasional effervescent glint of light reflecting in Omar's sparkling eyes. The turquoise sleeveless jacket that Omar was wearing over his white linen shirt and dark trousers, gave his eyes a bluish tinge.

Omar took a deep breath as Ira's jasmine perfume wafted across, reminiscent of the little islands of allure that Omar would at times encounter walking down a busy Mumbai Street, from a wicker basket displaying strings of jasmine flowers for sale, bringing with them, the pangs of Ira's memory.

"Before the movie, I have two things to do. Do I have your permission?"

"Permission for what Omar?" Ira muttered flippantly, engaged in blithely sampling each of the fascinating dips.

"One, can I show off a bit and two, can I ask your opinion on something?" Omar's eyes were shining.

Ira wagged a carrot baton at him.

"Since when did you start waiting for permission to talk, Omar? In fact, it looks like that's what you've done for a living, all these years – talk! And given your fame, it looks like it's worked for you!" Ira snorted.

Omar began, "Remember I used to feel inadequate in *Ajji*'s show-off room?"

"Omar, don't be saucy, especially with dead people! That was her study, home of her demi-Gods, not a show-off room! Please!" Ira shook her head indignantly.

"Of course, she called it that. But it made people like me with no illustrious ancestors feel like nobodies. Today, I'm going to show off. If I include Jewish people across the world, we will be here all night singing their eulogies. But I'll restrict myself to Jewish people with connections to India. Gandhi's first Ashram in South Africa was established on Tolstoy farm donated by his Jewish friend Dr. Herman Kallenback. Later in India, Dr. Abraham Solomon Erulkar, a Bene Israel Jew from Mumbai, became his personal physician and relocated with him to Ahmedabad in 1915. Then we had Jacob-Farj-Rafael Jacob, the Chief of Staff of the Indian Army's Eastern Command during the 1971 Bangladesh Liberation War." Omar rattled off nuggets from his Jewish community fact-finding mission.

"Interesting," quipped Ira, nibbling at the assortment of breads and dips.

"By the way, the first ever Miss India (1947) was Jewish - Esther Victoria Abraham, who took on the stage name of Pramila. She was one of India's first female film producers and an alumnus of Cambridge University. Esther's daughter Naqui Jahan became Miss India in 1967 and her son is the actor Haider Ali. There were two more Miss Indias of Jewish origin, Fleur Ezekiel in 1959, and Salome Aaron in 1972.

There was a time when Hindu and Muslim actresses wouldn't accept certain Bollywood roles and our Jewish actresses took them on. There was Florence Ezekiel (Nadira) and Ruby Myers (Sulochana) who was honoured with cinema's highest honour the Dada Saheb Phalke award in 1973. She was quite a spirit, driving a Chevrolet down Mumbai's streets with earnings, allegedly, higher than the Governor of Mumbai. And then more recently, the actors David Abraham, Pearl Padamsee, and her son Ranjit Chowdhury."

Omar beamed proudly.

"That's cool. We Bollywood aficionados did not know that!" Ira exclaimed.

"Your ethereal glow, exquisite smile and the mesmerising jasmine my lady…why would I not be enamoured," Omar cupped his chin and looked at her languorously and then, quipped,

"But yes, here's finally a match among equals! I have illustrious lineage too. And in stark contrast to your incestuous localised family tree which barely crosses the Mumbai-Pune Expressway, mine is a spicy, juicy global one! Omar raised his glass, in appreciation of his own attempt at dark humour. The 45-year-old woman slightly greying at her temples, plummeted into the deep chasm of love all over. After an eon that had lasted over two decades, her smile reached her eyes again.

"If your dear *Ajji* was alive, she would have likened my story to Lord Krishna's and his biological mother Devaki's eighth baby girl, swapped and whisked away so that Krishna could live as an adopted child in Gokul! Omar's eyes twinkled at the memory of the iron lady, supervising Abdul and Jamila's preparation of her religious festivities.

"Now that we have established, I am a reincarnation, it brings me to the question – who should I engage for the wedding?" he enquired, suppressing a cheeky grin.

Omar's non-stop prattling and attempt at an outlandish connection between Indian mythology to the fantastic story of his lineage had Ira's eyes watering with laughter.

"Don't spoil my eyeliner, Omar. We promised no tears tonight, even if they are tears of laughter. My make-up is not waterproof. Engage who, what wedding?" she put her fork in her mouth.

"Dr. Iravati Godse, I'm asking you who I should engage for the wedding, a Rabbi, a Catholic priest, a *Kazi* or will your priestess aunt be willing to do the honours?"

Ira plonked her goblet of Prosecco on the table.

"If you don't tell me quickly what kind of wedding you want, we might just have to first do the world-tour, which was to be our honeymoon, and then get married. I've lost the world map from school with our cities to visit marked in red. Every time we read about a new city; I would put a dot against the place to visit with you. We have all the Shakespearean sites to visit – Rome, Venice…" Omar broke off. Ira picked up the thread where he left off, "Oh yes, Georgia, Atlanta for "Gone with the Wind" and the outback from "Thorn Birds" and after all this, you would want to visit Israel." Omar interrupted,

"Yes, you've got the drift Dr. Ira Godse. Back to the present. If you don't tell me where you want to get married and how, it will have to wait till

In the name of LOVE again

after the world tour. Considering that Sameer and Cahya are on holiday, we might even have wailing grandchildren interrupting the proceedings at our wedding. So, make it quick!"

"Omar, did you just propose to me?" Ira quipped, leisurely picking at an olive stuffed with cheese and red pepper.

"What's this big deal about proposing? We've established that I could be any of the following – Muslim, Jewish, Christian, half Indian, may be half German. What I'm certainly not, is British. But it is you, who have become so English. After producing a son with a man who is sonorously, hopelessly, and passionately in love with you, you are still waiting for the man to go down on his knee and offer you a ring. I don't get this concept. This is overriding strong English influence after all! But I'm not going to do that. I'll go by what the movies of our impressionable 80s planted in our heads:

Asking a girl out for a coffee = declaring your love in public

Asking a girl out for a movie = proposing to the girl

A girl allowing you to hold her hand = girl agreeing to marry you

So, Ira, will you watch a movie with me?" With the dramatis persona of a conjurer, Omar flung the movie tickets in the air.

Omar and Ira were together at a movie again, in a small 70-seater cinema inside Warsaw's Ujazdowski Castle. The movie was not much to write home about. But it starred Christopher Plummer, now in his 90s, the star of the first movie Ira and Omar had watched together, when their teacher had bundled up her entire class of eight-year-olds on a school bus and carted them off for the grand Mumbai release of *The Sound of Music* in 1982. The popcorn was now caramelised, served in an elegant cardboard tub. Instead of the clink of a stubby glass bottle, the cola in its diet version came in a tumbler. In a country that had transcended so much sorrow, in a city that could not care about differences any longer, no scarf was needed for Ira, no obstacle course over knobbly knees to get to her seat in a cinema hall.

As the music faded on the giant screen, Omar held out his left palm and Ira's smaller one, slipped into his once again. Both knew, as they had always known but never dared to hope, that it could never ever have been any other way.

Glossary

A

- *Aadaab:* (Urdu) Polite, formal greeting with an upturned palm
- *Aagraha:* (Sanskrit) Insistence as a demonstration of hospitality
- *Aai:* (Marathi) Mother
- *Aaji:* (Marathi) Grandmother
- *Ajoba:* (Marathi) Grandfather
- *Aarti:* Prayer songs
- *Aatya:* (Marathi) Aunt – father's sister
- *Aamti:* (Marathi) Spiced lentil curry
- *Aapa:* (Urdu) Elder sister
- *Aapalyaat:* (Marathi) Amongst us
- *Ahimsa:* (Sanskrit) Nonviolence
- *Allah:* The Prophet Mohammed as per the Islamic faith
- *Alwan:* (Marathi): Maroon cotton garment covering the entire body except the face worn by Maharashtrian Hindu Brahmin widows in ancient India
- *Am Spiegelgrund:* (German) The Playground - Euthanasia clinics established by German forces during the holocaust
- *Apni:* (Hindi/Urdu) Own
- *Arbeit:* (German) Work
- *Arbeit Macht Frei:* (German) Work sets one free
- *Ashrit:* (Marathi) Dependent

B

- *Bai:* (Marathi) Lady
- *Baappa:* (Marathi) God
- *Baabu/Babua:* (Hindi) Boy
- *Barfi:* (Hindi/Marathi) Milk sweetmeat cut into squares
- *Bhaaji:* (Hindi/Marathi) Vegetable
- *Bhaji:* (Hindi/Marathi) Fritters
- *Besan:* (Marathi/Hindi) Chickpea flour
- *Besan laddu:* (Marathi/Hindi) Chickpea flour sweet balls
- *Beta:* (Hindi/Urdu) Son
- *Beti:* (Hindi/Urdu) Daughter
- *Bhaakri:* (Marathi) Jowar (Sorghum) or Bajri (Pearl millet) flour flatbread
- *Bhajan:* (Marathi/Hindi) Song sung in praise of God by Hindus
- *Bhaarat:* India
- *Bharatiya Janata Party* (BJP): Ruling party in India since 2014
- *Bhaat:* (Marathi) rice
- *Bharli Vaangi:* (Marathi) Stuffed aubergines
- *Bhau beej:* (Marathi) / *Bhai dooj* (Hindi), a festival during Diwali celebrating the brother-sister bond
- *Bhavan/Bhuvan:* (Sanskrit) House
- *Bhoomi:* (Sanskrit) Earth
- *Bhraatashri:* (Sanskrit) Elder brother
- *Biryani:* (Urdu) Spiced lamb or chicken rice
- *Bola:* (Marathi), *Bolo* (Hindi): Speak
- *Boltoy:* (Marathi) Speaking
- *Brahmin:* (Sanskrit) Priest caste of Hindus
- *Burkha:* (Urdu) Black outfit covering all parts of the body except the eyes

C

- *Chaal: (Marathi)*, *Chawl* (Hindi) Humble tenement typical of Mumbai
- *Chahaa:* (Marathi), *Chai* (Hindi) tea
- *Chalo:* (Hindi/Urdu) Come
- *Chachaa:* (Urdu/Hindi) Uncle – Father's younger brother
- *Chaas:* (Hindi) Buttermilk

- *Chitpavan:* (Sanskrit) Brahmin sub-caste from Maharashtra
- *Chivda:* (Marathi) Savoury snack
- *Chunri/Chunni/Dupatta:* (Hindi/Urdu) long scarf

D

- *Daal:* (Marathi/Hindi) Lentil
- *Daal khichadi:* (Marathi/Hindi) Lentil and rice cooked with spices
- *Daasi:* (Sanskrit) Maidservant
- *Dakshina:* (Sanskrit) Donation
- *Daye/Daayne:* (Hindi) Right
- *Dev:* (Sanskrit) God
- *Dev ghar:* (Sanskrit) Mini temple
- *Dhan:* (Sanskrit) Wealth
- *Dhanyavaad:* (Marathi/Hindi) Thank you
- *Dharma:* (Sanskrit) Duty and religion
- *Didi:* (Hindi) Elder sister same as *Tai* (Marathi) and *Aapa* (Urdu)
- *Dil:* (Hindi/Urdu) Heart
- *Dilwale:* (Hindi/Urdu) People with a heart
- *Dulhania:* (Hindi/Urdu) Bride

E

- *Eid:* Muslim festival

F

- *Faraal:* (Marathi) Snacks

G

- *Gajraa:* (Marathi/Hindi) String of flowers
- *Ganesha/Ganpati:* (Marathi/Hindi) Elephant headed Hindu God
- *Ganpati Bappa Morya:* (Marathi) Glory to the Elephant God Ganpati
- *Gau:* (Sanskrit) Cow
- *Gau Rakshak:* (Sanskrit) Protector of cows
- *Ghagra:* (Hindi/Urdu) Floor length skirt
- *Ghya:* (Marathi) Take
- *Goad:* (Marathi) Sweet

Glossary

- *Gujia:* (Hindi) Boat shaped pastry filled with sweetened chickpea flour
- *Gul/Gud:* (Marathi/Hindi) Molasses/Jaggery
- *Guru:* (Sanskrit) Teacher and mentor
- *Gurukul:* (Sanskrit) Residential school
- *Gut:* (German) good

H

- *Haldi:* (Sanskrit) Turmeric
- *Haldi kunku:* (Marathi) Social gathering for married Hindu women from Maharashtra
- *Hari:* Hindu God Shri Vishnu /Krishna
- *Harijan:* Children of God, a term introduced by Mahatma Gandhi for *Dalit* castes
- *Henna/Mehndi:* Designs painted out of the dye extracted from the Lawsonia inermis
- *Homa:* (Marathi/Sanskrit) *Havan* (Hindi). Symbolic holy fire

I

- *Immie:* (Hebrew) Mother
- *Indian National Congress (INC):* Political party established in 1885.
- *Itar:* (Marathi) Others

J

- *Jaa:* (Hindi/Urdu/Marathi) Go
- *Jaati:* (Sanskrit/Hindi) Caste
- *Jaenge:* (Hindi/Urdu) Will go
- *Jana:* (Sanskrit) People
- *Janata:* (Sanskrit) Public
- *Jee:* (Hindi/Urdu) Live
- *Jeera:* (Hindi/Marathi) Cumin seeds
- *Ji:* (Sanskrit) Honorific
- *Jindagi:* (Hindi/Urdu) Life

K

- *Kadhi:* (Curry) made from yoghurt and chickpea flour
- *Kaahwa:* Traditional tea from Kashmir
- *Kaka:* (Marathi) Uncle- father's brother
- *Kaku:* (Marathi) Aunt – wife of father's brother
- *Kamdhenu:* (Sanskrit) *Kama* (desire) and *Dhenu* (cow)
- *Kabab/Kebab:* (Urdu) Minced meat grilled snack
- *Kazi:* (Urdu) Muslim cleric
- *Kameez:* (Urdu) Shirt
- *Karanjis:* (Marathi) Stuffed boat shaped pastry
- *Karma:* (Sanskrit) A person's actions
- *Karma Bhoomi:* (Sanskrit) Place where one's constructive actions flourish
- *Khaala:* (Urdu) Aunt (Mother's sister)
- *Khadi saakhar:* (Marathi) Sugar cubes
- *Khandaan:* (Hindi/Urdu) Ancestral family
- *Koi:* (Hindi/Urdu) Anyone
- *Koknastha:* (Sanskrit) Hindu Brahmins sub-caste from the state of Maharashtra
- *Koshimbir* (Marathi) salad
- *Kshatriya:* (Sanskrit) The warrior caste of the Hindus
- *Kurta-* (Urdu/Hindi) Knee length upper garment

L

- *Laddu:* (Marathi/Hindi) Sweet balls
- *Laksham:* (Sanskrit) External indicator or symbol
- *Lashkar-e-Toiba:* (Urdu) Organization funded by Osama bin laden
- *Le:* (Hindi) Take

M

- *Macht:* (German) Make
- *Madrasa:* (Urdu) School for religious teaching on Islam
- *Maha:* (Sanskrit) Grand
- *Mahasabha:* (Sanskrit) Grand gathering
- *Mahar:* Hindu scheduled caste
- *Maharashtra:* One of the largest Indian states of which Mumbai is the capital

- *Mangal:* (Sanskrit) Auspicious
- *Mangal sutra:* (Sanskrit) Black and gold bead necklace worn by married women
- *Marathi:* Language spoken by the people living in Maharashtra
- *Masale Bhaat:* Maharashtrian spiced rice
- *Maunj:* (Marathi) ceremony marking a child's initiation into student life
- *Mavshi:* (Marathi), *Khaala* (Urdu) Mother's sister
- *Mee*: (Marathi) I or me
- *Modak:* (Marathi) sweet, steamed rice flour dumpling
- *Mohalla:* (Urdu) Locality
- *Moharram:* (Urdu) Islamic festival
- *Mood:* (Marathi) rice upturned into a plate using a mould
- *Mud:* (Hindi) Turn
- *Morya:* (Marathi) Glory
- *Motichoor:* (Hindi/Marathi) Fried chickpea flour balls soaked in sugar
- *Muhurta:* (Marathi), *Mahurat* (Hindi): Auspicious time for any ceremony
- *Mumbai kar:* People from Mumbai
- *Muh:* (Urdu) Mouth
- *Muh bole:* (Urdu) Unrelated individuals who develop close relationships
- *Munafa:* (Urdu) Profit
- *Muttor:* (Marathi/Hindi) Peas

N

- *Naan:* (Urdu) Soft leavened refined flour flatbread
- *Naanaa:* (Hindi/Urdu Maternal grandfather
- *Naani:* (Hindi/Urdu) Maternal grandmother
- *Namaste/Namaskar:* (Sanskrit) Folding of hands in greeting
- *Nath: (Marathi/Hindi)* Nose ring
- *Nau:* (Marathi) Nine
- *Nau wari:* (Marathi) Nine-yard saree worn by Maharashtrian women
- *Nahin*: (Hindi), *Naahi* (Marathi) No
- *Naivedya:* (Sanskrit) food offered to God as gratitude for one's good fortune
- *Nirupan:* (Sanskrit) narration of philosophical/religious tales

P

- *Padar:* (Marathi), *Pallu* (Hindi) Edge of a *saree* over the shoulder.
- *Pagdi:* (Marathi/Hindi) Silken head dress worn by men
- *Paithani:* (Marathi) Pure silk gilt woven saree from Paithan in Maharashtra.
- *Panha:* (Marathi) Raw mango drink
- *Papad:* (Poppadum). Sundried lentil pancakes fried or roasted
- *Panji:* (Marathi) Great grandmother
- *Parsi:* People of the Zoroastrian faith
- *Pedhas:* (Marathi/Hindi) Milk sweetmeat balls to celebrate good news
- *Pheta* (Marathi): Turban worn by men
- *Phirni* (Urdu): Rice pudding flavoured with rose water
- *Phodni* (Marathi), *Tadka* (Hindi): Heated oil, mustard seeds, asafoetida and turmeric
- *Phopa* (Urdu): Husband of father's sister
- *Phopo* (Urdu) Father's sister
- *Poli, chapati* (Marathi), *Roti* (Hindi): Wheat flatbread
- *Phulka* (Marathi) Thin wheat flatbread
- *Puri* (Marathi) Small round flatbread deep fried in oil
- *Pohe* (Marathi), *Chidva* (Hindi) Flattened rice snack culturally associated with "Bride viewing" ceremonies in the arranged marriage process.
- *Prasad:* (Marathi/Hindi): Food offered to God and distributed
- *Pooja:* (Sanskrit): Prayer ceremony
- *Pune kar:* (Marathi): People from Pune

Q

- *Qawwali:* (Urdu) Energetic musical performance of Sufi Muslim poetry
- *Qubool:* (Urdu) Agreed

R

- *Rajya:* (Sanskrit) Rule
- *Rastriya:* (Sanskrit) National
- *Rashtriya Swayamsevak Sangh (RSS):* Hindu nationalist volunteer organisation founded in 1924.

- *Rakhee:* (Marathi/Hindi) Friendship band that a sister ties on to a brother's wrist signifying a brother's promise to look after his sister
- *Raksha Bandhan:* (Sanskrit) The bond of protection (the festival)
- *Rava:* (Marathi/Hindi) Semolina

S

- *Saade:* (Marathi) Half
- *Saadi/Sari:* (Hindi/Marathi): Garment draped by women (6 yards)
- *Saati:* (Marathi) Seven
- *Saade Saati:* (Marathi) Seven and half years. There is a belief that there could be a period of seven and half years in a person's life that is difficult, ridden with multiple obstacles. Once this period of *Saade saati* is over, circumstances improve
- *Sadhu:* (Sanskrit) One who has renounced comforts
- *Saadhvi:* (Sanskrit/) Woman who has renounced comforts
- *Sabha:* (Sanskrit/ Gathering
- *Sabudana:* (Marathi) Sago, a starch from the pith of tropical palm stems
- *Sabudana Khichadi:* (Marathi): High energy sago snack eaten by Hindus during fasts
- *Salwar:* (Urdu) Loose trousers
- *Salwar Kameez:* (Urdu) Loose trousers worn with a long shirt
- *Samosa:* (Marathi/Hindi) Triangular wheat pastry with spiced potato filling
- *Sangh:* (Sanskrit) Organization
- *Sankranti:* (Marathi) Hindu festival occurring in winter
- *Sannyasa:* (Sanskrit) Fourth of the life stage of renunciation (ashramas) recommended by Hindu philosophy. After fulfilling the duties of the first three stages Brahmacharya (celibate student life), Grihastha (family responsibilities) and Vanaprastha (forest life).
- *Saransh:* (Sanskrit) Summary
- *Satori:* (Marathi) Flatbread stuffed with sweetened semolina
- *Satya:* (Sanskrit) Truth
- *Satyagraha:* (Sanskrit) Prevalence of the truth
- *Sena:* (Sanskrit) Army
- *Shaniwar*: (Sanskrit) – Saturday

- *Shaniwar Peth:* (Marathi): Area of Pune, with localities named after each weekday
- *Shevaya kheer:* (Marathi) – Vermicelli pudding
- *Sriram/Ram/Raghuveer/Raghu:* Hindu God, ideal king of Ayodhya
- *Sheera:* (Marathi) Sweet snack made from semolina, raisins and saffron
- *Sheer khurma:* (Urdu) Vermicelli pudding made in Muslim households for *Eid*
- *Shiva:* Hindu God
- *Shudra:* (Sanskrit) The caste traditionally engaged in manual labour
- *Soad:* (Marathi) Leave/let go
- *Stree:* (Sanskrit) Woman
- *Sutra:* (Sanskrit) Thread
- *Swarajya:* (Sanskrit) Self rule
- *Swayamsevak:* (Sanskrit) Volunteer

T

- *Tai*: (Marathi) elder sister
- *Tathastu*: (Sanskrit) So be it
- *Tel*: (Marathi/Hindi) oil
- *Teli*: (Marathi/Hindi) oil presser
- *Thecha:* (Marathi): Crushed chilli chutney with lemon and garlic
- *Tikli*: (Marathi), *Bindi* (Hindi) Coloured dot on the forehead
- *Til*: (Marathi/Hindi) Sesame seeds
- *Tilgul*: (Marathi) Sweetmeats made of sesame seeds and molasses
- *Tilgul ghya god bola* (Eat this sweetmeat and exchange sweet words round the year)
- *Tup:* (Marathi), *Ghee* (Hindi) clarified unsalted butter

U

- *Upama:* Savoury semolina snack

V

- *Vaan:* (Marathi) Gift given to Hindu married women
- *Vaangi:* (Marathi) Aubergine
- *Vadi:* (Marathi) *Sweet or savoury canape sized snack*

Glossary 225

- *Vaishya:* (Sanskrit): Hindu merchant/trader caste
- *Varan:* (Marathi) Boiled lentils with salt, asafoetida, and turmeric
- *Vedas:* (Marathi) The four scriptures of Hinduism

W

- *Wada:* (Marathi) A large house/tenement with a single entrance housing a single large or multiple small families. A typical feature of old Pune.